Discover the Only Way
of Successfully

ESCAPING YOUR FALLEN NATURE

Entangling Your Life and
Blocking Your Way

DAVID PIPER

Copyright © 2019 by David Piper
All rights reserved. No part of this book may be reproduced, scanned,
or distributed in any printed or electronic form without permission.
New Edition: September 2019
Printed in the United States of America
ISBN: 645505197
ISBN: 9781645505198

Scripture passages quoted are from the King James Version of Sword Searcher Bible program. Quotations referring to Strong's are from Strong's Talking Greek & Hebrew Dictionary, and those referring to Vine's are from Vine's Expository Dictionary of Old Testament and New Testament Words.

Credit Line: Thank you to Shutterstock for the Beaver Dam shutterstock_283590908 image and to Stockfresh for the stockfresh_6718526_breaking-brick-wall stock photo.

TABLE OF CONTENTS

Part 1. STEPS THAT WILL LEAD TO YOUR ESCAPE 1
    Chapter 1.   Understand Your Fallen Nature 3
    Chapter 2.   Examine Your Heart's Condition 13
    Chapter 3.   Reject the Ways that Seem Right 22
    Chapter 4.   Realize What Born Again Is Not 36
    Chapter 5.   Appreciate the New Birth Process 47
    Chapter 6.   Show a True Heart of Repentance 57
    Chapter 7.   Confirm with a Public Confession 68
    Chapter 8.   Release the Fullness of the Spirit 77
    Chapter 9.   Corroborate with a Changed Life 94

Part 2. ATTITUDES THAT SIGNIFY YOUR ESCAPE 109
    Chapter 10.   Moves on from Pre-salvation Grace 111
    Chapter 11.   Listens to Warnings on Backsliding 124
    Chapter 12.   Testifies to God's Power to Restore 143
    Chapter 13.   Tests if Heading in Right Direction 154
    Chapter 14.   Perseveres to Fulfill Commitments 169
    Chapter 15.   Resists Nurturing a Victim Mentality 183
    Chapter 16.   Refuses to Justify Quitting on Life 194
    Chapter 17.   Draws Inspiration from Conquerors 203

Part 3. PROOFS THAT JESUS IS YOUR ESCAPE 215
    Chapter 18.   Demonstrated Superior Nature 217
    Chapter 19.   Validated His Trustworthiness 231

Chapter 20. Repulsed at the Stench of Sin......................242
Chapter 21. Identified with Your Infirmities...................254
Chapter 22. Exemplified the Way of Escape....................264
Chapter 23. Delivered You into a New Life.....................276

PREFACE

My first attempt at conveying what the Lord laid on my heart to write was the book entitled Make a Way for Your Rescue and which was published in October 2017. But believing that I could do much better to make my writing more readable, adding about 25 more personal stories, I rewrote the whole book and gave it the new title, Escape Your Fallen Nature. In the April 2019 publication of this new edition I wrote in the preface of how I came to believe that God wanted me to write it. But in this September 2019 publication, where, in the title, I changed Escape to Escaping, I decided to include a few extra details on how the Lord prepared me for the writing of this book.

I've been working for 100 Huntley Street prayer lines in Ontario, Canada, since 1994. In my April 2019 version I shared that in the mid to late 1990s a caller from Winnipeg Manitoba said that she had a message from the Lord of a prayer partner being hypocritical. I acknowledged that this reproof was meant for me. Many months or even a year or so later, another lady, also from Winnipeg, called to deliver a message. This second lady told me that God instructed her to tell the person answering the phone that he was to write a book on salvation and that this was a task that He assigned specifically to me. She stressed very strongly that this book must be on salvation.

Though I said "hypocritical" in the preface of my first edition to summarize this first caller's statement, in fact, she said the word "hypocrite." Though it was honest of me to agree that I had been hypocritical, I didn't want to repeat this same word she used to describe my spiritual condition because the more concise word, "hypocrite," carries with it a much stronger sting. Though it was hard to accept, but because it came from the Lord, I decided this revelation of me must be accurate.

> [23] Search me, O God, and know my heart: try me, and know my thoughts: [24] And see if there be any wicked way in me...**Psalm 139:23-24**

In response, I examined my heart to see what was in there that needed to be cleaned out.

> [19] Nevertheless the foundation of God standeth sure, having this seal, The Lord knoweth them that are his. And, Letevery one that nameth the name of Christ depart from iniquity... [21] If a man therefore purge himself from these, he shall be a vessel unto honour, sanctified, and meet for the master's use, *and* prepared unto every good work. **2 Timothy 2:19, 21**

Before giving me this revelation about my hypocrisy, the Lord already knew that He was later going to give me a revelation about writing. But before He could use me to write this book, it was necessary that He first prompt me to do some purging.

> [1] Judge not, that ye be not judged... [5] Thou hypocrite, first cast out the beam out of thine own eye; and then shalt thou see clearly to cast out the mote out of thy brother's eye. **Matthew 7:1, 5**

It was because I am often critical in my heart of the faults of others while at the same time failing to recognize and correct the weaknesses in my own life that I believe, in retrospect, was one of the reasons that God sent me this reproof of declaring me a hypocrite.

It's because I haverequested readers to examine their hearts that the Lord wanted me to examine my own heart about my inclination of judging. I needed this correction so that years later when I finally obeyed His call to write, I would be careful to make sure that the difficult things He put on my heart to speak I would say with the right attitude. Though many times I still judge others when I shouldn't, the Lord knows that these statements in this book that appear to be judgmental, I have tried very hard to consistently share from out of a pure and compassionate heart.

The reason for detailing that first phone call is that it provides the proper context for the second call. How could I expect readers to believe that God had inspired this second lady to inform me of writing a book, and yet, not disclose that He had previously used another caller to rebuke me. To purposely leave this detail out, because of its sting, would, again, make me a hypocrite. I felt that I could not have it both ways. Either I leave out both narratives or I include them both.

It was essential that I tell my readers that it was God that initiated the book's writing. It is He, not me, who has shown them the way in escaping *their fallen nature*. I know I wrote this book solely for the purpose of pleasing the Lord. The only reason I did not give in to the temptations to stop advancing toward publication is because I knew that stopping would greatly displease Him.

It humiliates me to think that God, through this caller, called me a hypocrite. If anyone else had told me this I would have argued with them. But, since I am now convinced that this message originated with God, then how can I argue against it? What more could I say? I could either argue and ignore or confess and plead for mercy. I chose the latter. Since I gave in to the temptation in the earlier version to minimize the sting of that first call, I know I've done the right thing by including these details in this final version of *Escaping Your Fallen Nature*.

In using this caller in my life, God fulfilled the scripture from 1 Corinthians 10:13, "God... will... make a way to escape." Because of His mercy in providing me a way in *escaping my fallen nature* (my propensity toward judging others before judging myself) I know God will use *Escaping Your Fallen Nature* to make a way for you, my readers, in *escaping your fallen nature* also. You will be successful in *Escaping Your Fallen Nature Entangling Your Life and Blocking Your Way* only when you ask Jesus to replace your fallen nature with His new nature.

One reason I became convinced I was the person God chose to write this book is because both these women, as was I many years before, were residents of Winnipeg. Since God could have inspired anyone in the whole country, it struck me that He chose a Winnipeg resident not just once but twice to make these impressions on me.

And yet there are plenty of reasons why I could argue that this was not a genuine call from the Lord: these ladies may have been mistaken; it is safer to believe the message is from the Lord when it comes from Him directly, not through other people; too many people are saying that "God told me to tell you," which sometimes they will say to help them win an argument.

All I know is that until that second lady called, I never had any kind of desire to write a book. It was after many years of resisting this message that I reluctantly agreed to explore this possibility of God calling me to write. Though it's possible the whole thing is a mistake, yet I had to make a decision. Finally, I did decide, after much prayer and contemplation, that this message was, indeed, of the Lord. And, thankfully, over the next 10 to 15 years since then the Lord has confirmed this calling in my heart many times in many different ways.

Ever since I first felt the call of the Lord to be involved in ministry, it was witnessing to others about their need for salvation that I found to be most compelling on my heart. The church I regularly attended in my youth was Calvary Temple in Winnipeg. On Wednesday evenings following an inspirational talk from one of the pastors, I would join others to go to people's homes. We went to those people who had attended the church for the first time the previous Sunday to provide them with follow-up ministry. If we learned they were not saved, we would give them the opportunity to accept Jesus.

Because the Lord put it on my heart to be involved with leading others to Him, in 1967, when Billy Graham came to Winnipeg for a crusade, I attended the pre-crusade counseling classes. Once a week for the five weeks prior to the crusade, I received training on how to lead candidates to accept the Lord as their Savior. Each night of the crusade, after people came to the front of the arena to receive Jesus, I would join with them to go to a large back room where I was assigned to a candidate. I also did this for a James Robison crusade in 1991 in Hamilton, Ontario.

After becoming a pastor, going from door to door to tell others about Jesus continued to be my emphasis. The churches where my wife and I did much door-to-door ministry were Shell Lake, Saskatchewan (1977–1979), Grandview Manitoba (1980–1986), and Weagamow Lake, Ontario (1991–1992). In each of these places, we went to almost all the homes to see if the residents there needed ministry.

In 2005, in studying the book of Hebrews, I began to sense what specifically the Lord wanted me to write. What most caught my attention was the tendency of people to be so occupied with the many cares of this life that they neglect the care of their spiritual condition.

> How shall we escape, if we neglect so great salvation... **Hebrews 2:3**

A few years after that, while going on a long walk with my brother-in-law, we talked about the permanence of a believer's salvation. We discussed if there were any possibility that believers could backslide and be lost. At that very moment I decided that I would present a study to inspire people to examine their hearts to determine if they are in a relationship with God.

But knowing I wasn't a writer, for a very long time I procrastinated. But over the next few years, I wrote several booklets ranging from fifteen to fifty pages in length. Since I was convinced in my heart that writing this book was the Lord's will, I knew I needed the practice in writing. In late 2014, I wrote *Jesus Is the Only Way*, which initially I had hoped was the fulfillment of what the Lord had asked me to do. But because I had not written about the need for people to examine their hearts (for fear of being judgmental) I then realized that I needed to write again.

Though research would have been valuable I limited the development of my thoughts to the books of the King James Version of the Bible, *Strong's Dictionary, Vine's Dictionary,* Holy Spirit inspiration, MSWord thesaurus, editorial suggestions, memories, and deeply rooted seed thoughts. It was over years of studying the scriptures and preparing messages that many of these thoughts, some of which are very different from what has been taught traditionally, took root in my mind. I believe God called me to write because He wanted these seed thoughts to be developed and shared.

The reader will observe that I've interpreted certain scriptural passages far differently from the usual interpretations. Also, what I said on some subjects, such as the baptism with the Holy Spirit, was introductory and was never intended to be a full-scale study of them. Thus, because many of my statements were without the benefit of cultural and historical context, I have risked leaving some thoughts hanging. Hopefully, the cross-referencing of scriptures is adequate, but for a more comprehensive explanation, the reader may want to consult a commentary.

Because this book is primarily a study and not a devotional, I have adhered, while relying on the Lord to inspire my thoughts, to Paul's admonition:

> Study to shew thyself approved unto God, a workman that needeth not to be ashamed, rightly dividing the word of truth. **2 Timothy 2:15**

Though I admit that I also hope to gain the approval of my readers, it is God's approval that has motivated what I have written. But I know I am not a better student of the Word of God than was Paul. And since Paul wasn't given an automatic pass on the correct interpretation of the Word of God but was held accountable by his listeners for what he said, I too must be held accountable.

> These were more noble than those in Thessalonica, in that they received the word with all readiness of mind, and searched the scriptures daily, whether those things were so. **Acts 17:11**

Even as these people searched the scriptures to see if what Paul spoke lined up with what was written, so also the reader with all readiness of mind must check on me. If what I have written the reader believes isn't true to the scriptures, then please contact me and point out with scriptural support the errors I have made. My e-mail address is in the last chapter.

> And I thank Christ Jesus our Lord, who hath enabled me, for that he counted me faithful, putting me into the ministry; **1 Timothy 1:12**

I am also grateful to my wife for being so supportive of me during these last 4 years, to the few who reviewed earlier versions of the manuscript, and to these professionals whose advice, especially of starting over again and adding stories, inspired me to make many improvements.

INTRODUCTION

Luke tells the story of Jesus getting after a very religious man, Simon, for his criticism of a woman who came into his house to express her love for Him (see Luke 7:36–50). Though it appears Jesus was judgmental when confronting him for his lack of courtesy, He was compassionately showing him the true condition of his heart (original fallen nature).

Like Simon, if you are religious or have a religious background, Jesus wants you to know the true condition of your heart and that only He, not your religion, is the remedy to bring it lasting healing. Through this book, He will challenge you, especially if you're at or near the end of your rope, to look to Him to overcome your heart's natural deficiencies and defects.

You have possibly heard messages leaving you with the impression that you can make it to heaven simply if your good works outweigh your bad. If that is your belief, then, besides doing good, you have acknowledged that you also do things that you consider are bad. So, no matter how many good and loving deeds you do, they don't cancel or eliminate your tendency to do bad things. The only way you can be free from evil inclinations is when your original corrupt nature is replaced with a new one. Only then will you be eligible to enter heaven.

The cover of Escaping Your Fallen Nature, in showing a beaver dam blocking the flow of water, illustrates the damage done in our lives when we build dams to block God's life sustaining grace.

Because it's our nature to be independent, we regularly resist His ways, entangling our lives with substitutes that impede His inspiring influences from reaching our hearts. Like this tree in the stagnant water with the appearance of death, soon to fall, if we are blocking the refreshing flow of God's "living water" (resisting the formation of Jesus in our hearts) then we also, because we are without nourishment and stability, will soon come crashing down.

But when you ask God to replace your corrupt heart with a born-again new one, this dam opens to release this living water. Though God makes it easy, this process of *escaping your fallen nature* becomes difficult only because you've refused to let go your alternative schemes of coping with life. But these scripturally based explanations plus the stories of how God always provides an escape will inspire you to let go of your flawed beliefs and inadequate substitutes, trusting that you *Escaping Your Fallen Nature* comes only through this living water.

In this book, I have presented truths about the necessity of receiving this new nature. I know that if you have no clear understanding about this brand-new heart, you will eventually be deceived into believing something about it that is not true.

To not study the Word of God is like refusing to take the vaccine which your doctor said is necessary to prevent disease and death. If you refuse the teachings of the scriptures, then your belief system won't have the necessary immunity to detect and fight off lies. As you read the many explanations in this book and come to understand the scriptural truths in it, you will develop a resistance to the untruths that previously prevented your afflicted and diseased heart from being healed. Only the truths of God's Word can heal the terminally ill heart.

You might already have a new heart but are under the influences of your old corrupt heart to backslide or to give in to discouragement. Or, it could be that you know you are saved but have no assurance that you won't lose your salvation. Or, you may know that you do not yet have this new heart and are concerned because you know that you are not yet ready for eternity.

When you have received a newborn heart and have learned about its durability, you then will be free from life threatening insecurities. Without this new heart, as you have already discovered, there will be the constant threat, when troubles come, of giving up or giving in. As you study the scriptural explanations in this book of what your new heart can do, your faith will arise to help you to overcome and recover from the damages caused by your old heart. When you follow these many scriptural teachings in this book, very soon you will be consistently *Escaping Your Fallen Nature*.

PART I

STEPS THAT WILL LEAD TO YOUR ESCAPE

CHAPTER 1

UNDERSTAND YOUR FALLEN NATURE

I heard the story of an adventurous hunter who found a cub tiger whose mother had been killed. He decided to adopt this tiger as a pet believing that he could train it to behave so that it would never be a threat or a danger to him. This tiger grew to adulthood under his expert care. But one day, when he was walking this fully-grown tiger through the forest, he nicked his hand on a thorn, drawing blood. This tiger immediately caught the scent of this blood. Though it was fully trained to respect its master and to obey instructions, this tiger turned on his master, killing him.

I also heard the story of a farmer who believed that his well-trained bull, who won an award at a competition, would always remain docile and never be a threat to turn against him. But again, like with the tiger, when the farmer least expected it, this bull did turn on him and killed him.

The mistake that both the hunter and the farmer made was that they believed good training would control and perhaps even remove the original tendency of these animals to be violent and that they then would become trustworthy. They did not realize that regardless of how much these animals are trained, the original nature within them cannot be removed.

I'm afraid that most authorities in our society are making this very same mistake. From what I can tell, there are many experts who believe that education, excellent treatment, and the creation of a good environment is all that is needed to prevent people from manifesting behavior that would betray the trust of others and that would do society great harm. Some even believe that a person's wicked nature can be changed through exorcism, that is, the casting out of demons.

But there are historical records that can easily prove that these theories are wrong. There are millions of examples where people with the best lineage, the best environment, the best education, and the best religious training who, after many years of convincing others that they are trustworthy, then showed what was really in their hearts by doing society unimaginable and permanent damage.

Though we are restrained from committing terrible deeds through better education, better treatment, and better environment, yet, as illustrated by the above animal examples, certain stimuli or temptations will draw out of our hearts the very corrupt behavior that we believed were fully controlled or even eliminated. All these restraints have been proven to be unreliable.

Though it is obvious that there is something wrong with our original human nature, most of society refuses to acknowledge this truth. Though many are preaching the truth that we have a very corrupt nature and that we need to turn to God to get it replaced with a new one, yet there are some ministries today that are telling us that we are basically good. Many years ago, I read a book named "I'm okay, You're okay." Considering that many preachers and writers don't want to acknowledge that we have a serious flaw in our human nature, denying the truth of the scriptures, it is no wonder that their audiences are now very confused.

It is so easy to get confused and disoriented. Usually, I have a very good sense of direction. When my younger sister and I together toured Europe for 6 weeks in 1976 I was confident that we could walk away from the train station in downtown Copenhagen in Denmark and not get lost. But after a while as we were getting further and further away, my sister became very concerned as to how we were going to find our way back to the station. For a long time, I did not want to take her advice to ask someone for directions. I was sure that I could work my way through the maze of streets and finally arrive at our destination.

Though it previously usually worked to pay attention to the sun so that I could determine which way was north and which was west, this time I some how became disoriented and got mixed up. Though my sister was quite patient with me, but because I could tell that she was somewhat nervous, I finally admitted that we were lost and agreed to ask for directions. I've heard it said by others that it is not unusual of men to often be very slow to ask for directions or slow to look on a map because of our overconfidence. Obviously, I was providing evidence of a man's fallen nature.

Many are asking the question, that if I am basically good and that education, training and environment is key to bringing out this goodness, then why am I unable to overcome my tendencies to think and do evil? Why am I not able to overcome these habits that are doing me so much harm?

Everyone who has not yet been set free, even those who are very religious, are very confused as to what they must do in *escaping their fallen nature*. But this escape begins only when we decide to stop making excuses for our bad behavior and finally accept responsibility for our own choices.

> So then every one of us shall give account of himself to God. **Romans 14:12**

The people who have refused to accept responsibility for their decisions are very happy to learn that much of the evil that they have committed, according to the experts, really isn't their fault.

We hear it all the time that the reason for someone committing horrific crimes, such as school shootings and other terrorist atrocities is because there is something drastically wrong with them mentally. Surely, as many would reason, no one in his right mind would do such a terrible deed.

Recently, a gentleman told me that the reason that he sometimes does evil deeds is because he has a chemical imbalance in his brain and therefore not to blame for his actions. Even believers are sometimes attributing people's bad behavior to mental illness, or, if not mental illness, then to generational curses, demonic oppression, or childhood trauma producing terrible memories, thus excusing them of personal accountability. While in some cases that's partly true, many believersare reluctant to agree that people's corruption primarily stems from their natural born fallen nature.

Often, courts show leniency toward certain crimes declaring that the accused is not guilty or is not criminally responsible due to mental illness. Though in extreme cases people are indeed not responsible for certain actions, many people are knowingly excusing their behavior simply because a doctor officially diagnosed them with a mental illness. When people have been diagnosed with post-traumatic stress disorders, though we feel for the weight that they are bearing emotionally, we are not helping them if we confirm that their only remedy torecovery is to take medication plus months or even years off from performing their regular duties. Though getting away can be restorative, an overly prolonged rest is an emphasis on being a victim, not on being a victor.

When professionals make excuses for people's corrupt behavior, declaring that they are not accountable for their actions due to memories of abuse or distressing experiences, then others will use the same reasoning to excuse their evil behavior also. Not taking responsibility for their actions is typical of those who are under the bondage of their corrupt fallen nature. Catering to the demands of their old nature for a release from accountability will ultimately make people numb to the fact that they do evil, not because of an illness to their minds, but because of an illness to their hearts.

It's because our society is making excuses for people's bad behavior that there are so many unchecked evil and terrible injustices committed against the innocent. Many of these injustices are getting worse because we believers, whom Jesus said are the salt of the earth and light of the world, have allowed ourselves to be intimidated and silenced by the threat of repercussions. I presume that the murder of unborn innocent children and the parading of aberrant life styles have taken a foothold in our society simply because there haven't been enough of us willing to speak up.

But I thank God for those people in influential positions who lately are doing their very best to stand up against the corruption and hypocrisy that is so rampant in religion, business, politics, and relationships. While Jesus mandated believers to stem the evil and wickedness in our society from corrupting the earth, it is so refreshing to know that there are some governments that are also trying to drive out corruption. We need to support them with our prayers and with our votes.

This book helps to bring to our attention the source of this corruption and what it is that we believers must do to prevent it from continuing to spew out its filth and pollution. The scriptures tell us that the source of all corruption in our society is found within our own hearts. We need to recognize our fallen nature and then turn to God, asking Him to replace it with His new nature.

> The heart *is* deceitful above all *things*, and desperately wicked: who can know it? **Jeremiah 17:9**
>
> ² Wherein in time past ye walked according to the course of this world, according to the prince of the power of the air, the spirit that

> now worketh in the children of disobedience: ³ Among whom also we all had our conversation in times past in the lusts of our flesh, fulfilling the desires of the flesh and of the mind; and were by nature the children of wrath, even as others.
> **Ephesians 2:2-3**

I'm sure most people are aware of the many con artists that use a multitude of ways to trick and defraud them out of their money. All of us can tell stories of how others have taken advantage of us. But if we're honest, we can tell stories of how we too have taken advantage of the vulnerable. How can that not be true since all of us have operated under the influence of our fallen nature.

While we may not call it a lie, but any time that we withhold information from others that we know will work to our financial advantage at their expense, then we have committed fraud. We are giving evidence of a fallen nature whenever we knowingly hold back from declaring in our tax returns sums of money that we earned or when we don't tell the prospective buyer of our house or car of problems that will make them either regret buying it or make them feel they paid too much.

Recently, after making a certain purchase, I decided that I had made a mistake. I then called and inquired of the sales lady if I might get a refund. Because I had entered into a contract that I believed was permanently binding and which had no refund policy my only hope of getting a refund was that this company show me good-will courtesy. In speaking to this sales lady, I allowed her to believe that I wanted it because of financial stress. But in truth, I asked to get out of the contract so that I could use this money to make a better purchase from a competing company.

Though I found out later that this company had a refund policy and thus had an obligation to grant the refund regardless of my motivation for asking, still, I felt guilty for having withheld this information because I believed I was taking advantage of their good-will courtesy. I felt so terrible that it was only about 15 minutes later that I called her back and after telling her the whole truth cancelled the refund request. Though I was sincerely repentant and had quickly made amends, my temptation to take advantage of the sales representative's lack of knowledge so thatI might benefit financially, was a clear demonstration of my own corrupt fallen nature.

In 1968 when I worked as an office boy at a construction company I took some pencils, pens, writing pads, and certain forms. It took about 2 months before I finally felt enough conviction to decide to go to my boss and not only confess that I had stolen these items but also to return them. I was very much surprised that instead of firing me he instead forgave me.

> [5] And when Jesus came to the place, he looked up, and saw him, and said unto him, Zacchaeus, make haste, and come down; for to day I must abide at thy house. [6] And he made haste, and came down, and received him joyfully. [7] And when they saw *it*, they all murmured, saying, That he was gone to be guest with a man that is a sinner. [8] And Zacchaeus stood, and said unto the Lord; Behold, Lord, the half of my goods I give to the poor; and if I have taken any thing from any man by false accusation, I restore *him* fourfold. [9] And Jesus said unto him, This day is salvation come to this house, forsomuch as he also is a son of Abraham. [10] For the Son of man is come to seek and to save that which was lost. **Luke 19:5-10**

Zacchaeus promised to restore fourfold because he was under genuine conviction, due to the very presence of Jesus, for his theft of other people's money. In my above examples, it was also the presence of the Lord within my spirit that brought me to the point of realizing that I was as much a thief as was Zacchaeus when I withheld vital information or took things that I had not paid for. Like Zacchaeus, I too felt an obligation to return what I had gained through fraud.

We observe that babies are very selfish. If they don't get their way, they'll make quite a fuss. Of course, we don't fault them for their selfishness because we know they're only babies. But this nature of selfishness is not eliminated simply because of growth and instruction.

One time when I was a child, I took a quarter I had found in the kitchen cupboard. When my Dad asked me if I had gotten that quarter from the cupboard, I told him no. A few years later, when I was playing baseball with other children, I swung my bat, and everyone figured I had missed for strike three. But I insisted that my bat had ticked the ball. Again, I knew that I had lied.

Why did I lie in those two instances? Was it because I hadn't paid attention when Dad and Mom were teaching us kids to always tell the truth? If I had better instruction and perhaps had been threatened with the consequences of lying, would that have prevented me from doing it? Does the threat of punishment always prevent children from doing things they shouldn't?

Because we know Jesus was a man and had a human nature, many believe that He had the potential to display these same traits of selfishness? If true, how was He able even when He was a toddler to overcome these characteristics? Because we know He needed and submitted to training (see Luke 2:51–52), was it His parents' instructions along with His connection to His heavenly Father that caused His good behavior. The obedience of Jesus (which I thoroughly discuss in part III), even as a toddler, had more to do with His nature than with his parental training.

After I was grown up, I remember my mother telling me that of all her children – at that time there were five of us – I was the quickest to obey her commands. She told me that when we children were outside playing, she would call for us and I would

Escaping Your Fallen Nature

immediately stop what I was doing and run to her. Did that mean I was better at obeying instructions than my siblings were? I'm not sure. But I certainly wasn't better at telling the truth.

When Jesus was growing up, He was noticeably different from other children. He did not tell lies or disobey instructions. The reason for my sometimes lying and Jesus never lying had nothing to do with our attentiveness and alertness to instructions from our parents or our willpower to overcome. Quite simply, I lied because unlike Jesus, it was in my heart to lie. I was born with a corrupt and deceitful heart, the natural condition of everyone's heart.

Before moving on to the next chapter I need to give one more illustration of the deceptive works of our fallen nature. Though I know I've already escaped my fallen nature when I received Jesus as my Savior and received from Him a born from above new nature, yet, like every other believer, I often struggle to maintain my victory over the dictates and demands of my old nature.

To maintain the deliverance that the Lord originally gave to me when I was born of the Spirit, it is my responsibility to follow the scriptures and make no provision for these unruly appetites. I understand that to mean that it's up to me to make up my mind that I won't let my fleshly cravings control me. And I do this by putting off my fallen nature and daily replacing it with my new nature.

Many believers, instead of taking responsibility for their mistakes and bondages, will blame their actions on generational curses, demonic oppression, mental illness, or memories of abuse. But it's only when we stop believing the lies that excuses us of our own accountability that we can then expect to get victory over the inclinations of our old nature.

When I got married in 1978, my weight of 195 pounds made it obvious that I had a problem with overeating. My wife married me for who I am and did not let my addiction discourage her from doing the Lord's will to marry me. But after we got married, she decided I needed her help to overcome my habit of eating more than what I needed.

I immediately agreed with her that I needed to curb my appetite and get my weight down. After 3 months, my weight was down to 165 pounds. But that didn't mean that I had eliminated my addiction. There were many times afterwards that I lost control of my discipline and indulged in overeating. This cycle has been repeated numerous times over our 41 years of marriage.

Recently, I heard a commercial on the radio from a weight control company that said, "If you could do it alone, you'd have done it already." They recognized that many are unable to get their weight under control unless they get professional help. For those of us who have this addictive behavior, our problem is that once we get started on a favorite food we don't know how to stop.

I credit my wife for helping me to get my appetite under control. But I often interpreted her encouragement as controlling. It was when I sometimes reacted to this "control", that I came to realize that instead of depending on my wife, I needed to learn self-discipline.

There is always the temptation to indulge the flesh and go beyond the natural boundaries established by God. But the believer's ability to stay within these boundaries comes through the help of the Holy Spirit generated new nature within us. Though oftentimes we fall back into old ways, we know it's the gentle convicting work of the Holy Spirit that inspires us to stop when we need to stop (even when we don't have our spouse around to hold us accountable).

These examples on how my old nature sometimes controlled me, even to the point where I gave in to the temptation to deceive and withhold vital information, or to give in to fleshly desires, demonstrates how important it is that we recognize the dangers of catering to our fallen nature. We must regularly examine our hearts to discover its true condition so that we won't be deceived into believing that we can manage okay, yet totally unaware of the heart disease that may be killing us.

CHAPTER 2

EXAMINE YOUR HEART'S CONDITION

In recent years, people have become increasingly concerned about their health. Some will not drink water from the tap out of concern it may have picked up pollutants. Some are anxious that surfaces around them have germs. As a precaution, many may drink only water that they know has been filtered and touch only surfaces that they know have been disinfected.

But do they show the same concern for the pollutants affecting their mental health as they do for the pollutants affecting their physical health? Are they aware that if the information they allow into their minds isn't factual and honest it can ultimately pollute their views on life? Will they discern truth from error concerning the many views and opinions about the purpose for living?

The purpose of this life is to prepare for the next. But many people give little thought to what is beyond the end of their lives. This need for preparation Jesus illustrated in a parable.

> [16]The ground of a certain rich man brought forth plentifully: [17] And he thought within himself, saying, What shall I do, because I have no room where to bestow my fruits? [19] And I

will say to my soul, Soul, thou hast much goods laid up for many years; take thine ease, eat, drink, *and* be merry. ²⁰ But God said unto him, *Thou fool*, this night thy soul shall be required of thee: then whose shall those things be, which thou hast provided? **Luke 12:16-17, 19-20**

This man believed that preparations for life meant only the years that he expected to live. He worked very hard so that he could enjoy the bounty of his labor in his sunset years. He put more value on the harvest of his crops, which could provide him with only a few decades of enjoyment, than he did on his soul, which is guaranteed to continue forever. Since he died early without having made preparations for the next life, all his hard work, said Jesus, was in vain. He didn't realize his soul was so valuable that even if he had traded it for the whole world, he would not have profited.

I have often observed in news reports that when famous people are close to death due to diseases and old age, the media will ask their audiences to remember them in their prayers so that they would recover. Since these reports neglect to say that death is a passage way into something new, they give the impression that it's a tragedy if these famous people don't squeeze out a few more years. And when they do finally die, the media become so obsessed with their goodness that the uninformed, those who believe that heaven is for good people only, are then easily duped into believing that this person must now be in heaven. Sadly, these listeners and readers, since they believe that they are good, are now convinced that their goodness will get them into heaven also.

Many times, I have gone into nursing homes or hospitals and talked to people who know that they are soon going to die. When I broached the subject of the next life, I was amazed at their lack of concern. They gave more attention to their present life, knowing full well that it will end in a cemetery and yet not willing to prepare for the never-ending life that continues after the grave.

Escaping Your Fallen Nature

If people would take time to examine the misinformation that has been influencing their beliefs and decisions, they would prepare for what is truly valuable. It is so sad when we come to realize that it was their lack of preparation and their refusal to examine their hearts, trusting instead the dictates of their fallen nature along with the influences of the media, that has cost them their souls.

I know you want to go to heaven and live there forever. But arriving there depends on the value you place on your life. You cannot expect to make it until you give attention to those things preventing you from becoming prepared. If you planned on going to another country, you would obtain an up-to-date passport. If you want to be sure that you will not be refused entry at heaven's gate surely you are aware it's only in this lifetime that you can make the necessary preparations. To spare yourself disappointment, before departing you would make sure that you have a passport and that your name is on the passenger list.

On its very first voyage in 1912 the *Titanic*, after hitting an iceberg, sank within just two or three hours. Initially, most of the passengers didn't believe the ship would go down. They had heard so much publicity on how well it was built that they believed the lie that it was unsinkable. But when they heard there was no expectation of keeping it afloat, they then hoped a nearby ship would come to their rescue. And when it became apparent that there would not be a rescue they then depended on the crew to put everyone on their lifeboats. How frightened they must have felt when they realized that there weren't enough lifeboats onboard to rescue even half the people!

And those who were fortunate enough to get a seat in the life boat, knowing that there was plenty of space to make room for others who after the Titanic sunk were in the water screaming for help, refused to pull them into the boat. They explained later that they were afraid that if they reached for these victims to help them get into the boat that the boat would capsize. Rather than showing an attitude of gratefulness by helping these who needed rescue, they gave evidence of the "me first" corruption of their natural born hearts.

Today, it's happening again. Many fear what they see coming. Like those on the *Titanic*, some people are convinced that their world belief system is unsinkable and that when there is trouble, there will be enough lifeboats to rescue them from tragedy. Though alarm bells are ringing all over our planet, they continue with their normal routine activities, refusing to give attention to these many alarm bells and warnings. In so doing they also are failing to help those who are uneasy about the extreme chaos that is evident everywhere.

Many years ago I read a book about the terrible holocaust in Europe and how it was the intent of the Nazis to uproot and drive out of Europe the Jewish people. For many years they had shown their hatred of them and had boldly preached their doctrine of racism and the need to purify their country of all the Jewish population. Many of the Jews, knowing that hard times were coming, did take heed to these threats and warnings and even persuaded others to join them in their attempt to escape the coming holocaust.

But the sad thing that I remember reading in this book was that the author said that many of these Jewish communities, though frightened and concerned, carried on with life as usual. They continued to go about their routine business with the attitude that the coming storm would not really amount to too much and that it would ultimately blow over. It was sad to see these people make no preparations to escape, ignoring and giving no heed to these signs of coming calamity.

You reading this book indicates that you're aware of the insecurities in this world and are seeking ways to escape. Instead of relying on belief systems that have betrayed your trust, having jumped off this sinking ship called humanism, you are now floundering in turbulent waters hoping to be rescued. Right now, a lifeboat is coming into your view. This lifeboat, the scriptural truths in this book, will bring within your reach the hand of your

Rescuer, Jesus. But it may be that you are very reluctant to take His hand because you remain unconvinced that He isn't like all the other belief systems that have let you down.

But if you're drowning in confusion and many troubles and are tired of these support systems that have left you with a sinking feeling, it's imperative that you trust Jesus as your Rescuer. As you study the scriptures and give attention to the preparations that God requires of you, you will discover that the journey of getting to heaven is not as complicated as you first believed. If you will give attention to the qualifications of Jesus, you will come to realize that He is not like those false support systems.

Jesus did not come to judge you for your sins but rather to deliver you from them. When you discover there is only one sin, not a multitude, that can prevent you from being rescued, you'll be encouraged. When this one sin (which I will discuss in a later chapter), is forgiven, the condition of your heart will be dramatically altered.

In communicating with you through this book, since I don't have the ability or tools, as a doctor would have, to listen to your heart, I can only make assumptions about its condition. The fact you are reading this book shows you have a concern about your nonphysical heart. I ask that you consider giving your spiritual heart a close examination. The truths that you study in this book are tools by which you can examine its true condition.

Through this checkup, you will learn if your heart is in good condition, needs a tune-up, needs to be revived, or needs to be replaced with a brand-new one. Your self-diagnosis will show you whether the medicine of God's Word is adequate to prevent heart failure or if this medicine is needed to help you have a successful heart transplant. When you agree to test your heart, you may very well discover it is diseased and has the potential to disrupt or destroy your life. This discovery will give you the occasion to find a remedy, a prescription that will bring you healing. This remedy is Jesus and the scriptural truths that will lead you to Him.

The following are descriptions that might possibly be describing the condition of your heart:

1. You are saved and have an excellent knowledge of scripture. The truths you have learned have already set you free and transformed your life. You have complete confidence in making it to heaven.

2. You are saved but not sure you will forever remain saved. You have a genuine relationship with the Lord, but you have made yourself vulnerable to deception. You have put much greater emphasis on feelings than on the study of scripture. You often experience fear and condemnation. You do not enjoy real peace. You fear that if you died before confessing all your sins, you would go to hell. Though you know the joy and peace of a transformed heart, still, you fear it's possible for you to lose your salvation.

3. You know you were once saved, but now, you doubt you are any longer on your way to heaven. You have neglected your relationship with the Lord and have allowed your heart toward Him to become dormant and lifeless. You're in a backslidden state because you permitted yourself to believe that God doesn't care and that the ways of the world are more fulfilling. You have now discovered this path brings you no more fulfillment than did the path you were on before. You're looking for a graceful way to return to the Lord hoping that He will revive your heart.

4. You may be saved but have become so discouraged that you're tempted to quit looking to the Lord for help. You are asking God why He would allow so much suffering in your life and are justifying your temptation to forsake Him and return to your earlier ways and beliefs. You are discouraged because you feel there is no evidence that God cares about your needs. But in the depth of your heart, you want to be rescued from this temptation.

5. You may think you are saved but are unaware that you're floundering in a sea of deception. You believe messages that tell you only part of the truth. They emphasize that the grace and love of God are the only guarantees you need for assurance that you're on your way to heaven. You have been persuaded to believe it isn't necessary for you to put faith in Jesus to experience God's forgiveness. But because you lack order in your life, you're beginning to realize your present belief system doesn't bring you the peace your heart yearns for. You're searching for the truth that you hope will have the power to transform your life.

6. You are not saved and know that you've rejected every opportunity to receive Jesus as Savior. You have decided to continue in your accustomed lifestyle. Because it requires total commitment, rather than accepting a relationship with God you prefer to forfeit the forgiveness of your sins. Regardless of the evidence, you are reluctant to admit that you have a diseased heart that needs to be exchanged for a new one. Earlier in your life, you ignored certain heart sounds, but you're now finding those sounds hard to ignore. They bring to your remembrance the advice of your Doctor who, because He diagnosed you with an irreparably damaged heart, recommended a transplant.

7. The seventh condition of the heart is that of a person whose heart is so hardened toward God that no amount of warning has an impact. Such a person would have no concern about dying in their sins and missing heaven. Due to a lack of interest in spiritual truths, a hard hearted person would never read a book such as this. You reading this far into this book is proof that your heart has not deteriorated to this condition and that you are yet capable of responding to the message of God's Word.

Other than the first or last conditions, if you are struggling with one of these other conditions and willing to seek a remedy, then you'll benefit from your study of the scriptures and explanations in this book. These truths, as you seek healing through them, will help you to
1. maintain assurance,
2. be revived from backsliding,
3. overcome the temptation to give up,
4. agree with newly revealed truth,
5. respond to an inner voice.

If you already are born again, your new heart has the potential
1. to provide you the assurance that will eliminate your fear of losing your salvation,
2. to come to life in time to rescue you from your backsliding,
3. to be durable enough to outlast your troubles enabling you to overcome the temptation to quit.

But if you are not sure that you have this new heart, or you know that you are not born again,
1. the condition of your heart, if it's healthy or sickly, genuine or fraudulent, is determined when you, in accordance with the scriptures, put it through a test,
2. you need to remember that Jesus is the Doctor whose voice (sounds) you have heard and who is now offering to replace your terminally ill heart with a new one.

Because you have read this far, I am sure you are familiar with the Christian vernacular. It is quite likely that your heart, in one way or another, is ailing and is in need of the medicine or prescription that will heal it. It maybe that all the misunderstood teachings that you have about Jesus are so entrenched in your mind that you are looking for further evidence. As you continue to read, these misconceptions will be cleared up, after which you will then know the real Jesus. This book will reveal the truth about Him. It will expose the previous deception that prevented you from examining your heart's fallen condition, showing you how you can escape its devastating effects.

CHAPTER 3

REJECT THE WAYS THAT SEEM RIGHT

Many people believe that they are going to heaven simply because they do good deeds.

> There is a way that seemeth right unto a man, but the end thereof *are* the ways of death. **Proverbs 16:25**
>
> Jesus saith unto him, I am the way, the truth, and the life: no man cometh unto the Father, but by me. **John 14:6**

They believe that the life of Jesus serves as an inspiration as to how to live and that patterning their lives after His is all that is necessary to get them into heaven. They interpret "the way" to refer to the way that Jesus lived His life. They believe that if they follow His exemplary life and care for the needy in the way that He did, then they must be saved.

> Then shall the King say... Come, ye blessed of my Father, inherit the kingdom prepared for you ...[40]And the King shall answer and say unto

them, Verily I say unto you, Inasmuch as ye have done it unto one of the least of these my brethren, ye have done it unto me... [44] Then shall they also answer him, saying, Lord, when saw we thee an hungered, or athirst, or a stranger, or naked, or sick, or in prison, and did not minister unto thee?[45] Then shall he answer them, saying, Verily I say unto you, Inasmuch as ye did it not to one of the least of these, ye did it not to me. [46] And these shall go away into everlasting punishment: but the righteous into life eternal.**Matthew 25:34, 40, 44-46**

When I was a pastor I would regularly attend ministerial meetings with the pastors of the other churches in town. In this one meeting that I attended the devotional passage on which one of the other ministers read and commented was this Matthew 25 passage. Based on it he explained why his church was so involved with ministering to the needs of people like those Jesus described. He believed that this passage was about the duty of his congregational members to minister to the practical needs of the desperately impoverished people in their community and that if they did minister to these needs, they then would be qualified to enter heaven.

Though following the example of Jesus to do good deeds is highly commendable and is what He wants us to always do, yet, the doing of them doesnot entitle any of us to enter heaven. This passage is not about what people must do to enter heaven but rather about the evidence that proves that certain people are already citizens of heaven.

Jesus said He will judge the nations on how they treated those whom He calls brethren. While the world right now is sensitive as to how religious groups are treated, especially of those groups who are opposed to Christianity, there is less sensitivity toward the extreme abuse and persecution of the followers and brethren of Jesus. While some religious groups garner much publicity even when critcal and unpleasant words are spoken against them, Christians all over the world, though treated with brutality by these same groups, draw almost no attention from the main stream media.

Though people of all nations, when they put into practise and strictly adhere to their religious principals, will be good to their own people, Jesus will show that the unwillingness of these same groups to show goodness to His brethren, to flow in genuine love toward them, is the evidence that proves that they are not fit for heaven.

> [21] Not every one that saith unto me, Lord, Lord, shall enter into the kingdom of heaven; but he that doeth the will of my Father which is in heaven. [22] Many will say to me in that day, Lord, Lord, have we not prophesied in thy name? and in thy name have cast out devils? and in thy name done many wonderful works? [23] And then will I profess unto them, I never knew you: depart from me, ye that work iniquity. **Matthew 7:21-23**

In times of fires, earthquakes, flooding and other disasters, people do not discriminate as to who they are going to rescue based on the religion of these victims. If we interpret the words of Jesus as saying that all who have done good deeds towards Christians, such as disaster relief, have done it as unto Him or in His name, then we would have to conclude that Jesus is saying that the basis of entering heaven is simply providing proof that they have done good. Since doing good to others is the principle teaching of all religions, therefore all who are faithful to their religion, even if they have rejected Jesus, will make it to heaven. Clearly, that is not what Jesus meant.

Having done a good deed toward a brother of Jesus because of his desperate need and then on Judgement Day claiming thatwe did it as unto Jesus and in His name is not the same as doing a good deed toward a person whowe know is a fellow believer. We ministered to their needs not because we hoped our acts of goodness would qualify us for heaven or becausewe were touched with their extreme infirmities, but rather because we know that they are family. Christians have a very special bonding with fellow believers (brethren) because we all were born of the same Father and entered into the Kingdom of God through the same birth canal.

> As we have therefore opportunity, let us do good unto all *men*, especially unto them who are of the household of faith. **Galatians 6:10**
>
> But if any provide not for his own, and specially for those of his own house, he hath denied the faith, and is worse than an infidel. **1 Timothy 5:8**

Typically, those who do not follow Jesus have no concern, except in times of community wide disasters, for the needs of those who do follow Jesus. Their claim of doing good, even to say that they did it as unto Jesus and in His name will not fool Jesus on Judgment Day. Though there's no proof that they are telling the truth when they make this claim, Jesus will remind them that the reason that He knows that they did not minister to His brethren as their own brethren is because, having rejected Jesus and refusing to be born again, they have no family connection with them.

> By this shall all *men* know that ye are my disciples, if ye have love one to another. **John 13:35**

Wherein they think it strange that ye run not with *them* to the same excess of riot, speaking evil of *you*: **1 Peter 4:4**

They went out from us, but they were not of us; for if they had been of us, they would *no doubt* have continued with us: but *they went out,* that they might be made manifest that they were not all of us. **1 John 2:19**

On Judgment Day, Jesus will tell these nations, who neglectedto care for the needs of His brethren, that though they will claim that they did many wonderful works in His name and followed His example, any acts of righteousness and compassion that they did do, did not originate from hearts that were truly connected to Him. Since He said that He never knew them, therefore, though it is possible, following a community wide disaster, that they helped victims that also included the brethren of Jesus, they didn't do so because these victims were brothers and sisters in the Lord.

I am sure most of us have heard these sayings, "Birds of a feather flock together" and "He's not heavy, he's my brother."

One summer my older brother and I went to visit with our grandparents in Comber, Ontario, when I was about 7 and he about 10. It was at that time that my brother was just beginning to show his dominance over the rest of us. In the following years his dominance turned into emotional and physical abuse which I will explain in further detail in a later chapter. But at the time of our visit with our grandparents I was only just beginning to develop a fear of him.

One afternoon he came back to the house telling us that he had encountered some other boys who were a bit of a challenge to him. But my brother was never one to show fear. Apparently, he indicated to these boys that he wasn't afraid of them and that he would see them again that evening. But as he was about to walk to the village center, surprisingly, he invited me to go with him.

I got the feeling that he invited me, not because I could help him if a fight broke out because I was not at all that kind of person, but because he knew that my presence with him would indicate to these boys that he had backing and that this would show strength in unity. As it turns out, nothing happened. But it made a very big impression on me that my brother, who was already beginning to cause me to fear him, knew that there is strength in the bond that exists between brothers.

So likewise, we as a Christian family, though we may have our squabbles at home, when we face the world and those who hate the truths that have divided us from them, and when we sense their opposition and threats, we will drop offenses and bond together knowing that we are brothers and sisters in the Lord. This bonding exists simply because we have in common, which the worldly people do not have, the same Father from which flows His love, righteousness and peace. The evidence, then, of being citizens of heaven is not the good deeds we've done for the brethren of Jesus, but rather our knowing that we are connected with them through our new birth experiences.

Jesus told another story of a man who asked Him as to what he needed to do to have eternal life. In it He illustrates how people have been misinformed about salvation. Many are of the belief that simply following the Ten Commandments and sacrificially using their own resources to care for the needs of others, which was exemplified by Jesus, qualifies them for heaven.

> [16] And, behold, one came and said unto him, Good Master, what good thing shall I do, that I may have eternal life? [17] And he said unto him, Why callest thou me good? *there is* none good but one, *that is*, God: but if thou wilt enter into life, keep the commandments...[20] The young man

saith unto him, All these things have I kept from my youth up: what lack I yet? ²¹ Jesus said unto him, If thou wilt be perfect, go *and* sell that thou hast, and give to the poor, and thou shalt have treasure in heaven: and come *and* follow me. ²² But when the young man heard that saying, he went away sorrowful: for he had great possessions. ²³ Then said Jesus unto his disciples, Verily I say unto you, That a rich man shall hardly enter into the kingdom of heaven. ²⁴ And again I say unto you, It is easier for a camel to go through the eye of a needle, than for a rich man to enter into the kingdom of God. ²⁵ When his disciples heard *it*, they were exceedingly amazed, saying, Who then can be saved? ²⁶ But Jesus beheld *them*, and said unto them, With men this is impossible; but with God all things are possible. **Matthew 19:16-17, 20-26**

This young man believed it was doing good things that would qualify him for eternal life. He thought his diligence in following the commandments meant he lacked nothing. Though Jesus said keeping them would give life, He wanted him to realize that keeping them, even with his best effort, was impossible. The commandments would reveal to him his sin so that he would become aware of his need for forgiveness. He then would come to understand that the purpose of these TenCommandments was to point him to a Savior. Apparently, he understood none of these truths.

Jesus proved to him that he was living contrary even to the very first commandment, that He did not love God with all his heart. God was not His primary resource. When asked to give up his wealth, which is what he relied on to carry him through life, he found it very hard to believe that to overcome his reliance on riches he needed to show a willingness to part from all of them. He walked away very sorrowfully because he had many possessions.

> ¹⁷ Charge them that are rich in this world, that they be not highminded, nor trust in uncertain riches, but in the living God, who giveth us richly all things to enjoy; ¹⁸ That they do good, that they be rich in good works, ready to distribute, willing to communicate; **1 Timothy 6:17-18**

Many people feel really good about themselves when they demonstrate genuine care for others. Because they are following the example set by Jesus, they believe God is so impressed with their loving deeds that He will reward them with eternal life. They find it equally as difficult, as did this young man, to believe that Jesus requires them to stop relying on doing these good deeds.

However, Jesus does not tell us to stop doing good. He merely tells us to stop relying on good deeds to get us into heaven. Many of us who rely on our abilities to keep the commandments may not understand that our own resources amount to nothing. Some of us have re-interpreted the words of Jesus to mean that our doing good, especially if done sacrificially, will entitle us to "enter into life" (Matthew 19:17). The response of Jesus to this man clearly demonstrates the futility of doing anything at all to impress God. Fulfilling even the first commandment is impossible.

Jesus used the illustration of a camel so that we would not misinterpret His words about the way into heaven. He said it was no more possible for a rich person, that is, any person dependent on the wealth of his own resources (abilities), to enter heaven than for a camel to squeeze through the eye of a needle. But many of us have turned His illustration of "impossibility" into possibility.

There are some who preach the doctrine that is often referred to as "Possibility Thinking." I am not saying that it is wrong to adopt this kind of thinking. It agrees with the scriptural exhortation to believe that we can do all things through Christ because He strengthens us. But sometimes these possibility thinkers want us to believe to be possible the things Jesus clearly said are impossible. Though He said it, we then turn around and try to make it possible through "possibility thinking."

For instance, the Bible warn us that evil communications will corrupt our good manners and that if we don't follow these instructions of God's Word, then we will reap negative consequences. Many are trying their hardest through possibility thinking to prove that admonition to not be true.

I know of women who, though they knew their boyfriends were not fully committed to Jesus, yet because they were willing to go to church with them and displayed a potential of becoming a believer in Jesus, decided to marry them. Deliberately ignoring certain red flags that indicated to them that their boyfriends were only pretending to have that potential, they decided to believe that with enough godly influence they soon would become believers.

While it does happen sometimes that the unbelieving spouse finally becomes godly, in most of these marriages, the godly mates either compromise their principals or they end up with broken hearts and broken marriages. These women discovered that their receiving evil communications and influences from others, did, even as the scriptures predicted, corrupt and do great damage to their lives.

Jesus said it's no more possible to enter heaven by keeping the 10 commandments than it is for a camel to go through the eye of a needle. It's because they don't want to believe this statement that many people will interpret the eye of the needle to mean something far different from what Jesus meant. Jesus was familiar with fishing and the fishing nets that fishermen needed. Though I am not certain of it, I presume Jesus was referring to the needle that was used to sew these nets.

But there are those who have come up with the theory that the eye of a needle that Jesus was referring to was this small gate in one of the walls bordering the city of Jerusalem. They believed that camels, if they were to be stripped of the load that was normally on them, could get on their knees and somehow wiggle and squeeze their way through this very small gate.

Interpreting Jesus's words this way allows these people, though it would not have been easy, to believe that they could take off their load of personal interests, get on their knees, and, like a camel, squeeze and wiggle their way through heaven's gate. They then could point to their scars and woundsas proof that they made great sacrifices,when using personal resources and talents, in their efforts to care for the needy and down trodden. They would then present these good deeds and the wise use of their resources to God as evidence that they are entitled to enter heaven.

I know ofsome people who believe that their deliberate sacrifices, especially if it involves much suffering and even the loss of their lives, will convince God to reward them with eternal life. I've heard stories where people believed that through their own sufferings, such as crawling a mile on glass, that they were identifying with the sufferings of Jesus and that in some small way they were contributing, along with Jesus,to the payment that bought them their salvation.

People who rely on sacrifices to win God's favor, believing that they did what this young man failed to do, will be very disappointed if that is their sole dependence on getting into heaven. They were trying to make possible what Jesus had already declared was impossible.

> [24] And when Jesus saw that he was very sorrowful, he said, How hardly shall they that have riches enter into the kingdom of God! [25] For it is easier for a camel to go through a needle's eye, than for a rich man to enter into the kingdom of God. **Luke 18:24-25**

Many will interpret this word "hardly" to mean that some people who are relying on their riches, though it will be difficult, will just barely squeeze their way into heaven. They will claim that though it can hardly be done, but with a strong sacrificial effort they will eventually get it done. But this word "hardly" is equivalent to asking how hard it was for a rich man to enter heaven. How hard was it? As hard as it was for a camel to squeeze through the eye of a sewing needle, which of course we know is totally impossible.

So, if we are feeling the squeeze in our effort to make it to heaven, then that is a very good clue that we are depending on our own resources instead of on God's. Though we may make great sacrifices and give up everything to serve God and our fellow man, we have no more advantage to getting into heaven than those who made no sacrifices. It is commendable when we expend our resources for worthy causes. But we must not forget that these sacrifices contribute nothing toward earning God's favor. Our salvation, we must remember, is a gift and therefore cannot be earned.

If we discover it's very hard to stop depending on our natural ability to love others, hopefully, we won't, like this young man, turn away sorrowfully deciding that if our efforts are not acceptable with God, then we won't rely on His efforts either. Some believe their resources and talents are so important to the growth of God's kingdom that they cannot imagine that God would expect them to stop depending on them. When they came to realize that God's estimation of the value of their talents weren't nearly as high as theirs, they then, like this young man, turned away sorrowfully.

Many times, I have heard stories from people who have told me that they either are no longer serving God or are tempted to quit on Him because all their blood, sweat, and tears over years of faithful dedication has left them with nothing. One man told me that he cannot any longer believe in a God that failed to warn him of a con artist that scammed him out of his money. Another man told me, though he intended to serve God through his medical and doctoring training, that he was angry at Him because He did not protect him from a car accident that seriously injured his brain, ending his career and his ability to produce an income. I've heard some people curse God because after serving Him for a long time, God did not spare their child from dying a tragic death.

> [25] When his disciples heard *it*, they were exceedingly amazed, saying, Who then can be saved? [26] But Jesus beheld *them*, and said unto them, With men this is impossible; but with God all things are possible. **Matthew 19:25-26**

The reaction of the disciples upon learning that this young man had no advantage to making it to heaven because of his riches is very revealing. The disciples seemed to believe that riches were proof of God's blessings and that poverty was evidence of His disapproval. They reasoned that if the rich, who have an abundance of resources to prove that they have God's favor, couldn't make it, then what hope was there for those who have no evidence of God's favor?

Like the disciples of Jesus, some of us will be "exceedingly amazed" to learn that our acts of kindnesses and love toward others provides us no advantage. Though imitating the life of Jesus is a beautiful way to live, relying on these good deeds to get us to heaven is a stumbling block that we must overcome.

Thankfully, God has given us enough light so that we can find the true way. Jesus said the way is narrow, but it's not so narrow that we must squeeze to get in. He said only robbers try to squeeze through a window. Children will use only the front doorway. What seemed impossible for getting into heaven, Jesus said God would make possible. The possibility of getting into heaven was through only one door, and Jesus alone is that door.

> Verily, verily, I say unto you, He that entereth not by the door into the sheepfold, but climbeth up some other way, the same is a thief and a robber. **John 10:1**
>
> ⁷ Then said Jesus unto them again, Verily, verily, I say unto you, I am the door of the sheep. ⁸ All that ever came before me are thieves and robbers: but the sheep did not hear them. ⁹ I am the door: by me if any man enter in, he shall be saved, and shall go in and out, and find pasture. **John 10:7-9** Page 33

What seemed impossible for getting into heaven God made possible when making candidates for salvation members of His family. The possibility of getting into heaven was becoming a child of God through the new birth. No longer would we need to impress God with sacrificial service.

> Then Peter said, Silver and gold have I none; but such as I have give I thee: In the name of Jesus Christ of Nazareth rise up and walk. **Acts 3:6**

Peter said that he has Jesus. The kindness that he showed to this crippled man was not so that he could impress God and then be entitled to enter heaven, but rather was the outflow of the new nature of Jesus in him which he received through the new birth. Though his old nature was capable of generating good deeds, he realized that since a corrupt tree can produce only corrupt fruit, these good deeds, if they came from his old nature, would be somewhat tainted and corrupted.

For instance, though a man's wife or sweetheart is thrilled to receive a bouquet of red roses from which comes a sweet-smelling aroma, if she didn't know at the time she received them, surely within a few days she'll come to realize that what she received, though it appeared to be alive, was already dead. Likewise, unless our good deeds flow from out of our relationship with God through Jesus, all the goodness that we share with others, though they may please the recipient, flowed from a heart that is dead (not connected to God) and ultimately will produce a rotten smell of death.

Peter knew he was going to heaven because the services that he sacrificially extended toward others did not spring from his original fallen nature but rather from the new nature that the Holy Spirit planted in his heart when he received Him just a few weeks or months earlier.

In this chapter we have learned that imitating the wonderful deeds of Jesus, following the commandments, relying on our resources, and making extreme sacrifices will never make us ready for heaven. We have come to realize that it is not our faith in the loving example of Jesus' life that saves us but is our faith in His sacrificial voluntary death on the cross (which I thoroughly explain in part III) that is the only way in which our old nature can be replaced with a born-again new nature.

CHAPTER 4

REALIZE WHAT BORN AGAIN IS NOT

The first step in the process of birthing Jesus into our lives, conception, begins when people hear the message of the gospel enlightening them of the condition of their diseased corrupt heart and of their need for a brand new one.

> Jesus answered and said unto him, Verily, verily, I say unto thee, Except a man be born again, he cannot see the kingdom of God. **John 3:3**
> ⁶ That which is born of the flesh is flesh; and that which is born of the Spirit is spirit. ⁷ Marvel not that I said unto thee, Ye must be born again. ⁸ The wind bloweth where it listeth, and thou hearest the sound thereof, but canst not tell whence it cometh, and whither it goeth: so is every one that is born of the Spirit. **John 3:6-8**

The phrase "born again" seems to be quite common in our society. From a survey conducted many years ago by a professional pollster, I heard from a reporter that of the sample group that was surveyed, about 45% of them considered themselves as "born again" believers. Thoughmany claim to be born again, I wonder how many understand what the born-again term actually means?

And if 45% of the population is born again and thus on their way to heaven, then what do we make of the words of Jesus who said,

> [13] Enter ye in at the strait gate: for wide *is* the gate, and broad *is* the way, that leadeth to destruction, and many there be which go in thereat: [14] Because strait *is* the gate, and narrow *is* the way, which leadeth unto life, and few there be that find it. **Matthew 7:13-14**
>
> Marvel not that I said unto thee, Ye must be born again. **John 3:7**

The reason that very few find the way of salvation is because they have not understood thetrue meaning of what Jesus said about born again. The truth that you most need to consider and be sure that you do not neglect is His statement, "Ye must be born again." He said the only ones going to heavenare thosewith the newborn nature. Since He said it's necessary for entering heaven, it is therefore paramount that you investigate to make sure you understand what it truly means.

> [9] *That* was the true Light, which lighteth every man that cometh into the world. [10] He was in the world, and the world was made by him, and the world knew him not. [11] He came unto his own, and his own received him not. **John 1:9-11**

By telling us that Jesus is the true Light that "lighteth every man," John is implying other lights in the world are not true. He explains that though Jesus came to His own – to those whom He created – yet we followed a light that led us away from Him. We have elected to follow lights that caused us to give our attention to idols.

> That seeing they may see, and not perceive; and hearing they may hear, and not understand; lest at any time they should be converted, and *their* sins should be forgiven them. **Mark 4:12**
>
> For the time will come when they will not endure sound doctrine; but after their own lusts shall they heap to themselves teachers, having itching ears; **2 Timothy 4:3**

Though they've heard the truth, when people don't truly understand what they have heard, they will come up with alternative interpretations and explanations as to why they didn't respond to it. Though I would like to think that I'm a very disciplined student, I know there have been times when I made it appear that I had listened carefully to a lesson, a sermon, or an instruction, and yet knew that I had not fully understood it.

In 1988 I lived in Edmonton, Alberta and worked in a hotel at the front desk. I assured the other front desk clerk, as he was training me, that I understood all his instructions. I wasn't willing to admit it then, but I didn't want him to repeat his instructions because that would mean that he would now know that I had not given him my full attention the first time. I had briefly let my mind think on other things even though I tried to make it appear that I had been listening carefully.

So, after he gave the instructions on what to do if the fire alarm rings, knowing that I did not understand it fully, I was hopeful that I would never have to deal with a fire alarm during my night shift. But it was only two or three nights after that that the alarm did ring. In the 10 months that I worked there as a front desk clerk and night auditor, that night was the only time the alarm sounded.

Apparently, this alarm was deliberately triggered by someone who had been drinking in one of the bars at closing time around 1 or 2 in the morning. When this happens, the alarm sounds only in the foyer area and not throughout the entire hotel. I was told that there would be a 2-minute delay after which it would then sound everywhere in the whole building. Since there was no fire, it was my responsibility to make sure that I had cancelled this alarm before it rung and awoke all the hotel patrons.

I remembered that I was supposed to go into the kitchen area and pull a certain lever or flip a switch. But when I opened the panel it was far more complicated than I had realized. That was because I had not paid close attention when I received these initial instructions. Remember, I had only 2 minutes from the time I first heard the local alarm at the front desk to the time that I had to flip this switch to prevent the general alarm from sounding. I was in the process of trying to figure it out when, indeed, the alarm sounded throughout the whole building, presumably waking up all the patrons.

The next day my boss phoned me at home to inform me that, indeed, all the residents in the hotel were awakened by these alarms. I was so surprised when he did not cancel my schedule as I thought for sure he was going to let me go. Afterward, I was very careful to follow all instructions. When he told me how to convince people, who were tempted to go elsewhere, to stay with this hotel, I followed his instructions exactly. A few months later he told me that I sold more rooms than any of the other front desk night clerks. He admitted that he almost was going to fire me over that fire alarm mistake but was now very glad that he had decided to give me another chance.

The one thing I learned is that we must not let our pride get in the way of asking for clarity when we are not sure. Most people who are not sure of the way of salvation and never do discover it, missed these truths that would've saved their souls simply because they were too proud to ask.

To make sure we understand who the people are who will be saved, we learn from John who the people are, who think they are saved, but, in fact, are not. Later, I will explain what being born again is. But right now, we will focus on John's explanation on what born again is not.

I have observed that people who wish to remain in charge of their own lives, and yet be known as born-again believers, will re-interpret born-again with an entirely different meaning. They believe that being born again has something to do with acquiring a good understanding of the nature of God. Because they think they understand Him, they believe it's not in His nature to keep out of heaven those who have at least acknowledged Him. Though they are following a path that has excluded Jesus, they believe that their confession of God as their Father (because He is Creator) is all that is necessary to get them into heaven. After all, the scripture teaches us that Jesus paid for the sins of the whole world:

> And he is the propitiation for our sins: and not for ours only, but also for *the sins of* the whole world. **1 John 2:2**

Propitiation means the wrath of God against us is placated or appeased – that the judgment that was poured on to Jesus has satisfied the justice of the Father. This scripture supports the view that since Jesus took all of God's judgment on the cross, therefore, no one in the whole world has to face His wrath. They believe every person entering eternity will in some way benefit from His sacrifice – especially for those who acknowledge this truth.

In other words, they believe everyone who trusts in the favor, the justice, and the mercy of God, even if they have no personal relationship with Him, are born-again. While these attributes about the nature of God are true, the people who choose to leave Jesus out of their lives cannot expect these qualities of God to deliver them. The favor, the justice and the mercy of God can work for their benefit only because of Jesus. Those who have turned Him away, unwittingly have also rejected the flow of these graces.

From our study of his gospel we will see if the apostle John agrees with these assertions that anyone who simply acknowledges or confesses their belief in these attributes of God, that that is proof that they are saved. The devil also concedesto the existence and power of God. Yet he and all the demons that work with him tremble at the thought of their future.

> [12] But as many as received him, to them gave he power to become the sons of God, *even* to them that believe on his name: [13] Which were born, not of blood, nor of the will of the flesh, nor of the will of man, but of God. **John 1:12-13**

Many people will remind us that they are connected to God because they are connected to people who are connected to God. But their claim to God's favor and to their entitlement to enter heaven because of these connections and family ancestry John counters with "**not of blood.**"

By producing genealogy or membership records, this group believed that they can count on special favor from God. They have confidence that no matter how they have lived their lives and how deserving of punishment, their earthly family's historic tie with Him would secure for them His favor. Since they believe they're God's children through these family connections, they believe that they will make it to heaven simply because they know that God would never refuse His own children. Their reasoning is that since we would never refuse our children no matter how badly they have misbehaved, then neither would God refuse us no matter how badly we have rebelled.

When I was in my teens, I remember having the feeling that I am safe simply because I knew that my parents were believers and that I regularly went with them to their church. I remember thinking that the people who did not attend our church are on their way to hell. I believed that it was only our denomination that taught the truth and that all other religions and denominations had been deceived into believing lies.

For a long time while attending this church, though no fault of the leadership, I felt my hope of being saved was my continued connection with this church or denomination. I believed I was safe because of my connection to my parents. It was a real shock when I came to realize, even after becoming an adult, that there are others outside of our denomination that were also saved. I was like Peter who, after preaching to the Gentiles, was shocked to see that they too had the Holy Spirit.

Because they belong to an "elite group" based on their ancestry or associations many church groups claim that that is why they have God's favor and access to heaven. They believe that they are secure simply because there are records that can prove that they are in good standing with their church and that they have done nothing to warrant the consideration of being excommunicated.

However, if there is no evidence that they are members of God's spiritual family, their claim of being related to Him is unfounded. God welcomes into heaven only those who are His children. And since no one is His child unless they have been born into His family through the new-birth experience, these who have not been born again will be denied entrance. They will have no more success in convincing God that they are His children than those, who reminded Jesus that they were the descendants of Abraham (see John 8:39), that they were God's children.

People will remind us that God is forever just and that He will always reward those who live according to His law. They concluded that they deserved God's reward because they had overcome the many tendencies and inclinations of their flesh and that their good deeds far outweighed their misdeeds and shortcomings. These who believe that they have earned God's justice and reward John counters with "**not of the will of the flesh.**"

It could be that John had in mind the Pharisees whom Jesus acknowledged as people who observed the demands of the law more scrupulously than any other group. They believed their good deeds would not go unnoticed, and that God would be obligated to recompense them.

Jesus told of one Pharisee, who, proud of his righteousness, thanked the Lord that he was not like sinners and tax collectors. Though he excelled at keeping the law, according to Jesus, the tax collectors and harlots were more likely to make it to heaven before him (Matthew 21:31-32).

So it is today. Some have lived upright, moral lives and have appealed to God's "fairness" hoping to make Him obligated to let them into heaven because of their good deeds. Others, instead of going through Jesus to access God's grace to overcome their fleshly habits, have joined 12-step recovery programs. They try to make a case that they deserve God's justice because of their success in overcoming addictions. But because they have not confessed their need for Jesus and the new birth, they will not be successful in persuading God to let them into heaven.

When I was pastoring in Shell Lake, Saskatchewan, I became acquainted with a man who had been an alcoholic for most of his adult life. But prior to my coming to his town he began to attend AA meetings. When I met him, he told me that he is now born again. He gave all the credit for his transformation to this AA program because they helped him to depend on a certain higher power to overcome his addiction. When I asked him if it was the power of Jesus to whom he was referring he said he did not believe in Jesus and that neither was it necessary to believe in Him.

And finally, people will remind us that they can count on getting into heaven because they know that God is forever merciful and will always grant forgiveness to those who request it. To those who relied on this kind of logic to convince God that He, because of His mercy, must allow them into heaven, John counters with **"not of the will of man."** No one will ever be successful in their efforts to reason with God that He must forgive them because of His nature of great mercy.

Jesus tells us that on the day of judgment many will present arguments to Him as to why He must show them mercy and allow them into heaven. To all these people, though they claim that they did many wonderful works in His name, Jesus will say,

> I never knew you, depart from me ye workers of iniquity.**Matthew 7:23**

God rejects their plea for mercy because all their lifetime they had rejected His plea to open their hearts to Jesus to receive His abundant mercy and grace.

These people will reason that a compassionate God could never turn anyone away simply because of their neglect to believe all the truth. They will remind Him that His mercy has always been from everlasting to everlasting. They have convinced themselves that if they can demonstrate a genuine sorrow for their mistakes and neglect, then God, because it is His nature to show mercy, must forgive them.

Though John probably wasn't thinking of him, Esau is an excellent example of this kind of thinking and reasoning:

> ^{16} Lest there *be* any fornicator, or profane person, as Esau, who for one morsel of meat sold his birthright. ^{17} For ye know how that afterward, when he would have inherited the blessing, he was rejected: for he found no place of repentance, though he sought it carefully with tears. **Hebrews 12:16-17**

Esau demonstrated that his desire for food was more important than his desire to hold on to the exclusive heritage God gave to him at birth. After he was deceived by his brother and sold his birth right to him for some porridge, Esau strongly appealed to his father to restore the blessing that he believed rightfully belonged to him. Though he expressed sorrow, even to the point of shedding tears, the Hebrews writer said there was no real repentance or change in his heart for selling his birthright. His poor regard for his spiritual heritage had not changed. Though he reasoned with his father, Isaac, that he was entitled to this blessing because he was the eldest, arguing that he had been deceived by his younger brother, Jacob, he could not persuade his father to change his mind.

Today people have as little regard for Jesus, the substitute for the punishment they deserve, as Esau had for his birthright. Since God's mercy flows only through Jesus, in rejecting Him they have dismissed His mercy and excluded themselves from their only way of being saved. They may tearfully sorrow over their destructive and corrupt nature, perhaps even reminding God that they did wrong because they were deceived or because others had convinced them that they were not accountable for their bad behavior due to mental illness. Though God invites them to reason with Him, this kind of rationale or appeal to His mercy will not persuade Him to change His mind. But He will change His mind when people, in humility and contriteness, come to Him through Jesus.

All these erroneous ways and beliefs that I described in the above paragraphs had the effect of aborting the born-again process of those candidates for salvation who had heard about the favor, justice and mercy of God. Although they've heard the gospel message, all these groups who have neglected to believe that God will never allow into heaven those who have refused escaping *their fallen nature* through the new birth, God must now block from entering.

In this chapter we have learned that John soundly refutes ideas about alternative ways of getting into heaven. Connection with God is neither by blood, nor by the will of the flesh, nor by the will of man, but only by the work of God's Spirit to produce the new born nature. Only to those who personally receive Jesus as their Savior does God recognize as members of His family.

If you have not already done so, God is pleading with you to call to Him for His mercy. When you respond to the drawing power of the Holy Spirit you will get through the deceptions and enticements of the world and become transformed through the new birth. The seed of God's Word will take root in your heart, overcome your resistance, and enable you to go through the birthing process until the formation of Jesus in you is completed.

CHAPTER 5

APPRECIATE THE NEW BIRTH PROCESS

Thankfully, God has made it possible for the new birth process to be completed.

> [25] Then will I sprinkle clean water upon you, and ye shall be clean: from all your filthiness, and from all your idols, will I cleanse you. [26] A new heart also will I give you, and a new spirit will I put within you: and I will take away the stony heart out of your flesh, and I will give you an heart of flesh. [27] And I will put my spirit within you, and cause you to walk in my statutes, and ye shall keep my judgments, and do *them*. **Ezekiel 36:25-27**
>
> [4] But God, who is rich in mercy, for his great love wherewith he loved us, [5] Even when we were dead in sins, hath quickened us together with Christ, (by grace ye are saved;) But now in Christ Jesus ye who sometimes were far off are made nigh by the blood of Christ. **Ephesians 2:4-5, 13**

We can see that our new hearts are the righteousness and the holiness of Jesus. Paul referred to it as our new creation, or new man.

> Therefore if any man *be* in Christ, *he is* a new creature: old things are passed away; behold, all things are become new. **2 Corinthians 5:17**
>
> ²² That ye put off concerning the former conversation the old man, which is corrupt according to the deceitful lusts; ²³ And be renewed in the spirit of your mind; ²⁴ And that ye put on the new man, which after God is created in righteousness and true holiness. **Ephesians 4:22-24**

That is why the transformation of our hearts is described as born again by the seed of the Word of God. As any farmer or gardener will tell us, there can never be a harvest of fruit until there has first been a planting of seed.

> Being born again, not of corruptible seed, but of incorruptible, by the word of God, which liveth and abideth for ever. **1 Peter 1:23**

Though initially we rejected Jesus, God mercifully gave us opportunity to receive Him.

> ¹² But as many as received him, to them gave he power to become the sons of God, *even* to them that believe on his name: ¹³ Which were born, not of blood, nor of the will of the flesh, nor of the will of man, but of God. **John 1:12-13**

Being born again is the work of the Spirit to produce a new creation. Jesus said you should not marvel at needing to become born-again any more than you would marvel at the wind. Though you cannot tell exactly how it happened, your new-birth experience, just like the wind, will compel you to acknowledge that the landscape of your life has been completely changed. God has declared that those who have received Jesus are His exclusive possessions. John affirms that they have been born by His Spirit into His family and are delivered from God's wrath.

> He that believeth on the Son hath everlasting life: and he that believeth not the Son shall not see life; but the wrath of God abideth on him. **John 3:36**

As mentioned earlier, our new birth has absolutely nothing to do with family bloodlines, human effort, or well thought out reasoning. If it did, our corrupt nature would just be replaced by another corrupt nature. Our becoming qualified for heaven is based entirely on God's grace and mercy. We don't deserve salvation as we can do nothing to earn it. It is a gift. We can receive it only when we humbly acknowledge that we are sinners in need of forgiveness and are totally dependent on God to show us mercy. And that mercy is channeled to us only through Jesus.

> [34] Then said Mary unto the angel, How shall this be, seeing I know not a man? [35] And the angel answered and said unto her, The Holy Ghost shall come upon thee, and the power of the Highest shall overshadow thee: therefore also that holy thing which shall be born of thee shall be called the Son of God. [38] And Mary said, Behold the handmaid of the Lord; be it unto me according to thy word. And the angel departed from her. **Luke 1:34-35, 38**

Jesus was conceived of a virgin to escape the corruption and curse He otherwise would have inherited had He been conceived by an earthly father. Since our believing the promise of God's Word totally excludes any human effort, we also are of a virgin birth. When we, like Mary, receive into our minds the announced Word of God, the Holy Spirit comes upon this planted seed to begin the new birth process. Though our initial reception of the Word of God is the conception of a new life, the life of Jesus beginning to grow in the womb of our hearts, it is only when this formation of Jesus in our hearts is completed that we become born again.

This process of birthing Jesus in us could take as little as nine seconds, as it did for Mary, or even as long as nine or more months as it is I suspect for most people, until we are finally willing to confess "be it unto me according to thy Word." I think for most people, who are now born again, the conception stage of the born-again process began when they were children listening to their parents or Sunday School teacher sharing with them the message of the gospel. It was only when they became adults many years later that the gestation stage of their spiritual "pregnancy" came to completion that they finally birthed the born-again new nature of Jesus.

In the bus ministry at the church that I attend, many children are picked up every Sunday and then put in classes where they hear a presentation of the gospel, the planting of the seed that begins the new birth process (conception), and which then grows in the formation of Jesus in them. Many people who rode the buses as children, after reaching their teens, strayed away from what they had learned. But then years later, after returning to the church, some have testified that what they learned in Sunday School played a significant role in bringing them to the point of finally confessing Jesus as their Savior and Lord.

When Peter preached the message of Jesus, his audience asked him what they must do.

> Then Peter said unto them, Repent, and be baptized every one of you in the name of Jesus Christ for the remission of sins, and ye shall receive the gift of the Holy Ghost. **Acts 2:38**

Peter indicated that if their repentance and belief in Jesus was genuine, they would receive the gift of the Holy Spirit.

> ⁴⁵ And they of the circumcision which believed were astonished, as many as came with Peter, because that on the Gentiles also was poured out the gift of the Holy Ghost. ⁴⁶ For they heard them speak with tongues, and magnify God. Then answered Peter, ⁴⁷ Can any man forbid water, that these should not be baptized, which have received the Holy Ghost as well as we? **Acts 10:45-47**

In this passage, Peter's emphasis was not on tongues but on his need to recognize, based on the evidence, that these people were indeed born again. Tongues simply made it easier for him, because of a similar recent experience (see Acts 2:1–4), to conclude that they had received the gift of the Holy Spirit and thus born again. Without this evidence, he would not have recommended water baptism (I will thoroughly discuss the evidence of the gift of the Holy Spirit and the purpose of water baptism in later chapters).

Peter needed evidence because he knew that for many coming to faith could be a very slow process. The planting of the seed of the Word of God in people's hearts is like that of planting a seed conceived in the womb to begin the process of becoming born. After this conception, many people have the faith to accept it as the truth and immediately are born again. Others may give the appearance that they truly believe, but as illustrated in the parable of the sower explained at the end of this chapter, only life's trials can reveal if they hadconception to birthing kind of faith.

While there are many who do not, most candidates for salvation who have been told of their need usually struggle with sorrow. After conception, deciding whether to surrender their lives totally to Jesus can be like the travail of a woman who is going to have a baby. Some agonize when contemplating the consequences of losing their personal freedoms. Many will agonize with this decision for a long while because, as we remember, salvation can happen only after we have denied ourselves and have fully surrendered our will over to the control and Lordship of Jesus.

> [21] A woman when she is in travail hath sorrow, because her hour is come: but as soon as she is delivered of the child, she remembereth no more the anguish, for joy that a man is born into the world. [22] And ye now therefore have sorrow: but I will see you again, and your heart shall rejoice, and your joy no man taketh from you.
> **John 16:21-22**

Jesus knew the disciples would face great tribulation when learning of His departure. He knew they would think He had forsaken them and would've felt sorrow like that of a mother with birth pangs (see John 16:22) once He had departed. The disciples needed His encouragement.

Jesus cheered them up by telling them the coming of the Holy Spirit would be like that of the arrival of a newborn. He said their sorrow would turn to joy the same way a laboring mother's distress turns into joy once she's delivered her baby. As she holds her baby and the two of them begin to bond, "She remembereth no more the anguish" (see John 16:21). Therefore, it was the arrival of their "baby," the Holy Spirit, that turned the sorrow of Jesus's disciples into joy.

A birthing into the kingdom of God is also like a woman's pregnancy. While initially the labor pains of a candidate for salvation are intense with months or even years of conviction, the Word of God continues to grow until finally the formation of Jesus in them is completed. And this formation of Jesus is only completed when, after much resistance, they surrender their lives over to Him totally. Because the joy of their newborn baby (the Holy Spirit generated born-again new nature) is so overwhelming, the sorrow that they experienced in getting to this stage is very quickly forgotten.

Though Jesus is beginning to be formed in the womb of our hearts, He is not birthed until we reach the stage where we willingly commit our lives to Him. During the incubation period after conception, we respond to Holy Spirit conviction to remove hindrances that steal the seed of God's Word conceived in our hearts. We eliminate anything in our lives that would interfere with the development of this seed of Jesus in us and that would otherwise cause an abortion or miscarriage.

> [19] My little children, of whom I travail in birth again until Christ be formed in you, [20] I desire to be present with you now, and to change my voice; for I stand in doubt of you. **Galatians 4:19-20**

When Paul preached God's Word under the anointing of the Holy Spirit, he indicated he took part in birthing new believers. However, what he initially believed to be genuine born-again experiences among these Galatians, he began doubting. Upon observing the condition of some of their hearts he suspected Christ had not been formed in them after all and thus were not born again. He figured he might have to start over again this process of birthing them into God's family.

> ¹⁵ For though ye have ten thousand instructors in Christ, yet *have ye* not many fathers: for in Christ Jesus I have begotten you through the gospel. ¹⁶ Wherefore I beseech you, be ye followers of me. **1 Corinthians 4:15-16**

Paul was also involved in the birthing of some of the believers in Corinth. Because these Corinthian believers gave evidence of being birthed into God's family, Paul, because it was the seed that he personally planted into the womb of their hearts through his preaching of the gospel, said he had begotten them in the same way that a father has begotten his son.

But when there was no longer any evidence to convince him that they were truly born from above, he became suspicious and doubtful of their new birth, at least of the Galatians, and that this born-again process of forming Christ in them, since the earlier pregnancy had been aborted, would have to be restarted or resumed.

When I say aborted, though it usually means the death of the baby, I simply mean that the birthing process which was within minutes of being completed, has now been stopped or put on hold. This birthing process may resume within a few days or it might be many years before the formation of the life of Jesus is finally completed to bring about this long overdue new birth.

Once candidates for salvation have received Jesus and have been born again, this newborn nature is in them permanently. Paul's comments indicated he thought that the new birth process in these Galatian candidates hadn't reached full term. The formation of Jesus in them appeared to have been sabotaged or aborted due to lack of commitment. More of God's Word anointed by the Holy Spirit would have to be planted in their hearts before they would commit. While for many, because of the hardness of their hearts the development of Jesus is very slow, forothers, when their hearts have been cultivated, the life of Jesus is formed in them quickly.

In my early teen years, I heard the message of salvation many times. A few times, I mouthed the prayer of inviting Jesus into my life but continued to resist Holy Spirit conviction in my heart. Though I said the prayer with my lips, I knew in my heart I hadn't fully surrendered the control of my life. While it's possible I was born again in one of those experiences, I cannot say for sure.It was in 1966 when I was nineteen and working at home on my grade-eleven assignment that I finally overcame my resistance to the Lord and gave my life fully to Him. It was only then that I had assurance that the many years of the formation of Jesus in my heartwas finally completed.

After the planting of the seed of the Word of God in the womb of my heartwhen I was a young child, the growth of the life of Jesus in my heart was slow and had even stalled for a few years. But when this conceived life of Jesus grew in me to the point where I was finally willing to say "be it unto me according to thy word," then this new life of Jesus in me was birthed.

Obviously, the natural and spiritual birth analogy has limitations. Though physically, life begins at conception, for this study I'm using the gestation or pregnancy period to illustrate the process leading to the new life experience. While conception begins when the seed of God's Word is planted in the heart, it's only at the end of the pregnancy, when this birthing process reaches its completion, that there is a new birth.

If there is an abortion in the natural process, an aborted baby's spirit goes to heaven. But in the spiritual realm, the candidate, whose birthing process is aborted, as illustrated in the parable of the sower, has no hope of making it to heaven until the formation and birthing stages have been resumed and completed.

In the parable of the sower,Jesus spoke of four categories of candidates for salvation (see Matthew 13:3–23). These first three candidates in this parable didnot make it to full term.

Theformation of Christ in them was aborted at various stages for various reasons.
1. Some allowed the enemy to steal away the seed of God's Word in their hearts, hardly giving their new "baby" a chance to get started.
2. Others endured their "pregnancies" for a while, but when they began to feel "morning sickness" (shallow, due to stony ground), they aborted, choosing to disregard God's Word.
3. Still others permitted the cares of their life (thorns) to choke out the Word, deciding that personal cares were more important than Christ being formed in them.
4. Only the fourth bore fruit. Since only the Holy Spirit can produce it, this fruit proves that the candidate endured to the end the travail of completing the birthing stages.

This parable describes the growth of the seed of God's Word in the hearts of candidates for salvation. It shows the various birthing stages and whether the formation of Christ in them:
1. has been aborted,
2. is still in the pregnancy prebirth stage, or
3. has been completed and birthed into the world.

In this chapter we have learned that if our receptivity to God's Word is weak and we abhor labor pains, it's likely we haven't yet endured all the stages to complete the formation of Christ in us. Though you may think you already are born again with a new nature, but if there is evidence to suggest that you are still dominated by your fallen nature and that all your efforts to escape your diseased heart has proven to be futile, then it is quite likely it is one particular sin, not a multitude of them that has interfered with your attempt to escape your old nature.

CHAPTER 6

SHOW A TRUE HEART OF REPENTANCE

Many years ago, I heard the song "Heaven is just a sin away." This secular song implied that if the couple overcame their temptation to commit adultery, they would be assured of making it to heaven. It is not uncommon for people to believe that it is their success in overcoming the tendency to indulge the flesh that will win God's approval and thus assure them of going to heaven.

It is essential that all of us come to realize that our diseased nature, unless it is replaced with the born-again new nature of Jesus, will continue to generate evil deeds. From the scriptures, we learn the good news that if we are willing to humbly admit that we are sinners, we can be healed of this terrible sickness that afflicts every one of us.

> How God anointed Jesus of Nazareth with the Holy Ghost and with power: who went about doing good, and healing all that were oppressed of the devil; for God was with him. **Acts 10:38**
>
> And the publican, standing afar off, would not lift up so much as *his* eyes unto heaven, but

smote upon his breast, saying, God be merciful to me a sinner. **Luke 18:13**

We have the assurance that Jesus is not at all judgmental. All throughout the Gospels, we see He was so loving toward sinners that He drew the fury and condemnation from the religious people for having anything to do with them. Jesus saw those who were in bondage to sin as sick people who needed a doctor to prescribe a healing medicine. For all who genuinely commit their lives to Jesus, their contaminated hearts will be replaced with a new one that is just like His.

> [10] And it came to pass, as Jesus sat at meat in the house, behold, many publicans and sinners came and sat down with him and his disciples. [11] And when the Pharisees saw *it*, they said unto his disciples, Why eateth your Master with publicans and sinners? [12] But when Jesus heard *that*, he said unto them, They that be whole need not a physician, but they that are sick. [13] But go ye and learn what *that* meaneth, I will have mercy, and not sacrifice: for I am not come to call the righteous, but sinners to repentance. **Matthew 9:10-13**

Jesus made it clear that we are sinners who need to repent of our sins. However, repentance is not so much turning from sin as it is in turning to Jesus. Most of us believe repentance means to stop sinning, but since we are beleaguered with a corrupt nature, how can we stop? It means that we make up our minds we want to stop and yet recognize we don't have the ability or power to stop. And if we're genuine in our desire to stop sinning, we will then turn to the one who will give us that ability to stop.

Therefore, repentance is our acknowledgment that we can stop sinning only when we allow Jesus to replace our corrupt nature with His righteous nature. It never works to try to overcome sinning through our own efforts. We need help. A 12-step addiction recovery program can do little more than to show us how deplorable our natural human condition is. The one-step program is the only one that works. It labors not with a multitude of sins but with just one.

The song was right! Indeed, heaven is only a sin away. But the sin that must be eliminated is not any of these sins people typically work hard to overcome. The Bible makes it clear that the only sin preventing us from seeing heaven is the sin of unbelief, the sin of refusing to accept Jesus as Savior. We learn about this sin and how we can overcome it from the words of Jesus:

> [8] And when he is come, he will reprove the world of sin, and of righteousness, and of judgment: [9] Of sin, because they believe not on me; **John 16:8-9**

If the work of Jesus and His Holy Spirit were to reprove us of each of our sins, then there would never be any end to our consciousness of our sins. We would always be keeping track of our progress as to how well we have done in overcoming sinful tendencies, only to discover we are either sensing inadequacy and guilt or self-sufficiency and pride. That is the description of religion, and we know that no one can ever be saved by or through their religion.

When people give in to the dictates of their flesh and have come to realize that they have done something that is likely to draw reproof or condemnation from others, though they may feel guilty, to deflect this guilt they will remind their loved ones that they are wrong to be judgmental toward them. It is this fear of condemnation from their loved ones that sometimes is the reason people are so reluctant to acknowledge their sins and to turn their lives over to Jesus.

But thankfully, Jesus sent the Holy Spirit to show us our sin of unbelief so that instead of feeling condemnation we will have the light that reveals His truth, and which will set us free from our constant attention on our fallen nature. When we respond in faith to the planted seed of God's Word in the womb of our hearts, rather than having religion we will have a relationship with God as one who has been newly birthed into His family.

Jesus won't condemn you for sin that you have no ability to overcome, but you leave yourself wide open for condemnation when you deliberately choose not to believe in Jesus.

> [17] For God sent not his Son into the world to condemn the world; but that the world through him might be saved. [18] He that believeth on him is not condemned: but he that believeth not is condemned already, because he hath not believed in the name of the only begotten Son of God. [19] And this is the condemnation, that light is come into the world, and men loved darkness rather than light, because their deeds were evil. [20] For every one that doeth evil hateth the light, neither cometh to the light, lest his deeds should be reproved. [21] But he that doeth truth cometh to the light, that his deeds may be made manifest, that they are wrought in God. **John 3:17-21**

The purpose of this light is to reveal that you have an utterly corrupt and evil nature. This revelation makes you aware that you need deliverance from this condition. This light also reveals that *escaping your fallen nature entangling your life and blocking your way* can come only through Jesus. Only then can you be free

Escaping Your Fallen Nature

from these lies that had created a sense of bondage and judgment in your heart.

If this is your need, the one and only step to escape your sinful and corrupt tendencies is to identify yourself with Jesus. Since the primary work of the Holy Spirit is to reprove unbelief, your decision to turn from your unbelief to belief is the only step that will bring you forgiveness and deliverance from all your sins. Repentance from individual sins without belief in the sacrifice of Jesus will subsequently either bring frustration because of your failures or bring pride because of your successes – neither of which will set you free from your bondages.

> For Christ also hath once suffered for sins, the just for the unjust, that he might bring us to God, being put to death in the flesh, but quickened by the Spirit: **1 Peter 3:18**
> And almost all things are by the law purged with blood; and without shedding of blood is no remission. **Hebrews 9:22**

Only unbelief prevents us from entering heaven. People who end up in hell are there only because of this sin, not because of a multitude of sins. Since the Holy Spirit's work is to reprove us of this sin, rejection of that reproof means rejection of the Holy Spirit. Choosing not to believe in Jesus is the same as blaspheming the Holy Spirit. Jesus confirmed this rejection of the Holy Spirit as the only unforgivable sin (see Matthew 12:31).

Paul warned that if we decide to reject the light that enables us to surrender to Jesus, God will send a powerful delusion that we might choose to believe a lie.

> [10] And with all deceivableness of unrighteousness in them that perish; because they received not the love of the truth, that they might

be saved. ¹¹ And for this cause God shall send them strong delusion, that they should believe a lie: **2 Thessalonians 2:10-11**

The sense in which God "sends" delusion is quite simple. He withdraws the truth that we have repeatedly rejected. Nothing remains for us to believe except the lies propagated by the world. If we refuse the truth of receiving Jesus, it's no wonder we're easily persuaded to believe that there are other ways of getting to heaven.

People are deceived into thinking that God in His great love won't allow anyone to go to hell. Indeed, God will not allow people to go to hell without first making a way for them to escape the enemy's enticements that draw them in that direction. In His great love, He gives everyone the opportunity to take hold of the hand of their Rescuer, Jesus.

God will help people to escape their sinful hearts through the gospel, but He leaves it up to each person to make their own choice. The choice is easy because He has put up hundreds of sign posts pointing to this path. He has even added hundreds of obstacles along the way making it harder for them to turn aside. He especially uses His servants through the sharing of the gospel to set up these signs and obstacles. We try our best to persuade those who are tempted to exclude Jesus to not give in to this temptation. Thankfully, many people do surrender to the light that has been shown to them.

In 1968, an employment agency sent me to work in the offices of a construction company. I was to distribute the mail, make pickups and deliveries to construction sites, and do various other duties. After a few months, I developed a friendship with one of the estimators. I began to share with him about my relationship with the Lord. Because I was fearful of causing offense, I said very little to him. But when I heard that an evangelist was coming to Winnipeg to hold meetings, I decided that these meetings would be a way of him hearing more fully the message that I was afraid to share.

I invited him to go with me but didn't expect a positive response. I was very surprised when he agreed. In fact, he went with me three nights in a row. Each night at the end of the service, the evangelist would invite people to come forward to demonstrate their willingness to receive Jesus as their Savior. I could tell he had listened carefully to the messages and was seriously considering going forward. Though I meant well, I think it irritated him that I offered to go with him. All three nights, he resisted and battled the drawing of the Holy Spirit on his heart.

But on that third night near the end of the call for people to go forward, without saying anything to me, my friend went to the front. After the evangelist led him and others in a prayer of commitment to the Lord, he was taken into a room backstage to receive counseling. I waited for about twenty minutes for him.

When he returned, I have never seen anybody with a more glorious glow on his face than I saw on his. He was a changed person. The light that had shone in his heart, but which he had resisted for two days was springing forth from his innermost being and shining brightly through his countenance. So dramatic was the change in his life, that a few days after his conversion he boldly witnessed to his fiancé to try to win her to the Lord. Sadly, she not only rejected his message but permanently rejected him also. But God had somebody much better for him. A few months later I had the privilege of introducing him to a godly woman whom he later married.

If you have not yet allowed the Holy Spirit to replace your corrupt heart with a new one, then you need to allow Him to shine into the depth of your darkened soul the light of the gospel which has the power to dispel this darkness and totally transform your life.

To open their eyes, *and* to turn *them* from darkness to light, and *from* the power of Satan unto God, that they may receive forgiveness of sins, and inheritance among them which are sanctified by faith that is in me. **Acts 26:18**

¹³ Who hath delivered us from the power of darkness, and hath translated *us* into the kingdom of his dear Son: ¹⁴ In whom we have redemption through his blood, *even* the forgiveness of sins: **Colossians 1:13-14**

For I am not ashamed of the gospel of Christ: for it is the power of God unto salvation to every one that believeth; to the Jew first, and also to the Greek. **Romans 1:16**

Jesus said that the people who have encountered the light of the gospel but have chosen to turn away from it would suffer greatly on the Day of Judgment. They have believed lies and are in danger of falling away. Since they have rejected the grace so abundantly poured out, it's possible that they may never get another opportunity to request forgiveness and receive Jesus. They have so immersed themselves in the lies of the world that the truth of the gospel can no longer prick their hardened hearts.

²⁰Then began he to upbraid the cities wherein most of his mighty works were done, because they repented not: ²³ And thou, Capernaum, which art exalted unto heaven, shalt be brought down to hell: for if the mighty works, which have been done in thee, had been done in Sodom, it would have remained until this day. ²⁴ But I say unto you, That it shall be more tolerable for the land of Sodom in the day of judgment, than for thee. **Matthew 11:20, 23-24**

This text indicates that it will be more tolerable on the Day of Judgment for Sodom and Gomorrah than for these people of His day (and of ours) who did not respond to the light. He implied that the terrible sins of murder and sexual deviancy is less deserving of judgment than a person's decision to turn away from the light that leads to the Savior.

When Jesus presents Himself to people as their Savior and they choose to reject His offer of forgiveness, I am sure He feels grief and disappointment, not judgment, over their decision.

> O Jerusalem, Jerusalem, *thou* that killest the prophets, and stonest them which are sent unto thee, how often would I have gathered thy children together, even as a hen gathereth her chickens under *her* wings, and ye would not!
> **Matthew 23:37**

But the writer to the Hebrews makes a serious comment about that rejection.

> ²⁶ For if we sin wilfully after that we have received the knowledge of the truth, there remaineth no more sacrifice for sins, ²⁷ But a certain fearful looking for of judgment and fiery indignation, which shall devour the adversaries. ²⁸ He that despised Moses' law died without mercy under two or three witnesses: ²⁹ Of how much sorer punishment, suppose ye, shall he be thought worthy, who hath trodden under foot the Son of God, and hath counted the blood of the covenant, wherewith he was sanctified, an unholy thing, and hath done despite unto the Spirit of grace? ³⁰ For we know him that hath said, Vengeance *belongeth* unto me, I will recompense,

saith the Lord. And again, The Lord shall judge his people. ³¹*It is* a fearful thing to fall into the hands of the living God. **Hebrews 10:26-31**

The writer expressed these remarks with a lot of emotion. He felt for the Father, who must now follow through and recompense or judge the people who made light of the sacrifice of His Son and have resisted His Spirit of grace. With God's incredible display of love and sacrifice thrown back into His face, these people certainly warrant a strong warning. It is no wonder the writer warned them about the possibility of falling "into the hands of the living God."

See that ye refuse not him that speaketh. For if they escaped not who refused him that spake on earth, much more *shall not* we *escape*, if we turn away from him that *speaketh* from heaven: **Hebrews 12:25**

The purpose of the Great Tribulation described in the New Testament will be to siphon out from the crowd believers who were careless about their salvation. Because of these hardships, for those who are truly saved there will come to the surface evidence of a relationship with the Lord that had been hidden in their hearts. They will consider these trials as God's tool of chastisement to draw out of them their new nature. These tests will cause them to acknowledge the Lordship of Jesus and to escape the effects and consequences of their fallen and corrupt nature.

However, for those who are not yet saved it is heartbreaking to learn from the scriptures that in response to these same tribulations, many will choose not to turn from their wicked ways: "And men ... blasphemed the name of God, and they repented not" (see Revelation 16:9). It is so sad to realize that though everyone will have the opportunity to escape their fallen nature, many will refuse to repent and instead continue to reject God's offer of an escape.

Some people fail to recognize the urgency of turning to the Lord even when threatened with death. Instead, they choose to ignore the care of their spiritual condition to preserve their physical and emotional life style. While it was said of those born again, "They loved not their lives unto the death," it was said of those who were not born again, "They repented not."

In this chapter we have identified the sin interfering with our escape from our fallen nature. We have discussed the importance of comprehending the light of God's Word and giving attention to its warnings.

Now that we understand what true repentance is and the seriousness of rejecting Jesus, we must fully identify with Him and show that we are committed to follow Him with our whole heart.

CHAPTER 7

CONFIRM WITH A PUBLIC CONFESSION

> Jesus answered, Verily, verily, I say unto thee, Except a man be born of water and *of* the Spirit, he cannot enter into the kingdom of God.
> **John 3:5**

Though Jesus may have been referring to the natural birth when saying, "born of water," I think the argument that He was referring to water baptism is much stronger. To suggest that He was referring to natural birth when He said, "born of water" would make Him to say that babies who die in the womb, and thus not born, cannot enter heaven. But neither did He mean that you will be denied entrance into heaven simply because you are not yet water baptized.

Since baptism in water was a convert's way of showing his commitment to John the Baptist's teaching, it is likely that when Jesus said, born of water, He was referring to John's baptism. From this scripture, some will say they are born again because they were baptized in water. But Jesus spoke of born of water because He knew that the new birth by the Spirit could not be confirmed as genuine unless it was accompanied with a spoken confession. And water baptism is the ideal platform from which a new convert can publicly and unashamedly make this confession heard.

> [9] That if thou shalt confess with thy mouth the Lord Jesus, and shalt believe in thine heart that God hath raised him from the dead, thou shalt be saved. [10] For with the heart man believeth unto righteousness; and with the mouth confession is made unto salvation. [11] For the scripture saith, Whosoever believeth on him shall not be ashamed. **Romans 10:9-11**

However, unless there is a heart transformation by the power of the Spirit, water baptism and the verbal confession that comes with it is meaningless if it stands alone. There is nothing special about water other than it being a tool through which a convert can demonstrate publicly how God washed away his sins through the experience of the new birth.

When converts submit to water baptism but provide no evidence that they have given their lives to Jesus, though they may be born of water, they have not been born of the Spirit. The hope of making it to heaven for many isn't their trust in what Jesus did but in their memory of what the water did. While faith in the flow of water impresses the church, it is only faith in the flow of Jesus's blood that pleases God.

Babies who died before they were born or in infancy will not be denied entrance intoheaven. Though they have the sin nature, until they reach that point in their understanding that they knowingly choose to reject the light that God has given to them, the blood of Jesus adequately covers their blemished hearts. Therefore, the baptism of babies, both dead and living, is not necessary to make them ready for heaven.

To help us understand why water is not enough to cleanse sin and produce a born-again nature, it is helpful that we consider what the audience of Jesus thought after listening to Him:

> It is the spirit that quickeneth; the flesh profiteth nothing: the words that I speak unto you, *they* are spirit, and *they* are life. **John 6:63**

Many were offended when Jesus mockingly said they must eat of His flesh and drink of His blood (see John 6:47–63). They agreed with Him when He said, "The flesh profiteth nothing." They knew eating His flesh and drinking His blood would bring no spiritual benefit. Therefore, they also would have had no difficulty in concluding that water on the flesh was incapable of cleansing the heart from sin to cause a spiritual rebirth.

Though not submitting to Jesus, they learned from Him that it was His words, not His flesh, that quickened believers unto new life. Since Jesus said eating His flesh and drinking His blood can contribute nothing toward the spirit and life of a true believer (except when they are symbols to inspire their faith), neither can water.

When Jesus said, "born of water," He was referring to the water baptism that symbolically demonstrates the work of the Holy Spirit to replace the believer's old fallen nature with their new nature. If, however, their confession doesn't agree with what they believe in their hearts about His death and resurrection, then there's been no new birth. In those cases, the water baptism celebrates the candidate's good intentions and is a pre-salvation grace that hopefully will eventually cause them to recognize their need for an inner transformation.

> Then Peter said unto them, Repent, and be baptized every one of you in the name of Jesus Christ for the remission of sins, and ye shall receive the gift of the Holy Ghost. **Acts 2:38**

Escaping Your Fallen Nature

The gift of the Holy Spirit comes upon believers as they repent and receive remission of their sins. Water baptism, Peter confirmed, gives believers the opportunity to declare that they are born again by the power of the Holy Spirit acting on their word (confession). In many cases, as Peter implied, the water baptism of declaring their faith is simultaneous with becoming born again. While water baptism does not save, it, like the exchanging of rings and vows at a wedding ceremony, clinches and confirms their previously confessed pledge of devotion.

In the mid-1990s my wife and son and I attended a church that believed water baptism in the name of Jesus and speaking with other tongues is necessary before a candidate for salvation can be declared or confirmed as being genuinely born again and receiving eternal life. After we had heard several messages and Bible studies on this subject we decided, though we had already been baptized years earlier, to submit to water baptism in Jesus's name just to be sure that we were saved. But upon thoroughly restudying the scriptures, I came to realize that since we were already baptized following our born again experience our rebaptism was not necessary.

It was a real surprise that this church took this position. The scriptures clearly teach that we are not saved because we were born of water. Water simply confirms that there's already been a work of the Holy Spirit to produce in us the new-born nature of Jesus. When people believe that water baptism is necessary for salvation they have decided that their salvation is dependent on their own performance rather than solely on the work of Jesus and the Holy Spirit.

Thus, it is important to know that born-again believers are saved even if they have not been water baptized. But if they've been taught from the scriptures and given lots of opportunities and yet continue to refuse to be water baptized, it is possible (but we must not judge) that they are not born again. But many will refuse water baptism because they were taught that going to the front of the auditorium (as in Billy Graham crusades) to make a public confession of their commitment to Jesus, also known as the sinner's prayer, is a legitimate substitute for a public water baptism.

While many can say the sinner's prayer privately and truly mean it to become born again, the point taught first by Jesus and then by Peter and Paul is that a genuine commitment to the Lord will produce in the new convert the willingness to identify with Jesus publicly. And since water baptism was the ideal way to communicate to the whole community their identification with Him, it follows that true believers would submit to water baptism, especially since Jesus commanded it.

In the years following Jesus's arrest and execution, many considered Him a revoltionary. They hesitated to publicly identify with Him because He had been convicted and crucified for the crimes of blasphemy and insurrection. To be identified with Him could have meant persecution or even death.

> And he said, I tell thee, Peter, the cock shall not crow this day, before that thou shalt thrice deny that thou knowest me. **Luke 22:34**

Because Peter was ashamed of what appeared to him as Jesus's defeat, on three occasions, in order to distance himself from Him and secure his freedom, he denied he knew Jesus.

In identifying those who were born again, John said, "even to them that believe on his name" (see John 1:12). The enemies of the disciples of Jesus warned them not to teach in the name of Jesus (see Acts 4:18, 5:28). After the authorities asked Peter by whose name and power had a certain man been healed, Peter, unlike before, boldly identified with the name of Jesus. He said there was no other name whereby we could be saved (see Acts 4:7–12).

Water baptism is the believer's opportunity to identify with Jesus. The willingness of people to publicly submit to water baptism gave demonstration that Jesus, not Ceasar, was Lord. Since their being baptized in Jesus's name identified them with a "criminal," their decision had to be genuine. Their ability to overcome fear demonstrated that their lives had been transformed, proving that they had the newborn nature of Jesus.

In 1972 or 1973, my identifying with the name of Jesus almost cost me my job. I was a dispatcher for the largest security company in Winnipeg and was responsible every week for making up the schedules for more than a hundred security guards. When I knew I was caught up with my dispatching duties, I would ask guards when they came in to ask for their paychecks or schedules if I could speak to them about the Lord. Once I had their permission, I would inform them what Jesus had done for me and that He was willing to do the same for them. Many of the guards nicknamed me "Bible Thumper."

Later, these guards complained to my boss that I had harassed them. When he called me in to his office, I was at first concerned he might fire me. When he questioned me, I told him that all my duties were always up to date and that I had the permission of the guards to speak. I also told him that since I saved my lunch breaks for the times when they came in, I wasn't wasting company time. I said it was only fair that since these same guards often would say the name of Jesus, but in vain, I should be allowed to speak His name as well. It's possible my boss would have let me go except that he had to acknowledge that he could find no fault with the performance of my duties.

In comparison to people who risk their freedoms and even their lives to speak and identify with the name of Jesus, my risking my job to identify with Him wasn't much of a risk. But as it turns out, taking that risk was well worth it. Years later, I learned that one of the guards to whom I had witnessed told another guard and who then sought me out and after finding me told me that my witnessing to this other guard had influenced him to accept Jesus as his Savior.

Following the departure of Jesus, the baptism with water of many of the believers occurred simultaneously or shortly after they were born again by the Holy Spirit. Water baptism is the same time as salvation whenever it acts as the final catalyst to produce faith in Jesus. When people refuse to be water baptized, they deny their identification with Jesus and possibly short-circuit their faith and abort the born-again process. Water baptism is a means of candidates giving witness to their decision to identify with Jesus in His death and resurrection.

Today, in places where there is no longer a threat of severe consequences to be identified with Jesus, people can submit to water baptism with no concern about whether their repentance is genuine. When repentance is honest, water baptism is an appropriate way of demonstrating faith. But for many, rather than it being a genuine representation of what is in their hearts, water baptism along with a spoken confession has simply become an action through which they hope makes them qualified for heaven.

But conversion in our speech, though it may appear to be genuine, is not necessarily proof of conversion in our hearts. I've been in churches where all the members of the congregation were asked by the leader to repeat a prayer of confession that they read off the church program bulletin. Though some may have truly meant it when reading these lines, this confessional prayer is no more a proof of salvation than people, whose hearts are far from God, just mouthing words of worship.

> This people draweth nigh unto me with their mouth, and honoureth me with *their* lips; but their heart is far from me. **Matthew 15:8**

Paul spoke of people who after receiving the grace that would've brought them into salvation chose not to appropriate it as God intended.

Receive not the grace of God in vain. **2 Corinthians 6:1**

Probably more often than we are willing to admit, we trust in the genuineness of a candidate's confession because it was accompanied with a great demonstration of emotions. We then allow the candidate to also believe that these feelings are proof that their confession of faith has produced the new born nature. But Jesus, in Mark 4, says quite the opposite.

> [16] And these are they likewise which are sown on stony ground; who, when they have heard the word, immediately receive it with gladness; [17] And have no root in themselves, and so endure but for a time: afterward, when affliction or persecution ariseth for the word's sake, immediately they are offended. **Mark 4:16-17**

Jesus seems to be implying that the true test of a candidate's commitment to Him is not their showing of emotions but of their endurance of afflictions and persecutions. If their emotions prove to be unreliable as a means of testing their commitment, then certainly their confession cannot be reliable either. If it's imperative that others know the true condition of our hearts, then we need to allow them to test or try our spirits. We cannot know for sure if a candidate's confession of Jesus originated from a heart of genuine commitment to Him until it has been tested through the trials of life. I will cover this testing in much greater deail in a later chapter.

In this chapter we have learned that the purpose of the water is to give us a tool whereby we can symbolically show that we understand that it's only the blood of Jesus that can wash away sins. Through water baptism, we have publicly identified with the name of Jesus and are declaring that we are willing, if necessary, to suffer because of His name.

Your willingness to publicly identify with Jesus is a very good indication that the new birth process of the formation of Jesus in you has now been completed. And because you have finally reached full term, then, just as a cry verifies the breath of life of a newborn baby, so also, from out of your mouth will come a "cry" that verifies the breath of life of a born-again new nature.

CHAPTER 8

RELEASE THE FULLNESS OF THE SPIRIT

While the previous chapter focused on born of water, this chapter focuses on born of the Spirit. Like oxygen for the physical body, the breath that sustains a newborn life is the wind of the Holy Spirit that flows from out of the new believer's born-again new nature.

> I indeed have baptized you with water: but he shall baptize you with the Holy Ghost. **Mark 1:8**

Some believe that when John the Baptist announced that Jesus would baptize with the Holy Ghost hewas referring to a work of grace coming sometime after the born-again experience.But it makes no sense that John would skip over the first and primary work of Jesus birthing people into His kingdom to announce a second work of Jesus empowering believers to flow in theSpirit. Peter's comments, as quoted in an earlier chapter, verifies that the gift and power of the Holy Spirit was the proof of having received salvation (see Acts 2:38; 10:45-47).

Jesus urged the disciples to ask for the gift of the Spirit (Luke 11:13). While preparing them for their upcoming work,

"... he breathed on them, and saith unto them, Receive ye the Holy Ghost" (John 20:22). His breathing on them was like Paul breathing out threats (see Acts 9:1). Jesus gave them a sampling or feeling that they would later recognize as the breath or flow of the Holy Spirit whom Jesus said they should receive after He sends Him.

Though Jesus had commanded His disciples to receive the Holy Ghost we know that this sampling of the Spirit's presence was not to be interpreted as actually receiving Him. Otherwise, Jesus would not have commanded them to wait for the promise of the Father. And neither was it, as some would suggest, the receiving of their new-born natures. We know this because there cannot be a new birth except the candidate is born of the Spirit and since we know the Holy Spirit had not yet been given, therefore there could not have yet been a new birth in the hearts of these disciples.

Though they already were believers, the disciples didn't receive the Holy Ghost generated newborn heart (promise of the Father) until after Jesus fulfilled His promise of sending the Spirit. Now that He has been given, believers today do not need to ask or wait. We received the Holy Spirit at the very moment when we were birthed into the kingdom of God.

> Not by works of righteousness which we have done, but according to his mercy he saved us, by the washing of regeneration, and renewing of the Holy Ghost; **Titus 3:5**

Jesus spoke of born-again believers as having within themselves this kingdom of God:

> [20]The kingdom of God cometh not with observation: [21] ...for, behold, the kingdom of God is within you.**Luke 17:20–21**

Escaping Your Fallen Nature

> For the kingdom of God is not meat and drink; but righteousness, and peace, and joy in the Holy Ghost. **Romans 14:17**

Paul's description of this kingdom of God is identical to the new nature within believers and is what John was referring to when he said Jesus would baptize them with the Holy Ghost.

The prophets referred to this new inner kingdom as the Father's promise of a new heart.

> ³³ But this *shall be* the covenant that I will make with the house of Israel; After those days, saith the LORD, I will put my law in their inward parts, and write it in their hearts; and will be their God, and they shall be my people. ³⁴ And they shall teach no more every man his neighbour, and every man his brother, saying, Know the LORD: for they shall all know me, from the least of them unto the greatest of them, saith the LORD: for I will forgive their iniquity, and I will remember their sin no more. **Jeremiah 31:33-34**
>
> ²⁶ A new heart also will I give you, and a new spirit will I put within you: and I will take away the stony heart out of your flesh, and I will give you an heart of flesh. ²⁷ And I will put my spirit within you, and cause you to walk in my statutes, and ye shall keep my judgments, and do *them*. **Ezekiel 36:26-27**

Jesus said this new heart spoken by the prophets was fulfillment of the promise of the Father:

> And, behold, I send the promise of my Father upon you: but tarry ye in the city of Jerusalem,

until ye be endued with power from on high.
Luke 24:49

This enduement, which I explainin further detail in a later chapter, was the righteous garment that candidates for salvation must put on for entering heaven.But Jesus not only referred to this new heart as that which the prophets described but also that this new heart was born of the Spirit.

> ⁵ Jesus answered, Verily, verily, I say unto thee, Except a man be born of water and *of* the Spirit, he cannot enter into the kingdom of God. ⁶ That which is born of the flesh is flesh; and that which is born of the Spirit is spirit. **John 3:5-6**

We observe that Jesus also spoke of this Spirit within us as living water.

> ³⁷ In the last day, that great *day* of the feast, Jesus stood and cried, saying, If any man thirst, let him come unto me, and drink. ³⁸ He that believeth on me, as the scripture hath said, out of his belly shall flow rivers of living water. ³⁹ (But this spake he of the Spirit, which they that believe on him should receive: for the Holy Ghost was not yet *given*; because that Jesus was not yet glorified.) **John 7:37-39**

In referencing an Old Testament scripture, Jesus was probably referring to Joel's prophecy (Joel 2:28-29) about the outpouring of the Holy Spirit (but see 1 Corinthians 10:1-4, Isaiah 12:3, Jeremiah 2:13).

> But whosoever drinketh of the water that I shall give him shall never thirst; but the water that I shall give him shall be in him a well of water springing up into everlasting life. **John 4:14**

Because people's thirst for the abundant life can be satisfied only through coming to Jesus we know that the apostle John was talking about salvation. Jesus told the Samaritan woman that the drink that she would receive would be a well of water springing up into everlasting life. Thus, the proof of salvation is a flow of living water, which Jesus said would be evident in all believers.

But John, by saying "this spake he of the Spirit," identified this well of water springing up into everlasting life as the Holy Ghost. He quoted Jesus as saying that any one who thirsts for this life and believes on Him would receive the Holy Ghost after which He would then flow out of the believer like a river of living water. But at the time Jesus spoke these words no one had yet received the Holy Spirit because Jesus had not yet sent Him.

> ⁴ And, being assembled together with *them*, commanded them that they should not depart from Jerusalem, but wait for the promise of the Father, which, *saith he*, ye have heard of me. ⁵ For John truly baptized with water; but ye shall be baptized with the Holy Ghost not many days hence. **Acts 1:4-5**

The sending of the Holy Spirit Jesus said was the promise of the Father. This promise of the Father is the same promise in Jeremiah and Ezekiel that speaks of the inward parts and the new heart. He also said that in sending the Spirit He was both baptizing them with the Holy Ghost and enduing them with power from on high. In other words, He was giving them their born-again new nature which would be manifested through the fullness and flow of Holy Spirit power.

Since both the baptism with the Holy Spirit and water springing up unto everlasting life are speaking of the same event (when the disciples received the Holy Spirit through faith in Jesus), we conclude, therefore, that salvation and the baptism with the Holy Spirit are the same.

Hopefully, the following list will help make clear the commonality of the new birth and the baptism with the Holy Spirit as both referring to the new heart of the believer:

1. Joel's prophecy appears to be the same event prophesied by Jeremiah and Ezekiel.
2. The promise of the Father refers both to a change in nature and receiving the Spirit.
3. The new nature springing up to everlasting life is the flow of Holy Spirit living water.
4. The enduement with power is also the righteous garment necessary for entering heaven.
5. The work of Jesus was both baptizing with the Spirit and beginning God's kingdom.
6. Peter claimed the Holy Spirit's power (new-birth) verified readiness for water baptism.

Please bear with me as I try to explain it one more time. Since this springing up of living water is the source of everlasting life, it's apparent that Jesus was speaking of candidates not only receiving the Holy Ghost but also of being born by the Spirit. Since the receiving of the new nature spoken of by Jeremiah and Ezekiel is the fulfillment of the promise of the Father, which John said is also Holy Ghost baptism, born of the Spirit is the baptism with the Holy Ghost. Since the new birth and the baptism with the Holy Spirit are both described as living water as well as the promise of the Father, we conclude, therefore, that the two are the same.

In Acts 2, because the tongues of fire and sound of wind (symbolizing the Holy Spirit's breath) inspired their faith, the disciples received the Holy Spirit and immediately flowed with power. This flow of living water, because it was unimpeded in its flow, was not only the baptism with the Holy Spirit but also the filling of the Holy Spirit.

But today, partly because believers are told it is a later work, many stop short of the fullness of the Spirit when accepting Jesus as Savior. Instead of a powerful river that Jesus said should flow out of all believers, the flow of living water coming from their innermost being is barely enough to produce even a very small yield of Holy Spirit fruit.

Because tongues were the initial physical evidence of the filling of the Spirit in the book of Acts, many seek the gift of tongues instead of seeking the filling of the Spirit and His fruitfulness.

> But ye shall receive power, after that the Holy Ghost is come upon you: and ye shall be witnesses unto me both in Jerusalem, and in all Judaea, and in Samaria, and unto the uttermost part of the earth. **Acts 1:8**

Jesus said the primary evidence of the filling of the Spirit and of the unimpeded flow of Holy Spirit living water is boldness, as displayed by the disciples, in being His faithful witnesses. That is the reason He told them to wait. It is when the Spirit is flowing from out of our born-again new nature to touch people with the flow of Jesus's love that we can say we are filled with the Spirit.

It was in 1972 while attending a sporting event that I first experienced this boldness and flow of Holy Spirit power. That winter, I drove to Virden, Manitoba, which is about a 3-hour drive west of Winnipeg, to watch a provincial curling championship. I have always found curling to be a very interesting game to watch as it involves deep strategy and precise execution.

I arrived there on a Saturday morning intending to watch the playoff games throughout the whole day. I then intended to sleep in my car overnight, so I could see the championship game on Sunday.

While watching the games on Saturday afternoon, because I liked talking to whoever was around me about the great shots, I became well acquainted with a young man sitting behind me. After the afternoon games were completed and intending to wait in my car until the evening game begun, this fellow invited me to go with him to his place for supper. I had a good time getting acquainted with his family. Learning that I intended to watch the championship game the following day, his parents welcomed me to come back to their place after the evening game was completed and to stay there for the night.

The next morning as I ate breakfast with the whole family I worked up my courage to share with them my experience with the Lord and how He had changed my life. Once I started speaking I was amazed as to my boldness and the flow of liberty in the words that I shared. Statements that I had not even thought about beforehand just rolled off my tongue. I think that was the first time I gave any evidence of Holy Spirit power flowing through me to be a witness.

That event greatly encouraged me. Afterwards I always had a sense I could count on the Holy Spirit, even as Jesus prophesied, to give me power, though many times I fell flat, to be His witness. And since then, both in house to house witnessing and talking on theprayer lines, this flow of the breath and power of the Holy Spirit has inspired me hundreds of times. That experience in Virden inspired me to believe that as we appropriate God's grace to remove hindrances, we can expect to come from out of our innermost being the powerful breath (fullness) of the Holy Spirit.

Though not seeing any evidence that this family responded to the gospel, several times when traveling through Virden, I stopped at the father's place of work, which was on the highway, to say hi. Three years later, between my second and third years at Bible college, this same place, Virden, Manitoba, was where I was assigned to a pastor (who used to be my pastor when I was a teen) to learn from him how to be a pastor.

These descriptions by Luke in the book of Acts of people speaking with other tongues were not doctrinal statements, such as those Paul put forth in Corinthians, but his observations. Many of these people who spoke with other tongues also flowed in Holy Spirit power to boldly witness to unbelievers of the life and resurrection of Jesus. From them was "a well of water springing up" from within their hearts, which Jesus said was the evidence that sets apart the believers from the unbelievers (see John 4:14).

There are believers who report flowing in power and boldness to speak about Jesus and yet do not speak with other tongues. There are others who report flowing in a powerful manifestation of speaking with other tongues, sensing God's presence to build them up (see 1 Corinthians 14) but have very little boldness or power to witness. Paul said that if we are not flowing in God's love toward needy people, then our speaking with other tongues is nothing more than a sounding brass and a tinkling symbol (see 1 Corinthians 13:1).

If you are struggling to receive the baptism with the Holy Spirit, be encouraged. When you asked Jesus to be your Savior and received His born-again nature, you received this baptism. Though baptized with the Spirit (new birth), you may not yet have experienced the filling of the Spirit (unimpeded flow) because of misunderstandings (as I explained in earlier paragraphs).

As you renew your mind on God's Word, your faith will grow to remove the logjam blocking this flow. When you praise God, Holy Spirit power will spring up from within your born-again new nature, like mercury in a thermometer, and flow in a love language that blesses others. Even as a pump above a well needs priming to cause water to spring up, so also praising the Lord and speaking with other tongues (see 1 Corinthians 14:2, 16) helps to draw out the Holy Spirit. When it reaches its peak and is unimpeded,this outflow is equivalent to being filled with the Holy Spirit.

> Speaking to yourselves in psalms and hymns and spiritual songs, singing and making melody in your heart to the Lord; **Ephesians 5:19**

In the book of Acts, we learn that the apostles heard there was a great work of the Holy Spirit in Samaria through the ministry of Philip. Their concern was that these new believers would also receive this fullness of the Spirit that they had experienced in Jerusalem (see Acts 2:4).

> [15] Who, when they were come down, prayed for them, that they might receive the Holy Ghost: [16] (For as yet he was fallen upon none of them: only they were baptized in the name of the Lord Jesus.) [17] Then laid they *their* hands on them, and they received the Holy Ghost. **Acts 8:15-17**

In this passage, we learn that though the people believed in Jesus and were baptized in His name, the Holy Spirit "was fallen upon none of them." Since He had already arrived on the day of Pentecost (Acts 2) in fulfillment of Jesus's promise to send Him, describing Him as fallen suggests, according to some people, that He had arrived a second time. But Jesus sent the Spirit only once.

According to *Strong's*, "fallen" comes from a Greek word meaning to "*embrace* (with affection) or *seize* (with more or less violence): - fall into (on, upon), lie on, press upon." When an epileptic person has a seizure, we don't figure the violent reaction came from a force pressing on him from without but rather a force pressing from within. "Fallen" happens whenthe new born nature,stimulated by truth,presses outwardly from within so that out of the believer's innermost being springs up or flows rivers of Holy Spirit generated living water (see John 4:14; 7:37-39).

From the apostles' point of view, since these believers were not yet flowing like a river (as the 120 did on the day of Pentecost), the receiving of the Holy Spirit was not yet complete. We know that they had already received the Spirit because "they were baptized in the name of the Lord Jesus" (see Acts 8:16). But Luke refers to this outflow as receiving because it was the final measure of being filled.

The apostles prayed that they might receive the Holy Ghost because this outward flow, since they expected this flow from all believers, was not yet evident. And it was the laying on of their hands that stimulated these new believers' faith to release from their born-again new nature this flow of living water.

> ¹ And it came to pass, that, while Apollos was at Corinth, Paul having passed through the upper coasts came to Ephesus: and finding certain disciples, ² He said unto them, Have ye received the Holy Ghost since ye believed? And they said unto him, We have not so much as heard whether there be any Holy Ghost. ³ And he said unto them, Unto what then were ye baptized? And they said, Unto John's baptism. ⁴ Then said Paul, John verily baptized with the baptism of repentance, saying unto the people, that they should believe on him which should come after him, that is, on Christ Jesus. ⁵ When they heard *this*, they were baptized in the name of the Lord Jesus. ⁶ And when Paul had laid *his* hands upon them, the Holy Ghost came on them; and they spake with tongues, and prophesied. ⁷ And all the men were about twelve. **Acts 19:1-7**

Though John had pointed them to Jesus, yet from what we learn in the last few verses of Acts 18 it appears that these Ephesian believers learned of the Gospel through the preaching of Apollos. But since Apollos preached to them an incomplete gospel (Aquilla and Priscilla had to expound to him the word of God more perfectly), it is quite likely that, though these Ephesians had heard John's message of repentance, Apollos' teaching had left them also with an incomplete understanding of the fullness of the Holy Spirit.

Because Paul asked these Ephesian disciples if they had received the Holy Ghost and then explained to them that the ministry of John was to point them to Jesus, it seems, because he probably had already learned from Aquilla of Apollos' earlier errors, that he was not convinced these Ephesians were born again. But after Paul made it clear that John's baptism was primarily that of introducing people to Jesus and showing them their need for repentance, their faith was inspired to be baptized again, but this time with the knowledge that Jesus had paid for their sins.

Then when Paul laid his hands on them, to baptize them, his touch had the effect of stirring up from within them the living water flow of the Holy Spirit causing them to prophesy and speak with other tongues. At this point Paul had no doubt and was finally convinced that they were, even as Peter proclaimed in Acts 2 and again in Acts 10 and 11, born again.

> [44] While Peter yet spake these words, the Holy Ghost fell on all them which heard the word. [45] And they of the circumcision which believed were astonished, as many as came with Peter, because that on the Gentiles also was poured out the gift of the Holy Ghost. [46] For they heard them speak with tongues, and magnify God. Then answered Peter, [47] Can any man forbid water, that these should not be baptized, which have received the Holy Ghost as well as we? **Acts 10:44-47**

Escaping Your Fallen Nature

Since we have the image in our minds that "poured out" is like water being poured out of a pitcher, we tend to believe the Holy Spirit came from without. But this same word in the Greek is translated in other places as "gush out," "shed," or "spill" (see Acts 1:18; Luke 22:20; Mark 2:22). These scriptures make it clear that what gushed out was shed or spilled from within. Thus, the pouring out, as described by Luke, was the springing up or the flowing out from within them of the Holy Ghost (John 7:37–39), which Jesus said would be evident in all true believers (John 4:14).

> [14] Who shall tell thee words, whereby thou and all thy house shall be saved. [15] And as I began to speak, the Holy Ghost fell on them, as on us at the beginning. [16] Then remembered I the word of the Lord, how that he said, John indeed baptized with water; but ye shall be baptized with the Holy Ghost. [17] Forasmuch then as God gave them the like gift as *he did* unto us, who believed on the Lord Jesus Christ; what was I, that I could withstand God? [18] When they heard these things, they held their peace, and glorified God, saying, Then hath God also to the Gentiles granted repentance unto life. **Acts 11:14-18**

We learn from these passages in Acts 10 and 11 that the household of Cornelius received the fullness and flow of the Holy Spirit when they believed. Observing that they were flowing with the Spirit and speaking with other tongues, Peter reacted with great excitement because this flow of power offered evidence that these people were born again (verse 18, "repentance unto life").

It was the laying on of the hands of the apostles that inspired the people in Samaria and Ephesus to believe for and to release from their new born nature the flow of Holy Spirit power and fullness. But for the people of Cornelius' household it was not the later work of the laying on of hands that stimulated their faith butwas the anointed preaching of Peter (when he first introduced to them the gospel) that inspiredthem to believe for and then release the fullness of the Spirit.

From these passages of Acts 8, 10, 11, and 19, we conclude thatwedo indeed experience the baptism with the Holy Spirit when we first believe.But the reason that the fullness and power of the Spirit does not immediately flow from us, like as we read in Acts 2 and 10, isdue to unbelief or misunderstandings. Though many do not experience this flow when baptized with the Holy Spirit (born again) it has always been God's intention that believers be filled with the Spirit at the very moment they first believed (not at a later separate time).

When I left Winnipeg to go to Bible School in Saskatoon in 1973, just prior to my departure, some members of the church that I had been regularly attending celebrated my sendoff by taking me to a restaurant. We had a really good time, and everyone wished me well. The Pastor of the church then drove me home.

On the way, we had a very serious discussion about the baptism with the Holy Spirit. I didn't mean to cause an offense, but when I told him that from my reading of the scriptures, I concluded that the baptism with the Holy Spirit and salvation was the same event, he was greatly offended at me. He and the church just gave me a great send off to go to Bible School and yet I dared to give an opinion that was contrary to their position. He was especially offended because he was widely regarded as the staunchest supporter of this traditional belief.

I regretted offending him because I knew he was a powerful godly man. But I shared what I believed because our discussion led us in that direction. Afterwards, I was always very careful as what I shared on this subject, especially after I had become ordained in this very same fellowship.

But then one would wonder how it is that I could become ordained considering I didn't agree with this denominational distinctive doctrine. When I was interviewed by their leadership, having learned of my position through the questionnaire, they simply required of me to read a certain book which they believed would persuade me to accept the official position. I did read it and was fully expecting another interview where I would then tell them that my position had remained unchanged. Instead of calling me in for another interview they sent me notice that I was scheduled for the ordination service.

Though I continued believing that the baptism with the Holy Spirit is the same as salvation I decided that as long as I was in an official position with this denomination as a pastor, I would never teach this aspect of our salvation. But now I am teaching this truth about salvation because it is a truth that I not only truly believe, but is a teaching that will help clear up a confusion over which many believers stumble.

Whenwe build up our faith through scriptures, through messages and testimonials, through praises to the Lord, and through speaking with other tongues, westir up the Holy Spirit generated fruits and gifts from within us, releasing them to penetrate the many untruths that previouslyhad impeded this flow. Though some of us are slow to increase in our understanding and to use these powerful tools that He has given to us, the Holy Spirit in His fullness is already within our new born hearts patiently waiting for our co-operation to release Him as a river of living water.

> [1] And Jesus being full of the Holy Ghost returned from Jordan, and was led by the Spirit into the wilderness. [14] And Jesus returned in the power of the Spirit into Galilee: and there went out a fame of him through all the region round about.**Luke 4:1, 14**

Since Jesus was born of the Spirit (see Luke 1:35), He was therefore baptized with the Spirit. Though already filled from His mother's womb, it was only after His water baptism that Jesus first gave full evidence of this filling. Jesus had not previously manifested the fullness of the Spirit to do mighty works because He had not yet begun His ministry. The Holy Spirit alighting on Him as a dove was so that John the Baptist would have confirmation that He was, indeed, the Son of God.

> [32] And John bare record, saying, I saw the Spirit descending from heaven like a dove, and it abode upon him. [33] And I knew him not: but he that sent me to baptize with water, the same said unto me, Upon whom thou shalt see the Spirit descending, and remaining on him, the same is he which baptizeth with the Holy Ghost. [34] And I saw, and bare record that this is the Son of God.
> **John 1:32-34**

It was John's responsibility to announce that the ministry of Jesus, baptizing people with the Holy Ghost, had begun (He was already filled with the Spirit). Thus, it was appropriate that this revelation, because it was a symbol of the Holy Spirit, be that of Him landing on Jesus like a dove.

The primary work of Jesus has always been to make a way for people's rescue from the works of the devil and to establish His kingdom in their lives (see Luke 4:18; Colossians 1:13-14; Acts 10:38, 26:18). We join Jesus in His powerful work of destroying the kingdom of Satan when we witness to unbelievers. We then become channels through which the power of the Holy Spirit flows (see Acts 1:8) allowing Jesus through us to baptize new believers into His kingdom.

> Who hath delivered us from the power of darkness, and hath translated *us* into the kingdom of his dear Son: **Colossians 1:13**

> For the kingdom of God is not meat and drink; but righteousness, and peace, and joy in the Holy Ghost. **Romans 14:17**

Righteousness, peace, and joy describe perfectly the newborn heart of new believers that the Father has delivered and translated into His Son's kingdom. All believers who have displayed these fruits have provided evidence that Jesus has not only baptized them with the Holy Ghost but has filled them to overflowing with Him also.

In this chapter, we have learned that the baptism with the Holy Spirit is the work of Jesus to place in all believers a Holy Spirit regenerated heart into a Holy Spirit generated kingdom. Theevidence of this baptism, while often impeded by misunderstandings about the use ofour tongues, is the living water flow of the Holy Spirit powerfully impacting the world with the love of Jesus.

Now that we understand that both "born of water" and "born of the Spirit" are "the two sides of the same coin" we can expect our lives, regardless of our troubles, to be completely transformed.

CHAPTER 9

CORROBORATE WITH A CHANGED LIFE

The power to overcome our deceptive nature doesn't come from us but from our Holy Spirit regenerated newborn hearts. This regeneration speaks of a new life we didn't previously have. We used to be dead, but because Jesus is now in us, we are alive with His resurrection nature.

> ⁴ But God, who is rich in mercy, for his great love wherewith he loved us, ⁵ Even when we were dead in sins, hath quickened us together with Christ, (by grace ye are saved;) ⁶ And hath raised *us* up together, and made *us* sit together in heavenly *places* in Christ Jesus: **Ephesians 2:4-6**
>
> ³¹ And the Lord said, Simon, Simon, behold, Satan hath desired *to have* you, that he may sift *you* as wheat: ³² But I have prayed for thee, that thy faith fail not: and when thou art converted, strengthen thy brethren. ³³ And he said unto him, Lord, I am ready to go with thee, both into prison, and to death. ³⁴ And he said, I tell thee, Peter, the cock shall not crow this day, before that

thou shalt thrice deny that thou knowest me.
Luke 22:31-34

The apostle Peter made a very bold statement, but he was very humbled when he realized that he did not have it in himself to overcome his temptation to deny Jesus. However, Jesus said that when Peter was converted, he would be entirely different in his behavior. And following his conversion, whenever he faced threats he boldly identified with Jesus and was an inspiration to his brethren, strengthening them in their resolve to also show this same boldness.

What made the difference? What did Jesus mean when He said "converted?" He said that He would pray that Peter's faith would not fail and that the day would come when Peter would be converted. This conversion was referring to the newborn nature that he received on the day that the Holy Spirit was given. He didnot develop a pattern of denying Jesus because he was no longer under the power of his old nature. He chose to obey God rather than wilt under the pressure of his enemy's intimidations (see Acts 4:12–20) because at that point he had been born of the Spirit.

Once we are born again, we have all the fruits of the Spirit as well as the same power that raised Jesus from the dead. Because our spirit man is the perfect nature of God, His Word is not nourishment and thus not necessary for the sustenance of our new nature. Rather than nourishing our newborn nature, the Word of God, as spiritual food, is necessary for our mind or soul.

> And be not conformed to this world: but be ye transformed by the renewing of your mind, that ye may prove what *is* that good, and acceptable, and perfect, will of God. **Romans 12:2**

Through God's mighty power in us, our minds, not our born-again spirits, are renewed day by day. Paul said the renewing of our minds on the Word has the effect of transforming our lives because it causes our minds to come into agreement with our perfect spirit man.

> For which cause we faint not; but though our outward man perish, yet the inward *man* is renewed day by day. **2 Corinthians 4:16**

It seems that many people believe that Paul, in speaking of this inward man, was referring to the inner born-again new nature. In the King James Version "*man*" is in italics which indicates that this is a word that was supplied by the translators and was not in the original text. Therefore, Paul, though in other passages (Ephesians 4:22-24, 2 Corinthians 5:17) his reference to the inner man was the born-again new nature, here, he was simply contrasting that which is not seen with that which is seen, as verified in the scriptures following this passage. Since the unseen included the soul, that is, the emotions and the mind, this "inward" that is renewed day by day is the soul or mind and thus agrees with Romans 12:2, "but be ye transformed by the renewing of your mind."

> ² Grace and peace be multiplied unto you through the knowledge of God, and of Jesus our Lord, ³ According as his divine power hath given unto us all things that *pertain* unto life and godliness, through the knowledge of him that hath called us to glory and virtue: ⁴ Whereby are given unto us exceeding great and precious promises: that by these ye might be partakers of the divine nature, having escaped the corruption that is in the world through lust. **2 Peter 1:2-4**

Escaping Your Fallen Nature

In mentioning divine nature, Peter was referring to the born-again new nature. Since we are sealed by the Holy Spirit, nothing of our new nature can be infected or corrupted. And because Christ is fully formed in us, producing a new birth nature, we are complete in Him.

> Which is Christ in you, the hope of glory: **Colossians 1:27**
> And ye are complete in him.**Colossians 2:10**
> After that ye believed, ye were sealed with that holy Spirit of promise, **Ephesians 1:13**

Our faithin God's promises will stimulate our new nature to release the outflowing of the gifts, the fruit, and the breath of the Holy Spirit (see John 4:14, 7:38–39). When we renew our minds on these promises our born-again new nature, which is made of the holiness of God (divine nature), will release spiritual power to nourish and transform our souls. This Holy Spirit outflow from within will cause usto escape the corruption of the world,of our fleshly appetites,andof the deceitfulness of our fallen nature.

Because Godenables us through faith in His promises to partake of His divine nature (which is the release of the fullness of the Spirit), we have confidence that He will keep us from falling. When waves of criticisms and temptations come against us these truths will anchor us to the Lord.

> Which *hope* we have as an anchor of the soul, both sure and stedfast, and which entereth into that within the veil; **Hebrews 6:19**
> Therefore, my beloved brethren, be ye stedfast, unmoveable, always abounding in the work of the Lord, forasmuch as ye know that your labour is not in vain in the Lord. **1 Corinthians 15:58**

When we have renewed our minds on the word of God, we will then be able to manifest the very nature and life of Jesus, to think and act just like Him.

> And be renewed in the spirit of your mind; **Ephesians 4:23**
> Let this mind be in you, which was also in Christ Jesus: **Philippians 2:5**
> Herein is our love made perfect...because as he is, so are we in this world. **1 John 4:17**

It is in this world, not in heaven only, that we can expect the character of Jesus to be fully manifested in our lives, enabling us to be victorious over our natural destructive nature. Knowing that we have the ability through our Spirit controlled new nature to live in this deceitful Christian hating world in the same way as Jesus lived is a great inspiration and encouragement to us. Because we have the divine nature of Jesusand His mind in us, then, once we've renewed our minds on His word, we have confidence that we can die to our old nature and overcomeits inclinations.

> ⁹ Whosoever is born of God doth not commit sin; for his seed remaineth in him: and he cannot sin, because he is born of God. ¹⁰ In this the children of God are manifest, and the children of the devil: whosoever doeth not righteousness is not of God, neither he that loveth not his brother. **1 John 3:9-10**

We can be sure we can defeat our temptations because our battle against them isn't through our corrupt nature but through the incorrupt nature of Jesus in us. Because we are born of God, it is Jesus's divine nature in us that John said cannot give in to the temptation to commit sin. This is how we can tell the children of God from those who aren't God's children.

That's not to say we can't sin. When we sin, our sin does not proceed from our new nature but rather from our failure to put off the "old man" or old nature. It is our responsibility to consider this old man, which Jesus took upon Himself when He was crucified, to be dead. Paul encouraged us to believe that we have power to put off our old nature and replace it with the new (see Romans 6:1–11, 2 Corinthians 5:17; Ephesians 4:22–24).

Since we are a new creation, when we go through trials, it's the very being of Jesus dwelling in us by His Spirit that is on trial.

> I am crucified with Christ: nevertheless I live; yet not I, but Christ liveth in me: and the life which I now live in the flesh I live by the faith of the Son of God, who loved me, and gave himself for me. **Galatians 2:20**
>
> These things I have spoken unto you, that in me ye might have peace. In the world ye shall have tribulation: but be of good cheer; I have overcome the world. **John 16:33**

Jesus assured His disciples that His new nature in them would make them overcomers. And they would receive this power when the Holy Spirit arrived to birth in them the born-again nature.

> And, behold, I send the promise of my Father upon you: but tarry ye in the city of Jerusalem, until ye be endued with power from on high. **Luke 24:49**

The word *endued* according to *Strong's* means to be clothed upon "in the sense of *sinking* into a garment." This same Greek word translated here as "endued" Paul translated as "put on" when referring to the new man that God created in righteousness (see Ephesians 4:24).

> And to her was granted that she should be arrayed in fine linen, clean and white: for the fine linen is the righteousness of saints. **Revelation 19:8**

It was the Holy Spirit, when enduing us "with power from on high," who convinced us to put on this garment of righteousness (the one which Paul refers to as "the new man."). This exchange of our corrupt nature for Jesus's righteous nature now makes us ready for heaven.

> That he might present it to himself a glorious church, not having spot, or wrinkle, or any such thing; but that it should be holy and without blemish. **Ephesians 5:27**

The only way we can be free from spot or wrinkle (sin) is to have on the spotless, unwrinkled garment we received when we were baptized (born) with the Holy Spirit. This garment will never wear out. The story of the king who put on a banquet for the wedding of his son illustrates the necessity for all who are invited and who want to enter heaven to put on this durable garment.

> ² The kingdom of heaven is like unto a certain king, which made a marriage for his son, ³ And sent forth his servants to call them that were bidden to the wedding: and they would not come. ⁴ Again, he sent forth other servants, saying, Tell them which are bidden… all things *are* ready: come unto the marriage. ⁵ But they made light of *it*, and went their ways, one to his

farm, another to his merchandise: **⁸** Then saith he to his servants, The wedding is ready, but they which were bidden were not worthy. **⁹** Go ye therefore into the highways, and as many as ye shall find, bid to the marriage. **Matthew 22:2-5,8-9**

Many who received invitations to this banquet decided not to attend. They are like many of us who for many years would have nothing to do with God or with anything that is religious. After hearing a clear presentation of the gospel, the life of Jesus was conceived in us, but not yet birthed. But then when we declined to exchange our troubles and burdens for the rest and peace that Jesus had offered to us, we were declaring that we can get through life without leaning on Him.

Having received invitations (pre-salvation grace), we know that all things are ready for each of us to attend the heavenly wedding feast. But, like the King in this story, God becomes grieved with those of us who make light of His invitation. Though the beginning stages of the formation of Jesus had already begun through the planted seed, our refusal to accept the invitation to have a relationship with Jesus indicates we don't want the new birth and thus have aborted this new birth process. Our rejection of this invitation shows that we don't believe in the necessity of going to Him and celebrating the work that He did to open a spot for us at His banqueting table.

¹⁰ So those servants went out into the highways, and gathered together all as many as they found, both bad and good: and the wedding was furnished with guests. **¹¹** And when the king came in to see the guests, he saw there a man which had not on a wedding garment: **¹²** And he saith unto him, Friend, how camest thou in hither not having a wedding garment? And he was speechless. ¹³ Then said the king to the servants, Bind him hand and foot, and take him away, and cast *him* into outer darkness; there shall be weeping and gnashing of teeth. **Matthew 22:10-13**

When those whom the King initially counted worthy to attend rejected his invitation, he then commanded his servants to invite everyone previously missed. It appears that these guests arrived in time for the wedding feast. Although scripture doesn't say so, it indicates thatthe King checked his guests to make sure that they were appropriately dressed. He then became very annoyed when he discovered that one of them had the boldness not to wear the required wedding garment.

This part of the parable illustrates those, who by responding to the invitation, have come to Jesus and have confessed Him as their Savior. But their refusal to exchange their dirty worn out clothing, their own righteousness, for the new white wedding garments of Jesus, His righteousness, is proof that they have not yet agreed to put on the born-again new nature.

Many of us think that our works are enough to get us into heaven. But it only makes sense that if we are going to attend Jesus's wedding that we first clothe ourselves with His righteous nature. If we choose not to, then we have shown that we did not truly commit to Him. Even as the King confronted the man who did not have on the wedding garment (see Matthew 22:12), we too must participate in the putting on of this garment of Jesus's righteousness.

> For as many of you as have been baptized into Christ have put on Christ. **Galatians 3:**27

If we ignore this requirement, thinking we can get into heaven without putting on this garment, then we are going to be greatly disappointed. God has no fault with us arriving just as we are but is grieved with us when we continue to believe we are fit for heaven by continuing to wear our filthy rags. He is offended when we don't put on the robe of righteousness which His Son purchased for us at the incredibly high cost of sacrificing His own life. It's only when we have put on Christ ("endued with power from on High") that we have put on this garment of righteousness.

It is an error to believe that there is a way to heaven other than through Jesus. We need to recognize the dilemma into which we have put ourselves if we don't put on the garment to which the Holy Spirit spent considerable time pointing. Where can we go where we can find the apparel that will make us appropriately attired for heaven? Is the garment of righteousness that we need available through someone else, or in some other way? Absolutely not!

Every Friday night since 1999 I've been working at a residence for Roman Catholic retired school teachers. They are part of the Sisterhood of Notre Dame. One Friday night while doing my usual cleaning duties I almost stepped on a mouse, after which it ran away but stopped near an exit door. After cornering it so it could not go down the stairs, I reached over to open this exit door and tried to get it to go out by saying, "this is your chance to escape, go, go, go, go, go."

But instead of going through the open door, it ran part way down the stairs. Because it had stopped, I was able to run past it and trap it from going any further. At that point I had a big decision to make. I really didn't want to kill it. But now that it refused the opportunity to escape for its own safety, I could not now let it escape with the possibility of it wandering all over the house to corrupt the residence and scare the Sisters. I got close and then stepped on it with the heal of my shoe, making sure that it was dead. Later, I gathered up its remains and cleaned up the floor.

In the same way I opened a door to allow that mouse to escape, God has also given every one of us an open door, Jesus, through whom we can escape His wrath. But when we give in to our fears, like this mouse, and run the opposite direction from the open door, because of our corrupt nature we will be barred from entering heaven. Even as I had to put that mouse permanently into the state of death, so also, if we refuse to put on the righteous garment of Jesus, the born-again new nature that He has provided for us, then we also will remain in a state of death permanently.

That squished mouse in all its grisly and hideous appearance is like our corrupt nature. Until we have submitted to the work of the Holy Spirit to wash and cleanse us of our ugliness and smelly corruption, replacing it with this new garment, then we have no hope of entering heaven.

The story of the ten virgins, who were also invited to a wedding feast, illustrates that those who want to go to heaven will not be ready until they are "endued with power from on High."

> ³ They that *were* foolish took their lamps, and took no oil with them: ⁴ But the wise took oil in their vessels with their lamps… ⁸ And the foolish said unto the wise, Give us of your oil; for our lamps are gone out… ¹⁰ And while they went to buy, the bridegroom came; and they that were ready went in with him to the marriage: and the door was shut. ¹¹ Afterward came also the other virgins, saying, Lord, Lord, open to us. ¹² But he answered and said, Verily I say unto you, I know you not. **Matthew 25:3-4,8,10-12**

Though oil usually represents the Holy Spirit, the oil in this parable represents the Holy Spirit generated righteousness of the nature of Jesus in new believers. Jesus implied that those who took no oil were those who, though they had verbally confessed Him

Escaping Your Fallen Nature

as Savior, didn't believe in their hearts the necessity of being born again by the Spirit. These five foolish virgins pleaded with the Lord to let them in, but He refused.

Since the only way to be clothed with the nature of Jesus is to be baptized with the Holy Spirit, those who have neglected to make sure they have been baptized will be refused entry. Only those who are dressed or endued with this Holy Spirit born-again garment of righteousness are ready for the return of the bridegroom. Those who think they are ready without this garment, if they were to get as far as the entrance of heaven, would immediately be consumed by the presence and holiness of God.

The temptation that many of us face and that threatens to destroy our assurance is to believe that we can commit a sin that could leave us not ready for Jesus's return. Considering the lies and temptations that is so prevalent in our society, we know that we're facing very severe persecutions because of our beliefs. I'm sure many of us have wondered if after we've been threatened with torture whether we will have the courage to resist the temptation to stop proclaiming Jesus as the only way of salvation.

We cannot be saved or even be assured of it unless we've supernaturally received from God His ability to endure. Those who aren't steadfast to the end demonstrate that they could not have been "endued with power from on High" of this born-of-the-Spirit new heart and nature of Jesus.

> And they overcame him by the blood of the Lamb, and by the word of their testimony; and they loved not their lives unto the death.
> **Revelation 12:11**

It should bring us great comfort, then, to know that we are among those believers who will overcome these threats and lies. The scriptures declare that we will overcome by the blood of the Lamb, by the word of our testimony, and by the ability of our new nature to endure the threat of death. So compelling is the character of Jesus in us that instead of fear we will have, like the disciples of Jesus, the boldness to resist our tormenters.

We have this confidence because this nature in us is the same nature that endured the severest temptation anyone has ever faced. Jesus's endurance through His tests proved there never was within Him even the remotest possibility of denying us our need for salvation:

> And ye shall be hated of all *men* for my name's sake: but he that endureth to the end shall be saved. **Matthew 10:22**

The primary way to determine if we are bornagain is to demonstrate that we have the character, likean unbreakable diamond, that "endureth to the end." When the hardships of life come at us from every direction and yet we endure, we can rejoice. Since Jesus is the diamond that cannot be broken, our remaining steadfast under pressure right to the finish is evidence that we have the new, born-from-above, never-dying spirit-man in us. Those who have endured temptation right to the end of their lives will receive the crown of life (see James 1:12, Revelation 2:10).

Those who endured unto death did so because they believed Jesus was God's Son. Because they believed, they were born of God and received His divine nature (see 1 John 5:4–5). When Jesus claimed He was God's Son, He was saying there was no possibility of Him giving in to the temptation to quit. So, when we confess with our spirit (see 1 Corinthians 12:3) that Jesus is the Son of God, we also demonstrate this same assurance that quitting is not part of our new nature.

So potent is our new nature that if we have backslidden and have allowed our new nature to become dormant, it will come alive in time to enable us to persevere. When we are forced to decide, either to return to Jesus or reject Him forever, God's grace in our new nature will deliver us from falling away:

> The Lord knoweth how to deliver the godly out of temptations, and to reserve the unjust unto the day of judgment to be punished: **2 Peter 2:9**

As mentioned in an earlier chapter, though natural conception and birth illustrate spiritual birth, they aren't a perfect analogy. In the physical, a baby cannot survive without proper care. But in the spiritual realm, those who were born from above will endure because the spirit man doesn't need outside nourishment. It is only prior to the new birth, during the gestation period, not after it, that a candidate for salvation may not be able to endure the temptation to quit on these graces of God. But those with the divine nature, though going a very long time without receiving sustenance to renew their minds, will survive lean times. In later chapters I explain in much more detail the ability of backsliders to bounce back from their backsliding.

When there has been no growth, as during backsliding, the new nature goes into dormancy. Because we know certain animals, such as bears, can survive for a long time without food, we can refer to backsliding as spiritual hibernation.

In May of 2018, I had quite the interesting experience with a bear, and it was not in a zoo. While driving down the highway returning from visiting my son and his family, my wife and I collided with a large bear which at that very moment decided to cross this 4 lane highway jumping over the median barrier. Since it was dark (around 11 p.m.) and the bear was black, I was not able to see it until the very last second. The collision with it produced quite the scare.

Immediately, I said to my wife "what was that?" after which I then said, "I think I hit a bear." Thankfully, I did not lose control of my car. I pulled off to the side of the road, and after inspecting the damage to the left front driver side fender, I walked back to see if indeed I had hit a bear. But I didn't get very far until the police came. The officer confirmed with me that I had hit a bear and that it was dead.

Because the car was severely damaged the police would not allow me to continue driving it. The tow truck driver took us to a near by hotel to stay for the night. The next day I walked over to a car rental agency, rented a car, went over to the compound to pick up things in my car and then went back to the hotel to pick up my wife. A few days later I bought a new car.

I'm not sure if black bears hibernate, but after experiencing this collision with one, I thought about hibernation. That bear survived the lean times of winter because God put into the nature of it the ability to draw nourishment, while it was sleeping, from its own body fat.

So also, in the spiritual kingdom, the born-again nature can survive because quite simply that's the abilityit has. And when it faces imminent danger and possibly death, that's when, like a bear, our new life will awaken out of its hibernation. That's when its spiritual adrenaline will take effect and enable it to come back to full life. This resiliency of our newbornnature is incredible.

In this chapter, we have learned that the ability of believersto endure hardships or return from backsliding to be ready for heaven, having been clothed with the righteousness and nature of Jesus, is due to their new nature's durability and resiliency. Now that you have an understanding of a believer's new nature, you need to examine yours. If you discover through your examination that you don't have this durability or resiliency to outlast your troubles, then you need to examine your heart to see whether you have *escaped your fallen nature.*

PART II
ATTITUDES THAT SIGNIFY YOUR ESCAPE

CHAPTER 10

MOVES ON FROM PRE-SALVATION GRACE

It could be that you aredisappointed with Christianity. Maybe you aretempted to give up believing in Jesus. Perhaps you're beginning to believe that faith in Him isn't necessary. If you are going through temptations, then the truths of the Bible and especially those in the book of Hebrews will make a way for you to escape them.

Possibly, you may consider the book of Hebrews as one of the most difficult to understand. But in it are passages offering you very useful advice to help you overcome your temptations. Though the task of drawing out the nuggets of truth beneath the surface seems very daunting, I decided the difficulty in digging them out wasn't reason enough to skip over them. Instead, I am asking the Lord to help me to explain and interpret them.

If you're tempted to quit on Jesus or quit pursuing the truth that leads to Him, I'm confident that as I make these passages understandable you will reconsider. If you stick with me as we dig for these treasures, what we will discover will encourage you to endure to the end and not give up.

During my first year of Bible college in Saskatoon, Saskatchewan, I was impressed with one of the teachers. He was teaching from 1 Corinthians and was emphasizing the work of Jesus to bring us forgiveness for our sins through His blood. What struck me was the powerful anointing that flowed through his speech as he explained some of the scripture verses. I have always greatly appreciated speakers who explain the scriptures well and pass it on as if it were a fiery torch whose light and heat would make an impact on me. After that, I always looked forward to his classes.

Even as the writer to the Hebrews believed a well thought out clarification of his teachings would make a huge impression on his listeners, I am being very thorough in the explanations of my thoughts also. This writer said that though his audience previously had been content to consume only milk, it was now time that they started chewing on the meatier revelations of truth.

He encouraged those who had come out of Judaism to escape this severe temptation to quit on Jesus. These Hebrew converts had given serious consideration to returning to their earlier ways of coping with life's trials. Disillusioned that faith in Jesus hadn't brought them freedom from persecution, they began to believe He wasn't the deliverer who had originally impressed them.

Throughout my explanations, I refer to these Hebrews the writer has written to as "converts." Though some think a convert is a born-again believer, according to *Vine's*, the word *convert* simply carries the meaning "causing a person to turn." I call these people converts because they had turned from their Hebrew traditions to embrace Christianity.

The writer sternly cautioned these converts to stand firm against the temptation to dismiss the truths that they knew about Jesus. Though they were tempted to stop following the Lord, he reminded them that if they were truly born again then the grace that is resident within their newborn nature would spring up, as Jesus promised, and thus escaping *their fallen nature*.

Escaping Your Fallen Nature

> ⁴ For *it is* impossible for those who were once enlightened, and have tasted of the heavenly gift, and were made partakers of the Holy Ghost, ⁵ And have tasted the good word of God, and the powers of the world to come, ⁶ If they shall fall away, to renew them again unto repentance; seeing they crucify to themselves the Son of God afresh, and put *him* to an open shame. **Hebrews 6:4-6**

From this text, we learn it would be impossible for those who have tasted of the Lord and have actively participated in the things of God, should they fall away, to be renewed again unto repentance. The writer warned that those of them who were contemplating quitting on Jesus were at the precipice over which if they fell, they would never again feel the draw of the Holy Spirit on their hearts. After the Holy Spirit has been repeatedly pushed away, the hearts of the candidates will harden and will no longer be responsive to His draw. At this point repentanceis impossible.

The writer seemed to be referring to born-again believers when speaking of the impossibility of being renewed unto repentance. Heseemed to be implying that if they backslid and failed to grow, they risked losing their salvation. Many students of the Word believe that these people were already born-again believers. They interpret thispassage about falling away as proof that born-again believers can lose their salvation.

But I'm going to show that that is a misinterpretation.A little explanation will help clarify the writer's intended meaning.While the writer was confident that some of his readers would respond to his teaching and grow to a maturity expected of believers, he couldn't be sureabout all of them. Though it appeared that he wasaddressing newborn believers, he was also speaking to those who,though they were committed to the church, were never fully committed to Jesus.

If you know you're saved but are struggling to overcome your fear of losing your salvation, relief from this fear will come as you grow in your understanding of this scripture passage. You need to be aware that these scriptures, which seem to imply that born-again believers can fall away, are not referring to true believers after all.

Though they had heard the gospel message and readily absorbed it in their minds, some of these people that the writer was warning had never accepted the offer of salvation in their hearts.

> ¹ Therefore we ought to give the more earnest heed to the things which we have heard, lest at any time we should let *them* slip... ³ How shall we escape, if we neglect so great salvation; which at the first began to be spoken by the Lord, and was confirmed unto us by them that heard *him*; **Hebrews 2:1, 3**

If we don't listen carefully, these words will slip away rather than dropping into our hearts to birth a brand new one. The writer warned that if we don't listen to his teaching, our rejection of it may mean that we hadnever been born again. If we neglect God's pre-salvation grace one more time, it's possible our hearts will become so hardened that we won't be able to or even want to make inquiry of the Lord again. Our hearts will no longer sense the drawing power of the Lord.

> No man can come to me, except the Father which hath sent me draw him: **John 6:44**

The writer encouraged his converts to put confidence in God's ability to keep them from falling away. He asked how they would be able to escape from further heartache and cope with their troubles if they chose to quit on Him. He urged them to reconsider Jesus. Since they had come from Judaism, the writer reminded them that Jesus was better than anyone else in whom they had previously had faith. He was better than any angel, better than the highly revered Moses, and even better than any high priest.

However, because they feared their persecution, these converts felt extreme pressure from the Jewish community to return to God's original belief system. Aggressive Jewish preachers had likely told them that they had forsaken Moses and the Law of God. If these new converts continued with Jesus, whom many Jews considered to be a blasphemer and a false prophet, they were told that they would incur very severe retribution from God Himself. Such a warning would have had a great impact on them.

The writer addressed these Hebrews as if they had completely missed the purpose of the Old Testament sacrificial system which was to help them to look forward to the coming of the Messiah. He maintained that they should have known these truths by that point. But because they were slow to grasp them, he would take time to now explain them in much greater detail.

He described how the old system of priests bringing blood sacrifices was a type of the ultimate sacrifice that would end all sacrifices. He explained how a new High Priest had performed a final sacrifice under an altogether new priestly system. This High Priest didn't qualify according to the criteria of the Aaronic priestly system but, instead, was qualified because He came from an earlier and far superior system which he referred to as the order of Melchizedek.

The writer declared Jesus to be this new High Priest and then showed how He had made the ultimate sacrifice of shedding His blood to cover their sins and had completely removed all their guilt. Through His sacrifice, He provided for each of them a new heart as prophesied by Jeremiah, one free of sin or corruption. Because God had accepted Jesus's sacrifice and had given them new hearts, they could now come free from fear into His presence.

They could come not once a year as under the old system but continually and without interruption forever.

> ¹⁰ For this *is* the covenant that I will make with the house of Israel after those days, saith the Lord; I will put my laws into their mind, and write them in their hearts: and I will be to them a God, and they shall be to me a people: ¹¹ And they shall not teach every man his neighbour, and every man his brother, saying, Know the Lord: for all shall know me, from the least to the greatest. ¹² For I will be merciful to their unrighteousness, and their sins and their iniquities will I remember no more. **Hebrews 8:10-12**

We observe that this passage talks about the newheart God promised (which earlier we learned is the promise of the Father) to all who put trust in Jesus as their Savior. It says the laws of God are now written not on stone as before but on "fleshy" hearts (see also 2 Corinthians 3:3). Why would these Hebrews return to the old ways of following laws if these laws were a part of their new, born-again, nature?

The writer of Hebrews acknowledged that these converts believed they had God's approval to return to their former religion. But he told them that instead of having His approval by quitting on Jesus, they would be subject to God's wrath. He brought to their attentionthat the purpose of the prior sacrificial system was to prepare them for the coming Messiah.

The writer showed that the priestly system that these Hebrews were tempted to return to was very inferior to the priesthood of Jesus. In defeating death, Jesus eliminated the need to continue their sacrificial system. They should have recognized that they no longer needed the former system that pointed to Him. Considering that they grew up with these truths, they had no

Escaping Your Fallen Nature

excuse for not knowing the signs that pointed to Him. They had no excuse for not recognizing Him.

John the Baptist was the last instrument in the old covenant that God used to point people to Jesus. John taught that he had fulfilled his role of introducing them to Jesus and that it was no longer necessary for them to have their eyes on him. In getting their focus on Jesus, their attention on the signs that pointed to him would steadily diminish. This attention on Jesus wouldincrease while that on John and all otherswould decrease.

These new converts could notsay thatthey had received the understanding and sympathy they needed from any of the priests on whom they had previously relied. Neither could they expect to get the kind of love and encouragement from former associates that they were nowreceiving from their new community of believers. There would be no point in departing from Jesus as He proved that He was far more interested in their troubles than ever demonstrated by these priests.

The writer demonstrated that Jesus, like none other, had the compassion to help them get through their suffering. He reminded them that the same temptation with which they were presently struggling, to quit, Jesus had also faced. And because He proved Himself to be an overcomer, He could help them in their battle to overcome also. While former associates pounced on them for having left Judaism, Jesus, withno ill feelings or judgment toward them, has completely identified with their temptation to quit on Him.

> [14] Forasmuch then as the children are partakers of flesh and blood, he also himself likewise took part of the same; that through death he might destroy him that had the power of death, that is, the devil; [15] And deliver them who through fear of death were all their lifetime subject to bondage. [16] For verily he took not on *him the nature of* angels; but he took on *him* the seed of

Abraham. ⁷ Wherefore in all things it behoved him to be made like unto *his* brethren, that he might be a merciful and faithful high priest in things *pertaining* to God, to make reconciliation for the sins of the people. ¹⁸ For in that he himself hath suffered being tempted, he is able to succour them that are tempted. **Hebrews 2:14-18**

The sufferings that Jesus experienced were no less a test of His character than the sufferings that these Hebrew converts experienced had been a test of theirs. Inspired by Jesus's example, they should not have been without the strength that they needed to overcome their temptation to quit.

Since Jesus identifies with our temptations and is thus able to help us through ours, the writer strongly exhorts us to consider Jesus's credentials: that He is far more worthy of our trust than any prior support system that we previously trusted and to which we are now tempted to return.

Jesus has proven Himself in every way to be the only priest or friend who can help us and feel for our infirmities during our times of temptation. He even welcomes us as His brethren. When we consider all the facts as these Hebrew converts were encouraged to do, how can we possibly not have the fortitude to overcome? The only reason strength would not be available is if we don't have within us His overcoming new nature.

When we go through times of discouragement, we need to remember that Jesus feels what we're feeling. Because of the weight of our burdens, many of us even right now are tempted to give up. Even as our temptation puts our commitment to the Lord to the test, Jesus's temptation not to complete His mission tested His commitment as well.

Whereas we may give in when stresses become too intense, Jesus remained faithful to the end. Because the intensity of His temptation was far greater, His victory over it (which I explain in greater detail in Part III) is a huge inspiration to us to continue. When we remind ourselves that we have His nature, the same one that endured the cross, we then realizethat we also have in our hearts this powerful grace for *escaping our fallen nature* (our temptations).

The writer then urged the converts from Judaism to move on from the sign posts pointing to Jesus to the point that they willembrace Him as their long-awaited Messiah.

> ¹ Therefore leaving the principles of the doctrine of Christ, let us go on unto perfection; not laying again the foundation of repentance from dead works, and of faith toward God, ² Of the doctrine of baptisms, and of laying on of hands, and of resurrection of the dead, and of eternal judgment. **Hebrews 6:1-2**

He instructed them to leave behind the beginning revelations that pointed to the Messiah, which earlier he referred to as milk (pre-salvation grace), and instead turn their attention solely on to Jesus. Since He has arrived, the pointer that had pointed to Him has fulfilled its purpose and is no longer needed. It was now time to get into the meat of what Jesus has done (see John 4:31-34).

What were these beginning revelations that they could now leave behind? Was the writer saying that repentance, faith,baptisms, laying on of hands, and the resurrection of the dead were elementary? Was he saying these were truths that these new converts no longer need because they have grown out of the baby stage of their born-again experience? That's not what he was saying.

Obviously, the truths that were a part of their daily spiritual growth should never be left out of their lives. These principles the writer recommended these new converts leave behind weren't the beliefs that would inspire them to grow; instead, they were part of their previous belief system.

When the writer spoke of not laying down again the foundation of repentance unto dead works, he was referring to the sacrificial system. He stated that no amount of shedding of the blood of animals or acts of repentance to turn from evil could by themselves remove people's sin and cleanse them from guilt and corruption. Since such works could not impart life, they must now be considered as dead.

He then, shockingly, said that they were to leave behind faith in God. When he made that statement, it's likely he had in mind the same thought that Jesus had in mind when He said,

> Ye believe in God, believe also in me. **John 14:1**

James said that people who believed in God were doing well. But then sarcastically, he reminded them the devil believes in God also. Thus, the writer didn't tell these Hebrew converts to stop believing in their understanding of God as revealed to them under the old covenant, but instead was encouraging them to move on from faith in God only. They needed to have a belief in God but more specifically as He was revealed to them through Jesus, their Messiah.

In the "laying on of hands," the writer was referring to one of the duties of the high priest. When he laid his hands on a goat, he transferred the sins of the people to this goat to carry them into the wilderness. But of course, the laying on of hands was symbolism and a means of pointing to what the Messiah would have done. Since the Messiah had arrived and had already taken on Himself all their sins, thus forever eliminating the need of more goats, it was time to move on.

The writer spoke to them as though they ought to have already known these truths about the purpose of the sacrificial system.

> ¹² For when for the time ye ought to be teachers, ye have need that one teach you again which *be* the first principles of the oracles of God; and are become such as have need of milk, and not of strong meat. ¹³ For every one that useth milk *is* unskilful in the word of righteousness: for he is a babe. **Hebrews 5:12-13**

He talked to them as newborns but not because he was convinced they had been born again. Rather, he believed the truths they had grown up on were the very seeds that when mixed with faith would have caused them to be birthed into God's family. But because some of them did not respond to these truths as God had intended, the formation of Jesus in them, instead of progressing toward newbirth, was on the verge of a miscarriage. Though babies (not fetuses) in the womb of their spiritual hearts, their nourishment continued to be the pre-salvation milk (grace) of the Word.

Many of us grew up with belief systems that in some way pointed us to God. Those in authority over us taught us to keep the Ten Commandments. Some of us were scolded when we did things on Sunday that they interpreted as breaking the Sabbath. We were taught never to steal or lie. We learned the golden rule of doing to others what we would have wanted them to do to us. We learned to love our neighbors as ourselves and give proper respect to those in authority. In a sense all this training, similar to the Jewish old covenant system, was a means of pointing us to something better. We now use this past training to inspire us to look beyond ourselves tothe One who can move us out of our bondages and forward into His liberty.

In my early years of knowing the Lord, I tended to be very legalistic. I was always concerned with doing everything perfectly according to the law. I was so rigid in my attempt to keep the commandments that instead of my relationship with Jesus giving me liberty, my focus on the law brought me to bondage. I was so hard on myself that for a short time, maybe one or two years, I applied the rule of keeping the Sabbath day rest very strictly.

Between my second and third year in Bible college, I interned in Virden, Manitoba, with a pastor to learn in practical ways how to be a pastor. While there, I became friends with one of the guys in the church. On one Sunday afternoon, he invited me to his place. It was a beautiful warm summer day – just right for playing baseball. He asked me to join him in playing catch. But because I was fearful of breaking the Sabbath-day commandment, I declined.

I was caught up so much with following the commandments literally that I forgot they were to act as signs pointing us to the one who would fulfill them. The Sabbath day of resting, while reviving us physically and mentally, showed us our need for the spiritual rest that we receive in Jesus. When Jesus on the cross said, "It is finished," He meant His work of paying for our sins was finished. We no longer labor to earn our salvation. Instead, we receive it as a gift.

Later, I was embarrassed to learn that resting from my labors on Sunday, because the Sabbath is Saturday, fell miserably short of what the commandment required. The ability to follow the Commandments, I discovered, came not through my efforts but only through the power I received when I received a new heart. Through this new heart, because flowing from it is the power and fruits of the Spirit, I am now able to keep the commandments.

> Love worketh no ill to his neighbor... love *is* the fulfilling of the law. **Romans 13:10**

These commandments are manifested not through rules and regulations but through God's nature of love as fruits of the Spirit. When these fruits of the Spirit, which are the very character and nature of Jesus, are flowing, no outside law is necessary (see

Galatians 5:18, 22-23). Now that Jesus has come into view, we should no longer pursue external laws that pointed us to Him; our focus should be on Him only. But like those Hebrew converts, some of us are slow in transferring our focus from the pointer to the one to whom the pointer points.

In this chapter, we have learned that those who listen carefully to instructions and warnings and who have reconsidered Jesus's credentials can have the confidence of moving forward. Those who have continually hardened their hearts to the gospel and who have not followed the signs that pointed them to Jesus have seriously increased their risk of falling away permanently.

CHAPTER 11

LISTENS TO WARNINGS ON BACKSLIDING

In several passages in this letter to these Hebrew converts, the writer warned them not to neglect their salvation. Considering the harshness and severity in the tone of his warnings, the writer had three groups of people in mind: the discouraged believers tempted to backslide; the believers already backsliding; and the unbelievers who, having neglected pre-salvation grace, were heading in the direction of falling away.

The author of Hebrews then used the analogy of the ground to illustrate there is no possibility for those who are no longer listening and are fallen away of being renewed again unto repentance.

> ⁷ For the earth which drinketh in the rain that cometh oft upon it, and bringeth forth herbs meet for them by whom it is dressed, receiveth blessing from God: ⁸ But that which beareth thorns and briers *is* rejected,and *is* nigh unto cursing; whose end *is* to be burned. **Hebrews 6:7-8**

Escaping Your Fallen Nature

After it's been soaked in the rain, the soil, as long it's been worked and cultivated, produces fruitfulness. But the cultivating of it must take place immediately following the rain. Otherwise, the moisture, being intercepted or diverted from the good seed, will produce briars and thorns.

When I was in my early teens my Dad required my younger brother and me to hoe or weed out the garden. It seems to me, if I remember correctly, that if we were regular in our weeding the garden, then the plants and vegetables did very well. But when we neglected to do our duties and were a few days late, then when we went back to the garden, much to our surprise, the weeds were everywhere and were choking out all the good stuff.

I suppose the reason why we let the garden go for a while was because since there had not been any recent rains, we believed that the weeds weren't as likely to grow so much. We found out that whatever small amount of moisture there was, if we didn't immediately hoe them out, then these weeds would intercept the moisture from getting to the plants and vegetables.

So likewise, when our hearts are weeded and receive the rain of God's pre-salvation grace that points to the Messiah, this rain will produce fruit unto salvation. When we respond to the convicting work of the Holy Spirit, we are cultivating or weeding our hearts and thus facilitating the growth of the seed of God's Word to form Christ in us. But when we neglect to respond to this conviction to remove (weed out) hindrances, we will then be giving an opportunity for these "briars and thorns" to continue growing, which will then interfere with the growth of the good seed.

> [14] The sower soweth the word. [15] And these are they by the way side, where the word is sown; but when they have heard, Satan cometh immediately, and taketh away the word that was sown in their hearts. [16] And these are they likewise which are sown on stony ground; who, when

they have heard the word, immediately receive it with gladness; [17] And have no root in themselves, and so endure but for a time: afterward, when affliction or persecution ariseth for the word's sake, immediately they are offended. [18] And these are they which are sown among thorns; such as hear the word, [19] And the cares of this world, and the deceitfulness of riches, and the lusts of other things entering in, choke the word, and it becometh unfruitful. [20] And these are they which are sown on good ground; such as hear the word, and receive *it*, and bring forth fruit, some thirtyfold, some sixty, and some an hundred.
Mark 4:14-20

The stony ground represents hearts that are not yet softened enough by the initial rain to allow the seed to take root. This rain of God's grace on the soil of our hearts is an occasion for us, who have chosen to consider God's offer, to complain and gripe. Because the beginning stages of the formation of Jesus in us hasn't reached far enough beneath the surface to establish stability, we doubt God's care. Because we believe God didn't provide us an escape from our tribulations and persecutions, we murmur against Him and become offended. Our offense is similar to that of the Israelites, who forfeited their "rest" because of their murmurings (see Hebrews 4).

The thorns represent hearts that don't have the commitment to guard themselves from the distractions of the world. The many cares and anxieties that we center our attention on and the deceitfulness of riches choke out the nourishment that is required for the continuing of the formation of Jesus. Our failure to weed these cares and deceitsout of our hearts cutsus off from this pre-salvation grace, leaving us malnourished and in danger of experiencing a miscarriage or abortion and thus making us to become unfruitful.

The deciding factor is what we do with the first rain. This first rain is our introduction to Jesus and learning how He has purchased our salvation and rightfully owns us. Will we be diligent to remove the stones and hoe out the weeds that cause us to resist His lordship over our lives? These stones and weeds are the quickly taken offenses and the easily captured anxieties that we allow to interfere with the growing of our faith. Unless our hearts are cultivated, these interferences usually become apparent following this first or former rain of God's pre-salvation grace.

But when we remove these stones and weeds, future showers will bring us the rest of the way to form Christ in us.

> His going forth is prepared as the morning; and he shall come unto us as the rain, as the latter *and* former rain unto the earth. **Hosea 6:3**
>
> For he hath given you the former rain moderately, and he will cause to come down for you the rain, the former rain, and the latter rain in the first *month*. **Joel 2:23**
>
> Behold, the husbandman waiteth for the precious fruit of the earth, and hath long patience for it, until he receive the early and latter rain. **James 5:7**

This "latter rain" of the Holy Spirit on us produces the newborn nature. But if we fail to remove these stones and thorns, they will prevent our hearts from becoming softened. Our sense of our need for Jesus becomes diminished.

When we reject God's pre-salvation former rain grace, we will become cursed and burned. These briars and thorns that sprout up will interfere with the latter rain grace of God that would have led us to salvation (see Titus 2:11). If our relationship with the

Lord is shallow or is of such little priority that the tribulations and cares of life render us unfruitful, we have reason to believe that possibly we are not yet born again.

In this parable of the sower, Jesus was showing that the ability to endure trials marks the difference between those who are fruitful and those who are barren. Jesus said the seed of the Word of God, if we allow it to be rooted in the depth of our hearts, can survive the hardships of life to produce fruitfulness. This seed of God's Word is so powerful that it will accomplish its purpose, not only to soften hearts but to harden them also (see Isaiah 55:11). Whereas the Word of God spoken by Jonah softened the heart of the king of Nineveh (see Jonah 3:1–10), the Word of God spoken by Moses hardened the heart of the king of Egypt (see Exodus 9:12, 34–35).

At the first, many will soak God's Word into their minds and souls and give the appearance that they are committed to the Lord. But it is their responses to the temptations and trials of life that will reveal their true level of commitment. Did they facilitate the journey of God's Word to reach the depth of their hearts or was it their failure to remove the stones and thorns on the surface of their hearts that caused the Word to be intercepted? Tribulations and persecutions, for some, revealed that they didn't allow the Word to get past the surface of their hardened hearts. For others, it was their many cares and the deceitfulness of riches that revealed, though the Word went beneath the surface, that they had not made room in their hearts for it to take root.

Those enduring only "for a while" became offended because they believed God deliberately allowed their troubles instead of preventing them. And though surviving initial troubles, those who "became unfruitful" revealed hearts that had allowed cares and deceits to "choke the word."

While persistent offenses and anxietiesare an evidence of beleaguered believers also, in this parable, Jesus distinguished growing Christians from those who hadnot been born again.

Escaping Your Fallen Nature

Though struggling with tribulations and distractions that reduce fruitfulness, the born-again believer can never be described as "becometh unfruitful" (see Mark 4:19).

Since it is only by the Word of God (see 1 Peter 1:23) that candidates can be born again, and since in the case of these 3 candidates the Word of God was stolen by Satan, blocked from reaching the depth of their hearts by offenses, and choked to death by worldly distractions, all of them failed to reach that point where the formation of Jesus could be completed to produce a new birth. This is verified by the statement of Jesus when He said that only the fourth candidate became fruitful.

Though we may backslide, returning to the Lord and enduring to the end proves fruitfulness. Any amount of fruitfulness, even as little as one-fold, is proof that the seed of God's Word fell on good ground (see Mark 4:20). But those people whose hearts produced zero fruitfulness were not of good ground and thus never were born again. The servant who received one talent but was unwilling to work it to produce a profit (see Matthew 25:26-30) illustrates unfruitfulness, after which he was cast into outer darkness, thus proving that those who are unfruitful were never saved.

These persecutions and deceits were not the cause of their fall and their turning away from the Lord. Rather, they were the occasion to prove that because their hearts were not cultivated, the planting of the Word had not taken root. This meant that the winds of life could easily blow them over.

> That we henceforth be no more children, tossed to and fro, and carried about with every wind of doctrine … they lie in wait to deceive.
> **Ephesians 4:14**

Though it's possible that Paul was referring to childish believers, I think it is more likely that he was referring to unbelievers. Those who are "tossed to and fro and are carried about with every wind of doctrine" is a description of the ungodly, not of newborn Christians who have surrendered their all to the Lordship of Jesus. When the winds of new doctrine appeal to their sense of pride and entitlement, it is the uncommitted who will show themselves to be unstable in all their ways.

Jesus illustrated this truth when He talked about the foolish man who had built his house on the sand. His house was blown over because it was not built on the rock. Likewise, the candidates for salvation who, when facing offenses and cares, are easily tossed to and fro to become unfruitful, have shown that their lives have never been grounded on the solid foundation of Jesus.

> [2] Every branch in me that beareth not fruit he taketh away: and every *branch* that beareth fruit, he purgeth it, that it may bring forth more fruit.
> [6] If a man abide not in me, he is cast forth as a branch, and is withered; and men gather them, and cast *them* into the fire, and they are burned.
> **John 15:2, 6**

Though these branches are now unfruitful, because they are connected to the vine, many believe this connection is proof that they are believers. But Jesus was trying to distinguish between the branch that "he taketh away" from the branch God purged "that it may bring forth more fruit."

Though there is no evidence that they bore fruit, many believe the branches taken away were believers and thus had lost their salvation. Paul used branches to indicate that Israel was also cut out of the tree because of unfruitfulness (see Romans 9–11). But they were cut off because it was their righteousness, not the righteousness of Jesus, that was hanging from those branches.

So also, Jesus illustrated that He would take away the branches in Him that were not bearing fruit. By saying "every branch in me," he was referring to the people who, though they don't know

Him personally, have experienced the draw of His pre-salvation former rain grace and in whom the formation of Jesus in its early stages in the womb of their hearts had already begun.

> For the grace of God that bringeth salvation hath appeared to all men, **Titus 2:11**

But because they have chosen not to abide in this grace, which would have brought them to salvation if they had properly cultivated their hearts and had not blocked it from producing genuine faith, they are taken away. Eventually, they end up in the fire to be burned. But the people who are born again are the branches that bear some fruit. They are never taken away but rather purged so that they may "bring forth more fruit." These same peoplewill bear different levels of fruitfulness: some at a hundred-fold, some at sixty-fold, and others at thirty-fold.

> ⁴ For *it is* impossible for those who were once enlightened, and have tasted of the heavenly gift, and were made partakers of the Holy Ghost, ⁵ And have tasted the good word of God, and the powers of the world to come, ⁶ If they shall fall away, to renew them again unto repentance; seeing they crucify to themselves the Son of God afresh, and put *him* to an open shame. **Hebrews 6:4-6**

Though the writer described these Hebrews as if they had newborn hearts, he has already concluded that among them were people on the verge of falling away.And since only unbelievers can be in danger of falling away, why is he suggesting that these believers may get to the point that they may not have any further opportunity for salvation? Did this writer make a contradiction? If these people are on the edge of falling away, why then, if they are not believers, is he also saying that they are enlightened, have tasted the heavenly gift, and are partakers of the Holy Ghost?

I'm sure many of us have seen people enlightened by the anointed Word of God and touched by mighty miracles who afterward walked away as if nothing had happened. Though they partook of the fruits of the Holy Spirit flowing from others, they resisted the wooing of the Spirit to make a decision for the Lord. When the writer described these people as being enlightened and having tasted, he did not say that this enlightenment had caused the transformation of the heart of every one of them. He was simply acknowledging that those who were on the verge of falling away had also been completely immersed in these Holy Spirit anointed meetings.

This uncertainty the writer had about some of these people is seen in several passages:

> ¹² Take heed, brethren, lest there be in any of you an evil heart of unbelief, in departing from the living God. ¹³ But exhort one another daily, while it is called To day; lest any of you be hardened through the deceitfulness of sin. **Hebrews 3:12-13**
>
> Let us therefore fear, lest, a promise being left *us* of entering into his rest, any of you should seem to come short of it. **Hebrews 4:1**
>
> Looking diligently lest any man fail of the grace of God; lest any root of bitterness springing up trouble *you*, and thereby many be defiled; **Hebrews 12:15**

But we notice that the writer also has commended them on their faithfulness to the Lord.

Escaping Your Fallen Nature

> For God *is* not unrighteous to forget your work and labour of love, which ye have shewed toward his name, in that ye have ministered to the saints, and do minister. **Hebrews 6:10**
>
> ³² But call to remembrance the former days, in which, after ye were illuminated, ye endured a great fight of afflictions; ³³ Partly, whilst ye were made a gazingstock both by reproaches and afflictions; and partly, whilst ye became companions of them that were so used. ³⁴ For ye had compassion of me in my bonds, and took joyfully the spoiling of your goods, knowing in yourselves that ye have in heaven a better and an enduring substance. **Hebrews 10:32-34**

But then he says he is not confident that every one of them is worthy of these compliments.

> ¹¹ And we desire that every one of you do shew the same diligence to the full assurance of hope unto the end: ¹² That ye be not slothful, but followers of them who through faith and patience inherit the promises. **Hebrews 6:11-12**
>
> ³⁵ Cast not away therefore your confidence, which hath great recompence of reward. ³⁶ For ye have need of patience, that, after ye have done the will of God, ye might receive the promise. **Hebrews 10:35-36**

The writer warned them that they should not be slothful or cast away their confidence. He told them to make sure God's pre-salvation grace wasn't ambushed by the many cares and deceits that continually attacked them. By encouraging them to be inspired by the patience they saw in others, he acknowledged the possibility that those who were struggling may not yet have had an experience of receiving thenewborn nature. He wrote thatit is only those who can endure all their troubles to the very end who have provided evidence that they have born-again new hearts.

> ⁶ But Christ as a son over his own house; whose house are we, if we hold fast the confidence and the rejoicing of the hope firm unto the end. ¹⁴ For we are made partakers of Christ, if we hold the beginning of our confidence stedfast unto the end; **Hebrews 3:6-14**

Only if they continued "firm unto the end" could they have confidence that they were a part of the house of Christ. If what impressed them enough in the beginning to turn to Christ didn't continue to sustain them to the end, that meant they never were born of the Spirit in the first place.

But this passage, again, seems to indicate a contradiction to what we earlier quoted this writer as saying. In Hebrews 6:1-4 he said that it was impossible for the partakers of the Holy Ghost, if they fall away, to renew them again unto repentance. But here, he says that the proof that we have partaken of Christ is that we will hold right to the end the initial evidences of our new birth. He seems to be saying that though we have partaken of the Holy Ghost, it is possible that we could fall away. Yet, at the same time he seems to be saying that if we have partaken of Christ, we have the assurance that we will hold out right to the end and will never fall away.

This seeming contradiction is resolved by realizing that these who have partaken of the Holy Ghost were partakers of the grace that was intended to lead them into salvation. However, if they did not continue with this grace to complete the born-again process, then they can never claim that they were partakers of Christ. And neither can they claim that they were ever partakers of Christ unless they endure right to the end. While candidates partake of the Holy Ghost prior to salvation, they cannot partake of Christ until after salvation – after they've come to accept Him as Savior.

It was to these whose commitment to remain steadfast to the end is in doubt that the writer was warning of the danger of permanently falling away. But if they sensed the conviction of the Holy Spirit due to these warnings, this was their occasion to escape their temptation to altogether fall away. This may have been their final opportunity to accept Jesus and receive a newborn heart.

The writer drew these conclusions either from personal encounters or from the observers who reported to him what they had seen. We can tell by his comments that he couldn't distinguish for certain the saved from the unsaved. He did not want to differentiate the discouraged believers as well as those already into backsliding from those who were at the point of falling away.

The writer put all these people in one group because they all had been exposed to the works of God and therefore had been enlightened, had tasted, and had partaken. All he knew was that these people, as a whole, were tempted to quit on Jesus, and hence his warning to them.

Everything I have said about this Hebrews church also applies to the seven churches in Asia to whom John sent messages from Jesus in Revelation.

To the church in Ephesus Jesus said that they needed to repent and return to their first love or else He would remove their candlestick. To the church in Smyrna He said that after they have proven themselves to be faithful unto death, He will give them the crown of life. To the church in Pergamos He said that there were people among them that were into evil ways and that unless they repent, He will fight against them. To the church in Thyatira He said that those among them who have refused to repent will go through great tribulation, but the rest He will spare.

To the church in Sardis He said that there were only a few of them who He knew would remain loyal to Him, but to the rest He warned to repent, or be lost. To the church in Philadelphia He commended them for their patience and said they would escape the tribulation and that their names would not be blotted out. To the church in Laodicea He said though they are lukewarm they still have time to surrender.

From all His statements to these churches we can see that Jesus never concluded that all the individuals within each church were saved. As in the Hebrews church, an examination of these churches reveals that there were individuals in them that either were at the brink of backsliding, already backsliding, or at the threshold of falling away. To most of them, Jesus issued a warning to certain individuals within them that if they didn't clean up their lives, they would be lost.

But He said it was the ability to endure and overcome that distinguished the saved from the unsaved. He gave no indication that those who were living an ungodly lifestyle, though they were regular attenders at their church, were saved. If they refused to repent or were unable to overcome their temptations, then that was proof that they did not have the born-again endurable new nature of Jesus in them – that they never were saved in the first place.

> ^{4} Nevertheless I have *somewhat* against thee, because thou hast left thy first love. ^{5} Remember therefore from whence thou art fallen, and repent, and do the first works; or else I will come unto thee quickly, and will remove thy candlestick out of his place, except thou repent. **Revelation 2:4-5**

Now for those in the church at Ephesus, Jesus indicated that everyone had left their first love. However, He did not suggest they would lose their salvation if they didn't repent. When He said that the candlestick of this church would be removed if they did not repent, He was saying that if they did not become more passionate in their service to the Lord to validate their claim that they truly loved Him, they would no longer be effective in their attempt to influence their communities.

> Follow peace with all *men*, and holiness, without which no man shall see the Lord:
> **Hebrews 12:14**

When we don't demonstrate a passionate love for Jesus and fail to give a clear testimony of the changes that He wrought in our lives, then the cities and communities to whom we are trying to be a witness won't see Jesus in us. For without a flow of Holy Spirit inspired peace and holiness among us, they won't see any evidence that proves that we truly care for them. We would then be no longer a candlestick lighting up the path that would lead sinners to the Savior.

These warnings applied not only to the Hebrew and Asian churches but also to the churches to which Paul wrote. Based on what he learned about the churches in Galatia, he seriously doubted that all were born again. For some, he was concerned that he might have to start all over again the process of birthing them into a relationship with the Lord (see Galatians 4:19–20).

Because Paul spoke very highly of those in the Corinthian church, saying that they had not come behind in any gift, many assume that he was saying that everyone in the church was saved. Though spending a major amount of his letter dealing with struggles that were common with many new believers, he did not mean to imply that all the people in the church were truly born again.

> ⁹ Know ye not that the unrighteous shall not inherit the kingdom of God? Be not deceived: neither fornicators, nor idolaters, nor adulterers,

> nor effeminate, nor abusers of themselves with mankind, ¹⁰ Nor thieves, nor covetous, nor drunkards, nor revilers, nor extortioners, shall inherit the kingdom of God. ¹¹ And such were some of you: but ye are washed, but ye are sanctified, but ye are justified in the name of the Lord Jesus, and by the Spirit of our God. **1 Corinthians 6:9-11**

After explicitly saying that people who continually demonstrated bondage to their evil nature would not inherit the kingdom of God, he conceded that some of them did not need such a warning.By emphasizing "such were some of you" reminding them that they were the ones that had already been delivered from these past bondages, Paul implied that many of them were not yet delivered and therefore not yet washed and cleansed. These peoplewere like many of them in the Hebrew and Asian churches who,though warned of the dangers that would befall them,continued to resist God's offer of pre-salvation grace (see 2 Corinthians 6:1–2).

Though many were warned of rejecting His pre-salvation grace, God assured those who had been rejecting His post-salvation grace that eventually they would respond and return to Him. An excellent illustration of God drawing and rescuing a backslidden believer is a story told by Jesus in the gospel of Luke about the son who demanded from his father his inheritance. This boy is referred to as the Prodigal Son because he went out and wasted all that he had received.

> ¹¹ And he said, A certain man had two sons: ¹² And the younger of them said to *his* father, Father, give me the portion of goods that falleth*to me*. And he divided unto them *his* living. ¹³ And not many days after the younger son gathered all

together, and took his journey into a far country, and there wasted his substance with riotous living. [17] And when he came to himself, he said, How many hired servants of my father's have bread enough and to spare, and I perish with hunger! [18] I will arise and go to my father, and will say unto him, Father, I have sinned against heaven, and before thee, [19] And am no more worthy to be called thy son: make me as one of thy hired servants. **Luke 15:11-13,17-19**

Nothing in this story indicates that when he repented, this son was responding to an outside influence. Scripture says, "He came to himself." He responded to his memory of the good things he had enjoyed when he was at home with his father. He realized the enticements of the world were nothing compared to what he had left behind.

The boy returned to his father's farm with contriteness and fear. He hoped that if he returned and admitted his error in leaving, his father would again provide him food and shelter and treat him at least as well as he treated his servants.

Instead, his dad greeted him with a great show of love and rejoicing. He discovered that the judgment that he had expected and knew he deserved was the furthest thing from his father's mind. His father and the servants threw him a party worthy of a prince because the Prodigal, who had been lost and counted as dead, was found and was alive.

Jesus told the story of this wasteful but restored son to illustrate how God restores to Himself all of us who have wasted away the resources He gave to us when we were born again. To everyone who has been born into His family, our heavenly Father has given to us grace as evidence that we belong to Him. We have been promised an inheritance and as a guarantee that He will always take good care of us we've been sealed with the Holy Spirit.

Unfortunately, we turn our attention at times to the things of the world. Like the Prodigal, we have wasted what we have inherited from our heavenly Father. Talents He has given us to draw people toward Him, we then have used for our own pleasure. Because of this waste, we've become every bit as prodigal as the Prodigal Son.

In the Old Testament, God's people who no longer lived to bring glory to Him and who did not continue to follow in His ways became known as backsliders. Christians who have struggled with habitual defeats and have gone into the world wasting their resources and making no further effort to please the Lord are also backsliders. Because backslidden Christians do not partake of spiritual nourishment, their newborn hearts have gone into dormancy or hibernation.

For those who appear to have quit on the Lord and yet are indeed born from above, what seems to be a falling away actually is backsliding. Because they have the Lord in their hearts, they will ultimately return to Him. It may take a crisis of betrayal and deceit along with memories, like that of the Prodigal Son, that will awaken them to return to the Father to escape eternal judgment.

Those Christians who are struggling to live victorious, overcoming lives but are continually defeated need to realize that they are just one step from giving in to discouragement. Though not altogether quitting on the Lord, they face the temptation of backsliding. If they backslide, it will be difficult for them, as well as others, to discern if they ever were truly born again.

> All we like sheep have gone astray; we have turned every one to his own way; and the LORD hath laid on him the iniquity of us all. **Isaiah 53:6**

Just prior to telling this story of the Prodigal son, Jesus spoke of a shepherd who had lost a sheep and a woman who had lost a

Escaping Your Fallen Nature

coin. Both persisted in their search. We are the sheep and coin that were lost. Jesus is the rescuer and seeker who, like the shepherd, will not quit until He rescues that sheep that had gone astrayand, like the housekeeper, finds that coin that had vanished.

The hope of a backslider in returning to the Lord and being saved from falling away is to "come to himself." Though he is a backslider, the born-again new nature and life of Jesus resides in him. A backslidden Christian comes to himself when he remembers who he is in Christ. And this memory of his newborn heart is refreshed when a believer intercedes for him in prayer.

Many with whom God is working aren't backsliders. Because they've never committed to Him, they continue to be candidates for salvation. Because the Lord does not want any to fall away, though they continually reject His pre-salvation grace, He holds off from withdrawing it. He is so loving toward them that He continues to extend His mercy to all those who are willing to listen.

The writerto the Hebrews expressed confidence that those who were genuinely born again but tempted to backslide would renew their commitment to the Lord. He believed that they would heed his warnings and that they would stop drifting further away from Him. But because some of the backsliders continued to attend the church to keep up appearances, it was hard for the writer to distinguish these backsliders and those tempted to backslide from those not yet born again.

Because they had no confidence that they were any longer born again, the writer's warnings caused these who were discouraged and tempted to backslide to examine their hearts. They, along with them already backsliding, weren't spiritually alert enough to know their hearts' true condition. Because of fear that they would fall away and not be capable of returning to the Lord, these alarms of the writer's warnings had the effect of reviving out of dormancy their born-again new nature.

But those who did not respond to these warnings continued to reject the pre-salvation grace that would have led them to accept the Lord. As far as the writer of Hebrews was concerned, this opportunity may very well have been their last. They were so absorbed with self that no amount of future Holy Spirit conviction would be able to prompt them to reconsider the Lord Jesus. God had cut them off and gave them over to a hardened heart and a reprobate or Christ-rejecting mind.

> He, that being often reproved hardeneth *his* neck, shall suddenly be destroyed, and that without remedy. **Proverbs 29:1**
>
> And even as they did not like to retain God in *their* knowledge, God gave them over to a reprobate mind, to do those things which are not convenient; **Romans 1:28**

If you are a backslider who has gone astray, be reminded that because you are still a son of the Father, He is faithful to make a way for backsliders to escape their temptation to quit altogether on Him. You can have confidence that He will draw you back because,

> The Lord knoweth how to deliver the godly out of temptations, and to reserve the unjust unto the day of judgment to be punished: **2 Peter 2:9**

In this chapter, we have observed the power of God's Word to change lives and to draw back those who strayed away from Him. We have learned that the Lord is faithful to give all people the grace that will reveal to them through His Word the true condition of their hearts. To those who are on the edge of falling away, are in a backslidden state, or are tempted to backslide, He gives warning and abundant grace to escape their fallen nature.

CHAPTER 12

TESTIFIES TO GOD'S POWER TO RESTORE

I have heard stories of car crashes in whicheveryonebut one is killed. It turned out that that one person was a backslidden Christian. That backslider, it was discovered, was often covered in prayer by a believing family member or by someone interceding on his or her behalf. A short time later, that backslider through God's post-salvation grace came back to the Lord.

In fact, that is my testimony. I have no idea who had been praying for me, but I know God rescued me from death so I could have further opportunity to return to Him from my backsliding.

In 1973, while living in Winnipeg, I was traveling during the winter via the United Statesto Windsor to visit relatives. I was about halfway between Chicago and Detroit and was going the speed limit,fifty-five, when I hit a patch of ice,causingmy car to spin out. The front end of my car dipped and hit something solid. Instead of crossing over the median into oncoming traffic, my carsomersaulted, I think two times, and landed in the median dividing the two directions of traffic.

Someone who stopped was shocked to see me alive. If my car had not somersaulted, it was possible I would've hit him. Having witnessed this horrific crash, he wondered aloud how anybody could have survived it. I knew the Lord had spared my life. But that wasn't the only mercy He showered on me throughout this experience.

My head was bleeding, and my back was hurting. The police came, and I sat in their cruiser while waiting for the ambulance. One officer wanted to give me a ticket for careless driving, but his partner said, "Can't you see he's got enough trouble? He doesn't need any more." I give thanks to the Lord for that mercy.

The ambulance took me about ten miles east to a hospital in Kalamazoo, Michigan. On the way, I saw at least a dozen cars that had also spun out due to the flash ice storm and had ended up in the ditches. I didn't need to stay in the hospital any longer than two hours, just long enough for X-rays and stitches for the cut on my head.

A taxi took me to a Holiday Inn, and the next morning, I called the Michigan State police to find out where my car was. They said it was at a service station about twenty miles west. I asked for a patrol car to take me there, otherwise, I would've had to hitchhike. They came about one hour later and dropped me off just outside of a town named Lawton. I walked a mile or so to the service station. One glance at my car, a 68 Renault, I knew I had a big task ahead of me to make this car ready for travel. I asked the manager of the service station for the keys to my car. He asked me how much I was willing to give him to take this lump of metal off my hands. But when I told him I had no plans of scrapping it but was determined to drive it back to Winnipeg, he scoffed at me.

The front windshield and the back window were laid on the backseat. The frame was very badly twisted and had many dents. I started the car, but it would barely stay running. I got out and pondered what to do. Sensing I needed the Lord's help, I prayed. I asked Him, though I was in a backslidden state, to send someone to help me.

Then came my answer. Not more than five minutes later, a stranger appeared. He saw I was in a daze wondering what to do, and he offered to help me. He gave his whole day to help me put the car together. With duct tape and rope, we were able to make the windshield, which was badly shattered on the driver's side, to stay in place. He helped me fix the car so that it would be drivable. Later, I met his family, had supper, and slept there for the night. I did not ask if he was a believer, but his hospitality sure demonstrated what we would expect of a believer (or maybe of an angel).

The next morning, I thanked him and left for Detroit. Since I couldn't go over fifteen miles per hour, I drove all day on the shoulder. I prayed that any patrol car going by would have concerns more important than worrying about an eyesore slowly driving along the side of the highway. It took me most of the day to go the many miles to get to the US-Canada border. I asked the customs officer who stopped me if he would allow me to cross so my car would become Canada's problem instead of America's. He had no objection to sending me across.

When I got to Windsor, I prayed that the Lord would help me find an all-night service station that would allow me to use their garage bay. I soon found one. The attendant graciously allowed me to put my car up on the hoist after which I spent the whole night pounding out dents. When the morning came, I then found a shop where a mechanic got the motor up to speed. Then in Toronto, I found a Renault dealer and bought a new windshield. I then continued my journey, arriving in Winnipeg a few days later.

I marvel at the mercy of the Lord. There I was in a backslidden state. That accident could've easily taken my life. Though I wasn't presently putting it into practice, because I had been born again years earlier, God considered me righteous. This righteousness was not mine as I inherited it from the Lord Jesus when I was born into His family.

Though I was backslidden, the events following that accident confirmed that God considered me His son. Just as the Prodigal finally came to himself and remembered to whom he belonged, my close call with death occasioned me to remember to whom I belonged. The story of the restored son is proof that God never gives up on backsliders. Jesus told this story of the Prodigal to reveal the rejoicing that takes place in heaven when a son of God who has gone astray returns to his heavenly Father. All the angels throw a party!

Only a couple of weeks after the Lord spared my life, I recommitted my life to serving Him. As I mentioned earlier, I was a dispatcher for a security company in Winnipeg. Becoming part of my recommitment, I made it my habit to talk to the guards about the Lord. As I talked to a newly hired dispatcher that I was training, he asked why I was in this job. He said I ought to be a minister. Because I knew I had been avoiding the call that the Lord had put on me years earlier, his comment struck me. A few weeks after that, I enrolled in a Bible College in Saskatoon, Saskatchewan.

God had demonstrated, as had the father of the Prodigal son, that He had confidence that a severe test would draw out of me what was truly in my heart. Though dormant, if the never-dying nature of Jesus weren't the substance of my heart, God wouldn't have swept the house or searched the wilderness to find and rescue me.

Conversely, those even without a hibernating newborn nature have no guarantee that they will want to escape their temptations. Instead, they may desire to remain in the world. Since they never were born into God's family, quitting on the Lord's pre-salvation grace was not backsliding.

When some believers experience a season of discouragement, they backslide. But since they are already born from above, they eventually return to the Lord. They will not lose their salvation.

Escaping Your Fallen Nature

But some have drifted so far from the Lord that they are unable to discern the true condition of their heart.

It is not likely that backsliders, even if they claim that years earlier they had been genuinely born again, can have confidence that they still belong to the Lord or have escaped the danger of going to hell. If they knew their spiritual condition and that they were out of fellowship with the Lord, they would also seriously doubt that they were even in a relationship with the Lord. After all, the Prodigal son doubted that his father would receive him back as his son.

But since backsliders are born again, their new nature will compel them to acknowledge the working of the Spirit in their hearts. Eventually, as I did following my accident, they will come to themselves as the Prodigal son had. They will at least have the hope that the heavenly Father will make them if not one of His children at least servants whereby they could "squeeze" into heaven. But squeezing doesn't work. Until they fully return to the Lord, they will never be comfortable.

On the other hand, those who think they are backsliders but yet are not truly born again, may deceive themselves into believing they can never lose their salvation and thus become content to continue in their ungodly lifestyle. Because of their self-confidence and their inability to discern the truth about their true spiritual condition they will probably ignore the warnings of believers.

In my late teens I knew a high school dropout who was very much into the ways of the world. I tried to warn him that if he continued the way he was going, he could miss heaven. He recalled that he had made a commitment to the Lord in his childhood. He said he knew that the scriptures teach that once people are born again, they were safe and could never lose their salvation. He said he didn't care if he arrived in heaven battered and bruised and barely making it. He didn't care about his condition because he already had the "assurance" he was going to heaven.

No doubt, some backsliders have deliberately quit on the Lord and gone back into the world. Though they may be born again, it's dangerous for them to assume that they will make it to heaven when they know they aren't right with God. Doing nothing to bring about restoration could just as easily indicate that they never were born again in the first place. It could be that their coldness toward God is proof that they are just one step from falling away from grace and that soon they would be beyond the possibility of being renewed unto repentance (see Hebrews 6:4).

If these who want to believe that they are in a backslidden state and yet have never been born again, then their departure from God's grace is not that of a saved person losing their salvation, butinstead is a rejection of the grace that would have brought them to the point of accepting Jesus as Savior. Those who deceive themselves into believing that a childhood experience is proof that they are safe are at risk of falling away.

The childhood experience that they are relying on as proof of their salvation, though it was genuine, may have been one of a series of steps that was working in their hearts to continue and then ultimately complete the formation of Jesus in them to cause the new birth. To rest on memory and to not seek restoration is a decision that terminates this formation of Jesus in them. To not allow the Holy Spirit to complete what many years earlier He had begun through the planting and wateringof the seed of the Word of God is to commit abortion (not necessarily to kill, but to stop the new birth process).

The fact that God intervened to spare my life is a good indication that His intervention is necessary to block backsliders from going to hell. If I had died in that accident and then went to hell, my previous experience in the Lord, though it may have produced good feelings, was not the new birth. Because I didn't escape hell, I would have to conclude that though I may have been heading in the right direction, I had neglected to make sure that I had genuinely surrenderedmy life to Him. For if my experience

Escaping Your Fallen Nature

had gone beyond the emotional to involve my will, then having received the new nature that is endurable to the end, rather than going to hell, I would've made it to heaven.

Since God knew that in my heart was His born from above new nature which was made after His righteousness and holiness (Ephesians 4:24) He knew that His intervention would allow me the opportunity to manifest what was truly already in my heart. Though I was backslidden, God knew thata severe crisis would get my attention and that I wouldrepent and seek His forgiveness. This thought of God's mercy toward me, even to spare my life so that I would have another chance to repent, overwhelms me with gratitude.

> [9] Do thy diligence to come shortly unto me: [10] For Demas hath forsaken me, having loved this present world, and is departed unto Thessalonica; Crescens to Galatia, Titus unto Dalmatia. [11] Only Luke is with me. Take Mark, and bring him with thee: for he is profitable to me for the ministry. **2 Timothy 4:9-11**

The Apostle Paul seems to believe that Demas, having forsaken him because of greater love for the world than for serving the Lord, has finally manifested what was truly in his heart. He quit on Paul because his commitment to the Lord wasnot genuine. Feeling the sting of losing Demas, the Lord brings tohis mind how John Mark, who many years earlier had also forsaken him, is now giving evidence that he, unlike Demas, is born again and is serving the Lord with his whole heart.

If a person is truly committed to the Lord and has the newborn nature in him there is just no way, should he backslide, that his backsliding would continue for years and decades. When people confess that they have been away from the Lord for many decades, it is probable that their earlier experience, which they thought was the new birth, was a step in the right direction to produce good feelings, but which did not involve a genuine commitment. For if it was genuine, then, because of the tenderness of their hearts, the next crisis, as it was for both me and for the Prodigal son, would have put a very quick end to their backsliding.

I'm not sure if Mark's departure from Paul (Acts 15:38) was backsliding or evidence that he was not truly committed to the Lord (not born again). But it is quite apparent that after he received a better understanding of the gospel and of the claims of Jesus on his life, either he quickly returned from his backsliding or the Holy Spirit continued the born-again process until the formation of Jesus in his heart was finally completed to produce the new birth. Since the Bible does not tell us whether Demas returned to the Lord, we cannot, therefore, draw any conclusion as to whether he was backsliding when he forsook Paul, or if this was him permanently falling away.

Now if I had gone to heaven even as a backslider, God's intervention to rescue backsliders at the point of death, as He did for me, would not be necessary. If true, remembering a childhood experience like the friend I described earlier would cause me to believe that I could not lose my salvation and thus would destroy any motivation to repent.

Many truly born-again Christians have been known to die tragically. Therefore, we mustconclude that God's purpose in saving the life of a backslider is not merely due to His favor and protection. Otherwise, why weren't these committed Christians protected from death?

Rather, God gives to the backslider another opportunity to "come to himself." As was the case with Lot, the Lord knows that with the right kind of stimuli, the backslider will return to Him proving that though it was dormant, he did have the born-again nature. This confirms what we will study in the next chapter that the Lord knows how to deliver the godly out of temptations.

Escaping Your Fallen Nature

But I am not inferring that among the Christian survivors of every tragedy is at least one backslidden Christian as we cannot possibly know that. But then what about the tragedies where dozens or even hundreds of people have died and there are no survivors. Does that imply, since none would have had the chance for a last-minute return to the Lord, that there were no believers in a backslidden state?

For people who we believe were in a backslidden state but did not survive the tragedy, we must conclude that either God had already dealt with their spiritual condition and rescued them before the tragedy began or they were not believers in a backslidden state after all. Though we may not know how God does it, we have confidence and are comforted when realizing thatHe, as He promised,knows how to deliver the godly out of temptations.

A few years ago, there was a Malaysian plane that totally disappeared off the radar screen and which investigators believe went down intothe Indian Ocean. But they needed confirmation. Apparently, every plane has a certain device on it that if the plane gets lost then this device will send out a signal to the air base so that rescuers will find it quickly. Since it is presumed that this plane may have sank to the bottom of the ocean, investigators were hopeful of picking up this signal so that they could locate it. But they needed to pick up this signal, or as they called it, ping, very quickly because the life of the battery in this device was good for only 30 days.

As born-again believers, when we go into the world and allow ourselves to be tempted with evil, at that point we have gone astray. For a while, because of the allurements all around us, we won't know how to find our way back to the Lord. But one of the qualities of the newborn heart of a believer is that weare forever attached to the Lord. Though we are in a backslidden state and buried in a sea of sin, always coming from our new nature will be a ping that reaches the ear of God. No matter how far we get away from God, His ear is always listening for the ping that is constantly beaming from our new nature. He knows who belongs to Him and as our Father, will, even at the very last second, deliver us from our temptations. But the danger of backsliding is that until we repent, we cannot be sure we have a born-again heart capable of sending out that signal.

Furthermore, it is because Jesus is our Advocate (see 1 John 2:1) that He will intervene to spare a backslider's life so that he will have the opportunity to repent. If no one else was praying for him, then Jesus, because He knows who belongs to Him, would intercede to arrange a rescue. His intercession on the backslider's behalf inspires the miraculous intervention.

But if "backsliders" are not backsliders with a hibernating Jesus nature in them, then, unless someone else is praying for their salvation, no intervention is likely. Instead, the candidates, having neglected their salvation, will reap what they have sown.

I need to make one thing clear. God does not continually spare the lives of believers until He is satisfied that we are no longer committing sins. None of us will ever reach that point in this life where we can guarantee ourselves that we will never sin again. Paul said that if we think we can, then we need to take heed lest we fall.

I'm sure many Christians have died and then went to heaven before they confessed a certain sin. It's because believers deliberately departed from God's ways, not because they succumbed to weaknesses and failures, that draws the attention of the Lord to arrange an intervention to give them another opportunity to repent.In the end times, when Christians go through the tribulation, I believe that every born-again believer who entered the tribulation in a backslidden state, because of the crisis that they will soon be facing, will repent of their backsliding and return to the Lord.

From this chapter, we have learned and conclude that those who have fallen away never were saved in the first place and that backsliders instead of falling away are eventually revived. I am so grateful that the Lord never gives up on any of us. I can personally testify to His faithfulness of providing for me an escape from backsliding, from physical death, and from eternal damnation.

In the next chapter, we learn that conclusions about the condition of a person's heart cannot be drawn until their lives have been tested. Though we won't study it, Romans 9 to 11 confirms that God works to restore backsliders. Once we have learned how God will restore the backslidden nation of Israel, we will agree with Paul's great statement:

> O the depth of the riches both of the wisdom and knowledge of God! how unsearchable *are* his judgments, and his ways past finding out!
> **Romans 11:33**

CHAPTER 13

TESTS IF HEADING IN RIGHT DIRECTION

While we marvel at God's grace to revive backsliders, we are disheartened to learn that some people who seem to be in a backslidden state are, according to the scriptures, fallen away.

> [21] For it had been better for them not to have known the way of righteousness, than, after they have known *it*, to turn from the holy commandment delivered unto them. [22] But it is happened unto them according to the true proverb, The dog *is* turned to his own vomit again; and the sow that was washed to her wallowing in the mire. **2 Peter 2:21-22**

In acknowledging that certain people who had departed from the church had "known the way of righteousness," many interpret Peter as claiming that they were born again. But if they had been born again, their returning to the world would be backsliding. However, Peter described them as though there was no hope of them ever being restored, thus proving that they could never have been born again.

> For if after they have escaped the pollutions of the world through the knowledge of the Lord and Saviour Jesus Christ, they are again entangled therein, and overcome, the latter end is worse with them than the beginning. **2 Peter 2:20**

But their fellowship and association with other believers has enabled them, due to thoroughly becoming acquainted with the graces of Jesus, to escape these pollutions of the world.

> ⁷ And delivered just Lot, vexed with the filthy conversation of the wicked: ⁸ (For that righteous man dwelling among them, in seeing and hearing, vexed *his* righteous soul from day to day with *their* unlawful deeds;) ⁹ The Lord knoweth how to deliver the godly out of temptations, and to reserve the unjust unto the day of judgment to be punished: **2 Peter 2:7-9**

Peter said that had these people been truly godly, they would have been delivered from their temptations. Though it appears that they fell from a position of salvation, it is only the unjust, those who have never known salvation, whom God has reserved for judgment and punishment. Though some backsliders appear to have gone too far into the world, Peter assures us that God, with Lot as an example, knows how to deliver the godly, though backslidden, out of temptation.

Though Peter informed us that Lot, the nephew of Abraham, was a righteous man, from what we read in the Genesis account, we know that he did not live righteously. Though Lot was not born again, his life fits the description of a backslider. Because he did not take God's announcement of coming judgment seriously, he did not follow the Lord's explicit instruction to leave Sodom.

But because of this crisis in which he could face severe judgment, in answer to Abraham's intercessory prayer, God sent His angels to coax Lot to leave. Because Lot was not born again, he needed the prompting of an angel to escape the coming wrath. However, since believers have new hearts, the prompting that we need to avoid God's punishment comes not from without, but from within by the convicting work of the Holy Spirit (as illustrated in the story of the Prodigal son).

Though he didn't comment on her, we learn from other scriptures that Lot's wife was just like these people who returned to the old life. Since she had set her heart and affections on the city life, she did not want to leave Sodom. Since her deliverance was dependent on her being near Lot, the lingering of Lot's wife meant she had fallen too far back. Though she was not righteous as Lot was, God, in His mercy, would've spared her if she had kept up with the delivering angel. Instead, she was caught in the firestorm and became a pillar of salt (see Genesis 19).

Knowing of Lot's escape and knowing God always delivers the godly, Peter reminds us that God knows how to set free every backslider from the corruption and pollution of the world. Peter has shown us the distinction between those who are fallen away and those who are backslidden. It is not easy for us, however, to correctly discern that difference.

Usually, we cannot discern until enough time has elapsed to allow trials and tests to reveal what is truly in the heart. Unless circumstances require it, we are wise not to try to discern people's hearts. If we do, we risk the possibility of passing unrighteous judgment (see John 7:24).

If they are ungodly, the time will come when they will be so irritated with the godly living of Christians that they will choose to go back to the old life they crave:

> They went out from us, but they were not
> of us; for if they had been of us, they would *no*

> *doubt* have continued with us: but *they went out, that they might be made manifest that they were not all of us.* **1 John 2:19**

Peter said it would have been better that they had never known the gospel than to have known it and then to have turned away from it. By using the term *known*, Peter acknowledged that these people were totally involved in the life and fellowship of the church (similar to what we studied about the Hebrews church). According to *Strong's, known* means "*recognize*; to *become fully acquainted with.*" Thus, *known* denotes someone who is thoroughly acquainted with and familiar with particular facts and characteristics.

These people had been enlightened, had tasted, and had partaken of all that came with the gospel message. They enjoyed the fellowship of other believers. They shared testimonies of the work of God in their lives. They experienced the presence and power of God. While appearing to be genuine, the evidence of change was the counterfeit version. Though receiving sufficient seed and grace to begin the new birth process, rather than committing their lives to Jesus to complete the formation of Him in them, they chose, as we learned from the parable of the sower, to abort.

Peter said it would be more tolerable for them in the coming judgment if they had never known and participated in these ways of righteousness. It would have been far better to have stayed in the old life than to have thoroughly explored all there is about the new and then deliberately abandon it. Because of their terrible decision they had put themselves in a position that would make their punishment that much more severe.

> *But it is happened unto them according to the true proverb, The dog is turned to his own vomit again; and the sow that was washed to her wallowing in the mire.* **2 Peter 2:22**

Peter did not say these people were saved. In returning to the pollutions of the world like a dog to its vomit and a sow to its mud, they showed that there never had been a real transformation in their hearts. Like Lot's wife, they preferred the old life to the new. They decided that rather than continuing on with true believers, they preferred to be with former acquaintances and friends. Their decision to quit on Jesus is the same falling away that was taught by the writer to the Hebrews.

From this passage, we learn that the confession by people of Jesus and their participation in the worship and services of the church are not necessarily proof that they trulyknow the Lord. The prospect of facing possible sufferings became an offense. This trial became the occasion to show that the commitment to the Lord was conditional. Had they not shown such desire, as Lot's wife had, to return to their old lifestyle Peter would not have indicated that they were beyond hope.

Their ease in departing from godly influences in the church suggested that they did not anylonger feel the conviction of the Holy Spirit. Choosing worldly ways at that point was worse than backsliding. As confirmed by the writer to Hebrews, giving in to the temptation to quit on Jesus is now a falling away. They will never again have the desire to repent.

Though they had a knowledge of Jesus and knew the way, did they know Him personally? We learn the answer from Jesus. He said these peoplewould claim on Judgment Day that they had done many wonderful works in His name. What they claimedcould be described as enlightening, tasting, and partaking (see Luke 13:23-28). But in response, Jesus would say He never knew them.

> [22] Many will say to me in that day, Lord, Lord, have we not prophesied in thy name? and in thy name have cast out devils? and in thy name done many wonderful works? [23] And then will I profess

unto them, I never knew you: depart from me, ye that work iniquity. **Matthew 7:22-23**

It should not come as a surprise that many who seem to be doing many wonderful works in Jesus's name are not saved. And we cannot claim they used to know Jesus and then having fallen from grace lost their salvation. Jesus made it clear that there was never a time when He knew them. He could not have said that if at any point in their past they had been true believers.

These people indicated that they would follow the Lord if they wouldn't have to give up too many of their comforts. They were like people pledging money to support a mission project. They make the promise based on a riveting emotional appeal, but after realizing the comforts they may need to sacrifice, they decide they cannot afford to give to this project after all. Giving no regard to the mission need that initially touched their hearts, they justify breaking their pledge.

Many people give no thought to the possibility that they're not born again. They are offended at the suggestion that they need to examine their hearts to see if they are in the faith. But according to Jesus, it will be on Judgment Day that many will find out for the very first time the true condition of their hearts. How sad it will be when they realize, but only after it's too late, that all their lifetime they had rejected the grace that would have led them to the Savior.

But thankfully, it's not too late. If you have no assurance of your salvation, then right now examine your heart. It may be that you will discover that you are not born again. But you will also discover that regardless of how long you have been resisting the Savior, He will give you another chance to receive Him. Then you won't ever need to fear hearing Him say, "I never knew you."

It isn't always a bad thing to lack assurance. It's like pain. When we feel pain, it prompts us to go to the doctor and find out why we are experiencing this pain. It is our built-in alarm system.

Pain gives us the occasion to submit ourselves to an examination to determine what we need to do to recover. Though it may not be pleasant we know that a test is necessary for our own good.

As in so many areas of life, the only way of distinguishing the genuine from the fraudulent is to put it through a rigorous test. We are used to this approach. Every new product is thoroughly tested before it goes to market. We often take it for granted that a legitimate authority has already done the testing and has given it its approval. None of us would risk driving a car or taking certain medicines that we knew had not yet been approved. While it is good that people accept us at face value, sometimes it works to our benefit that we allow them to test what we have declared. At the very least it will increase our confidence in what we believe.

If an employer needs to fill a secretarial position, to spare him from interviewing people who would not have the skill to keep up with the demands of his office, he would advertise that no one need apply unless they can type at least 75 words a minute. If the people who are applying for this position claim that they can type at this speed the employer's decision as to whether he should hire them is made much simpler when he puts their typing skills to the test.

> And thou shalt remember all the way which the LORD thy God led thee these forty years in the wilderness, to humble thee, *and* to prove thee, to know what *was* in thine heart, whether thou wouldest keep his commandments, or no.
> **Deuteronomy 8:2**

When we lead people to accept Jesus, we need to tell them thatafflictions and temptations are necessary to determine if their confession reflects what is truly in their hearts. If they confessed Jesus butdid not realize that there is also a cost to their commitment to Him, then how can they have a genuine assurance of their salvation?

Though the scriptures support their confession, if no one has explained it, they won't know that teaching alone cannot provide assurance. Teaching without the testimony of a changed life is like a water baptism without the work of the Holy Spirit to produce a new nature. Or, it is having all the facts to support an allegation against someone only to discover that these incriminating facts have been attributed to the wrong person. It is only after new converts have gone through the trials of life that they then would know if these scriptures of assurance apply to them also.

Because many new converts are not aware of the necessity of trials, they are content to settle for a version of salvation that may be counterfeit. Though they weretold that they are now born again due to their confession, the follow up teaching, though intended to give them assurance, is not sustenance for their spiritual growth. Rather, this teaching is the continuation of a series of steps where these candidates for salvation continue to receive pre-salvation grace to allow the life of Jesus to be formed in them until this formation is completed andready for birthing.

Jesus said that before making a commitment and confession of faith to Him, the candidate for salvation should first count the cost. He cautioned people about the hardships that they will have to endure if they choose to follow Him. Though there are benefits there are also costs.

> And Jesus said unto him, No man, having put his hand to the plough, and looking back, is fit for the kingdom of God. **Luke 9:62**

If they are reluctant to surrender the old life, it is evident as I taught in an earlier chapterthat they were not endued or clothed with power from on high. Though they put their hand to the plough to receive and contemplate God's pre-salvation grace,

Jesus said that their looking back is evidence that they had never fully committed to Him. If they had commited to Him and thus had put on His garment of righteousness, then Jesus would not have said that they weren't fit.

When persecutions came, many of these converts blamed God for not protecting them. Their negative attitude, like that of the children of Israel murmuring against God and refusing to believe His promises, showed that their diseased hearts had not yet been healed. This proved that when they confessed Jesus as Savior, they had not understood the implications of their decision.

To illustrate, while I was a dispatcher for a security company in Winnipeg, I had to send many security guards to very unpleasant job sites. There was this one site, a slaughterhouse, that was particularly hard to keep guards at on a steady basis. Guards were required to make forty-eight clock punches throughout the plant every two hours. Many times, guards would learn the duties expected of them and then wouldn't stay for the remainder of their training.

When booking new guards to go there, I usually told them it was not the normal kind of security site. I let them know what they could expect. I wanted guards to decide before arriving at the site, not after, whether they would agree to the unpleasant conditions. By telling them ahead of time, I had far more success in convincing them to accept and remain on the job.

Having not counted the cost, what many of these candidates for salvation experienced, which appeared to be the newbirth, was the abundance of God's pre-salvation conception grace. These mercies were to persuade them to fully commit their lives to Jesus. By responding, they would be *escaping their fallen nature* and over coming their temptation to give in to discouragement.

Though it didn't take root, their initial confession of faith wasn't necessarily false. Though it didn't reach the depths of their hearts, they were heading in the right direction. They may have become discouraged and felt God had abandoned them, but the

Escaping Your Fallen Nature

words of truth that they quoted from the scriptures pointed them to Jesus. The hardships that exposed the condition of their hearts has given them the occasion to realize that they were not quite there yet in becoming born again.

That does not mean that they are hypocrites pretending to be somebody that they are not. They truly want to get free from their corrupt way of living. But the reason that they are not yet *escaping their fallen nature* is because, though they have heard the message of the gospel and have even confessed Jesus as Savior, they have not truly committed to Him with all their heart.

Many people who are interested in receiving Jesus as Savior, when learning that they may have to face severe troubles and persecutions will endure only for a while. Eventually they willconsider these costs of following Jesus too high. If problems become so severe that they become offended, they,because they've not endured, have aborted the newborn birthing process.

If others want to determine if we can be trusted, they will exercise discernment. Their first impression may be that our confession is suspect, but they won't want to make a rash judgment. To avoid making the mistake of judging us, they will take us at face value. If there are no red flags or extenuating circumstances, it is likely that they will believe that our conversion is genuine.

But when people give us responsibilities and leadership roles or trust us with their resources, especially their children, we can understand why they are careful in making their decision. They will judge us based on evidence that our faith confession originates from hearts that genuinely trust God. They will give us enough time for our commitment to be tested. Will the trials of life reveal evidence of a new nature producing fruits of the Spirit, or will it show that the newborn life that we claim that we have doesn't even exist?

Building on what I've said previously, the candidate's difficulty of making a commitment to the Lord is a pain they must endure until the formation of Christ in them reaches its completion. This birthing process is a truth that many people haven't understood and have relegated as not very important. But not to warn them that troubles will come is like a mother telling her pregnant daughter that there won' be any discomfort at all during the development and birthing of her baby.

Thus far we have learned that though many give the appearance of being committed to the Lord, yet because of their attachment to the world, they are not. Though for many of them their commitment to the Lord is conditional, their continual exposure to the gospel is leading them in the right direction and may yet lead to their salvation. It's when they allow the trials of life to prompt them to examine their hearts and to test the genuineness of their beliefs and confessed commitment that they then will have the assurance that they are *escaping their fallen nature*.

We are often plagued, especially after failures, with the anxiety-filled question of whether we are truly saved. Sometimes, even if we read authoritative scripture passages, hear inspiring sermons, and receive compassionate encouragement, we continue to lack heartfelt assurance.

Jesus promised that tribulations and troubles will come to all believers. Though new converts are sincere in their repeating of the sinner's prayer, it's up to them to make sure their commitment can withstand the storms of life. It's possible that they did make a true commitment to the Lord with their initial confession of Him and were indeed born again. But if that's true, then their subsequent troubles are a means of testing and verifying their commitment.

Of course, it's only when we are agitated enough within our hearts to seek answers to our disturbing questions that we will be willing to submit to an examination. And to draw any benefit from this examination of our hearts, we need to show a willingness to rejoice when we encounter the pain of trials. It is from these testings that we will get answers to our questions.

Escaping Your Fallen Nature

When I was seventeen years old, I performed a test that saved my life. Because Dad decided to move from the outskirts of Winnipeg to the city center, my younger brother and I were assigned the task of painting the kitchen in our new house. Earlier, Dad told me that the previous owner of the house had shut off all the electrical power. Therefore, we did our painting during the daytime hours so that we could use the light that was coming through the windows.

A very heavy wire that was the electrical connection for the stove was protruding near the baseboard that I was painting. And at the end of the wire were two strands that were covered except at the very ends. Because the wires were in the way of my brush, I decided to tie these ends together to help get them out of the way.

Not giving it any thought, I took hold of the exposed end of one wire and reached for the other wire. My fingers were no more than an inch from the bare end and suddenly, at the very last second, I asked myself, *are these wires live?* Though I trusted Dad's report that all the electrical power had been turned off, I decided that I needed to do a simple test. I put my hands one on each strand on the covered portion below where the wires were bare. I then carefully touched the bare ends together to see if there would be a spark.

There was indeed a spark. It illuminated the whole room. I was so shocked at what I saw that I fell back. Other than the sun, I had never seen a light that bright! It also caught the attention of my brother who was painting at the other end of the room.

Later, when I shared the story, someone told me that if I had touched both ends of the wire, and I was only one inch away from doing so, I would have been fried to a crisp. What had saved my life was a sudden decision, which I think was of the Lord, to conduct a simple test. I'm sure many people's lives have been saved because they took the time to ask questions and sought for an answer through a test.

When we go through one of life's trials or testings, we often experience much pain. When we feel the pain that a lack of assurance brings, that's our signal that we need to ask some questions. We need to examine ourselves to see just where we are at in our spiritual condition. Paul said:

> *Examine yourselves, whether ye be in the faith.* **2 Corinthians 13:5**

In the context of what we have learned thus far from our study, we assist ourselves in the examination of our hearts when we sincerely seek answers to the following questions.
1. If we think we are backsliding, how do we know our new birth was genuine?
2. How do we know for sure we are backsliding and not on the verge of falling away?
3. If we're not living for the Lord, how can we be certain our assurance isn't false?
4. Do we realize that neglecting to actively pursue truth leaves us vulnerable to deception?

We also need to ponder the following statements!
1. Upon examination, we could discover that behind our lack of assurance and peace is a problem with the condition of our hearts. We may find out that we never were truly born again, or we may discover that we are backsliding or on the threshold of going into it.
2. If following severe testing we have the assurance that our endurance of these tests fulfills the teachings of the scriptures, then our salvation will never be lost. On the other hand, if our testings reveal that these scriptures don't apply to us, then to continue having assurance that we are saved means that we have been deceived.

3. If we are backsliding, we need to examine ourselves to see if our original experience of being born again was genuine. Because backsliders are in a backslidden state, they are no longer alert to their true spiritual condition. They are unable to discern if they are saved. Some will mistakenly think they are backsliding because of a memory of a childhood experience. And if they were never born again after all, their living in the world means they are on the edge of falling away.
4. Backsliders whose original confessions of the Lord, even as children, were genuine cannot know for sure that they will return to the Lord before the end of their lives. Though saved, if they had assurance that they are saved, they may not have the motivation to get right with God before dying. It's the lack of assurance – apainthat acts like an alarm system – that motivates backsliders to return to the Lord.
5. The fear of losing their salvation drives backsliders back to the Lord. If they have assurance but no desire to return to the Lord, their assurance is false. They are the ones to whom the writer to Hebrews warned that if they didn't stop their neglect,theywould have no escape, thus proving that they were not backsliders after all. But if they are true believers but in a backslidden state, they have God's Word that they will return to the Lord before they die.

In this chapter, we have learned that regardless of our stand, it's the courtroom of life's trials that will cross-examine our confessed position. No matter what the outcome, the verdict will work for our good. If the examination and testing reveal that we are born again,our trial, especially if it is very severe, becomes the occasion of removing our doubts to give us assurance of our salvation. It also gives us the occasion to greatly rejoice (see 1 Peter 1:6-9).

But if the examination reveals we aren't born again or that we are backsliding, that too works for our benefit as we'll now know the true condition of our hearts. If we have been alerted of our neglect through the gift of pain, we can be grateful that our testings have given us an opportunity to respond to God's pre-salvation or post-salvation grace.

CHAPTER 14

PERSEVERES TO FULFILL COMMITMENTS

If the answers that we have discovered through our examination of our hearts has helped us, then to be certain that we maintain our relationship with the Lord, we must develop the trait of perseverance. When we persevere to fulfill our commitments, we are drawing from our new nature the grace that enables us to escape the temptations that have been stirred up by our fallen nature.

We all know what it is to be tempted to give up on commitments we have made to God, to others, or to ourselves. Many of us make New Year's resolutions, but because we seem to have difficulty in following through with them, most of us break them within a month or so. Of course, if our commitment is only to ourselves and involves no one else, breaking our promises is our own business and shouldn't stir up condemnation.

But when we quit on an unconditional commitment that involves others, that probably means that we were insincere when we gave our word and made our promise. There may very well be circumstances that justify breaking our word, but it's usually an undisciplined character trait that flows from out of our fallen nature that makes us feel justified in doing this.

Weshouldnot take on a project or commit to an agreement with someone without seriously considering whether we have the resources to follow through with our plans. Quitting midstream distinguishes those who were never committed from those who intended to follow through. But in fairness to those who have quit midstream, there are circumstances that justifiably allows them to get out of certain commitments.

For instance, when an agreement is made between two parties and a major component of the agreement is based on a deception or a lie, then that is a good reason to break the contract. When a couple are engaged to get married and then it is discovered that one of them is already married, then that is grounds for breaking the engagement or, if the discovery is made after they are married, grounds for an annulment. Certainly, any agreement where valuable information has been withheld is a betrayal of trust and therefore a justifiable reason for terminating it.

I'm not saying that those who don't follow through on their word aren't saved. Many of us will quit on overcoming addictions, fighting discouragement or depression, pursuing career goals, or saving friendships or marriages. Being in the habit of giving up doesn't necessarily mean we don't have the born-again nature of Jesus. But by the same token, there is no clear evidence that we are who we claim to be.

If we have very little ability to escape the temptation of quitting on family, friends and fellow citizens, then why are we so sure that we won't also quit on Jesus when we become inundated with severe troubles. If we claim that we will endure because we have the born-again nature of Jesus in us, the nature that has a built-in quality of endurance, then why does this endurable new nature not work in our relationships with other people?

One of the greatest evidences that we are truly born again and are committed to following Jesus is our flow of the fruits of the Holy Spirit toward other believers. Jesus said it is by our fruits

Escaping Your Fallen Nature

that we are known and also by our love for one another that people know that we are His disciples.

By my mid-teens I had developed the habit of quitting whenever I thought circumstances were getting too hot to handle. I quit school shortly after starting grade ten because I was afraid of the initiation gimmicks pranksters pulled on new high school students. I took on three or four jobs all of which I quit after working only a few weeks. I left without giving any notice. One time when I was working in a factory, I quit after making a mistake because I was too scared to face the boss. I just walked out without a word to anyone. I didn't even go back to collect my pay.

In early 1964, I left Winnipeg and lived with my grandparents in southern Ontario. I worked on a farm all summer and then went back to school in the fall. At the end of December, once again I quit school and then returned to Winnipeg. In the early winter of 1965, I joined the Canadian Armed Forces and was stationed at a base near Montreal, Quebec for basic training. After just six weeks, I decided the military wasn't for me and once again I quit.

After leaving Quebec, I then went back to Winnipeg and took a job delivering telegrams by bicycle. On the second day, I had to ride my bike eight miles in driving rain and cold just to get to work. Again, I quit. But that night, I thought about how I was always messing up my life and was so prone to giving up and quitting when I became discouraged. I made a decision that turned out to be one of the most important decisions of my life. Since the company didn't know I had quit, I changed my mind. The next day, I rode my bike to work vowing never again to be a quitter.

I was determined to break free from that terrible habit of quitting. Having worked all spring and summer, in the fall of that year (1965) I switched from full time to part time. I worked for that company every weekend for four years. I rode my bike in all weather, even during snowstorms and when it was thirty below. If I had not made that decision, my life would've been a disaster.

I went back to school and for the third year in a row started grade ten. This time, I finished high school and didn't return to the habit of quitting. After that, whenever I did quit something, it was always for legitimate reasons.

Overcoming the habit of walking away from commitments started with one simple decision. There were times afterward that I was very strongly tempted to quit, but the memory of that decision and my commitment to it carried me through. I thank God that He inspired me to make up my mind to adopt the attitude of perseverance and never giving in to quitting.

The following year, whenI was in grade eleven, I received a sense of the Lord calling me to go to Bible school. Though I don't know for sure if I previously had been born again, I finally committed myself to fully following Jesus. But after I had completedmy high school, though I had not forgotten my commitment, I put it off each summer for the next four years.

Finally, in the middle of 1973, I enrolled in a Bible college in Saskatoon intending to attend for just one year. After graduating from the one-year program Ireturned to Winnipeg and resumed my job as dispatcher at the security company where I had workedthe previous three years. During a time of prayer at a mid-week prayer meeting, I knew the Lord was once again speaking to me. I felt that He was telling me to go back to Bible school and enroll in the three-year program.

About two months after I made the decision to go back in September, my boss asked me to take over as chief dispatcher. I told him that had he asked me sooner, I might have considered it. In the previous three years, three different chief dispatchers were so stressed by the job that each of them, at the advice of their doctors, resigned. On all three occasions when the job was vacant, I let my boss know that I very much wanted that position.

But I was turned down because the security company wanted only people who had military experience. Since I was in my mid-twenties,they also considered me too young. Had I not already agreed in May to accept the Lord's calling, then in July when my boss approached me, I'm sure I would have accepted his offer. The Lord's timing was perfect. Otherwise, my life would have gone in a different direction. It was only because I knew this was of the Lord to go to Bible school that I decided to turn down this promotion.

In the middle of my second year in Bible school, I was tempted to quit. I was so discouraged over a disappointment that I seriously contemplated giving up on trying to find God's will for my life. Though I did not know where I stood spiritually, I did consider the possible consequences. I realized that if I did what I was tempted to do, I might never return to the Lord and thus be giving evidence I may never have been saved. But the Lord, in His reminding me of my commitment to not quit and His stirring up the new nature within me, enabled me to not give in to discouragement.

The Lord also used a fellow student to encourage me. Probably because he heard me crying due to the dorm walls not being soundproof, he came to my room and told me that the Lord had sent him to encourage me to hang in there and not give up. I was very thankful to the Lord for that timely confirmation. Though I still struggled with disappointment, no longer did I struggle with the temptation to quit.

That temptation to quit and then God giving me the grace to help me make a way to escape its pull encouraged me to believe that I had developed the character trait of perseverance. Yet even now, because I haven't arrived at perfection, I know that there always remains the possibility that I could return to that habit. When discouraging circumstances arise, I must not forget that God will always, through the born-again nature in me, make a way for me to escape these temptations.

I learned as a child from a message preached by my pastor that we must not make vows unless we commit to keeping them. I interpreted that to mean that the Lord wanted me to keep my promises. Years later, I finally applied these lessons to my life. The principle of being true to my word has remained with me ever since. It has influenced hundreds if not thousands of decisions I've made. I can give two examples.

After planning a trip to Europe in the fall of 1976, I promised my landlady in Saskatoon that I would be back at the end of November. I returned in the middle of October, spent time in Winnipeg with my younger brother, and went to southern Ontario to visit my uncle and aunt. In Windsor, my uncle introduced me to a very sweet girl. I became interested in her and was tempted to stay there and pursue a possible relationship.

But because I remembered my promise to my landlady, I decided not to go back on my word. I went back to Winnipeg and then on to Saskatoon arriving there before the end of November as I had promised. I considered staying for a while and then going back to Windsor.

Instead, at the end of the church service on my first Sunday back, a fellow Bible school student told me she had served as an interim pastor that summer at Shell Lake, ninety miles north of Saskatoon. She knew from our years at the Bible college that I was very timid and fearful. She said the church in this village needed a pastor. She felt it would be a good fit for me because the people were very loving and would likely accept me even though I was just newly out of college.

She didn't know about my temptation to quit pursuing becoming a pastor. Though I had taken three years of pastoral training, I didn't think any church would want me. If I hadn't learned of that opportunity on that Sunday morning, it's likely I would have returned to Windsor.

I had to wonder if that meeting was the Lord's way of helping me overcome my fears and inspire me to take the first step toward fulfilling His calling on my life. I hadn't seen anything in me whatsoever to make me believe I was pastoral material. Since I had fulfilled my promise to the Lord to go to college, I felt free to

Escaping Your Fallen Nature

do what I wanted. But the encounter with my classmate radically shifted my direction. I had to decide between interpreting that as the leading of the Lord or continue to pursue selfish interests.

I spent several weeks praying about it. In January 1977, I phoned the pastor of the Leask church (about thirty miles from Shell Lake) who was also covering the services in Shell Lake. We set a date when I could preach there to see if the congregation would be impressed with me enough to give me a call. Anticipating that they wouldn't be interested, I thought going there would give me justification that I could never be a pastor.

Knowing that I did horribly in my preaching, I had no confidence that they would consider me. But after the service, the board members got together for a discussion and theninformed me of their decision. Very much to my surprise, they invited me to become their pastor.

Because I hadn't anticipated their invitation, I wasn't ready to give a response. I told the board that I would decide later and would let them know. As I traveled with the other pastor back to Leask, the Lord spoke to me. Truthfully, Ihad gone there only to give myself justification to quit this idea of becoming a pastor. But I couldn't deny that the Lord had impressed upon my heart to accept the call to go to Shell Lake. Finally, I discerned the Lord was indeed calling me to be their pastor.

But I told no one. Instead, I went for three weeks to Calgary to visit my twin sister. I hoped the Lord would reveal to me I had misread Him and didn't want me to go to Shell Lake after all. Instead, as I continued to pray, He gave me confirmation in the depth of my spirit. I wrote to the church board and gave them a date when I would arrive.

Once there, I felt like quitting almost every Sunday after I preached, but the church was very gracious and patient with me. Their encouragement pulled me through. On one occasion, however, a member was so upset with me that I could tell he would have been quite happy if I had quit. It was a real test of my commitment. Though discouraged, I knew quitting was not the answer. It was my recollection of how the Lord brought me to Shell Lake that sustained me when feeling the impulse to run away. My decision to remain faithful was confirmed about a year later when I visited people on the reserve north of Shell Lake for it was there that I met my wife.

The second example of keeping a promise was when the Lord reminded me of a promise I had made a year earlier. After I had pastored in western Canada for eleven years, my wife and I moved to Kitchener, Ontario, in 1988 so we could live near her dad. At the same time, we were told of a pastoral position in Weagamow Lake, Ontario. Because my wife's dad's health was failing, I decided I would be open to going there only if and after her dad had died.

We lived not far from my wife's dad, so we regularly visited with him. I worked in a factory for half a year making brake pads and then drove truck for about three quarters of a year. It was during that time, about ten months after we moved to Kitchener, that my wife's dad died. A few months later, I got the opportunity to drive for Greyhound bus lines. Just as I was to begin driver training, the director of this northern Ontario mission informed us of the need for a couple to go to Weagamow Lake. A year earlier, I had promised that if this native community needed us, I would become their pastor. I knew that my commitment to go there, should they need me, was made first.

I admit that it was a great temptation to not follow up on either of those commitments. It would have been easy to justify not returning to Saskatoon so I could pursue a possible relationship or not to go to that Native community so I could drive bus. But the alternative would have devalued my integrity and the importance of keeping my word.

It's critical that we, with God's help, get free from any habit that prevents us from being faithful to our own word. If we don't, we may be setting ourselves up for a fall. If we find ourselves quickly and easily and without remorse quitting on our promises to others, how can we be confident that we have the new nature enabling us to keep our word to the Lord?

John asked how someone who claims to be a Christian could fail to love those in need.

> [17] But whoso hath this world's good, and seeth his brother have need, and shutteth up his bowels *of compassion* from him, how dwelleth the love of God in him? [18] My little children, let us not love in word, neither in tongue; but in deed and in truth. [19] And hereby we know that we are of the truth, and shall assure our hearts before him. **1 John 3:17-19**

If failing to meet the needs of others brings into question whether the born-again nature of God (His love) is in us, it's legitimate to ask that question when we betray people's trust. If our showing genuine love assures us that we have God's truth in us, then our following through on our word to others should, in like manner, give us confidence that we are of the truth and are truthful.

> But above all things, my brethren, swear not, neither by heaven, neither by the earth, neither by any other oath: but let your yea be yea; and *your* nay, nay; lest ye fall into condemnation. **James 5:12**

James was saying it is an error if the only time we make sure we keep our word is when we have sworn an oath. We should take seriously every promise we make. When we do, we remove the hindrance that would prevent us from continuing to persevere when unpleasant situations arise.

> ¹⁰ He that is faithful in that which is least is faithful also in much: and he that is unjust in the least is unjust also in much. ¹¹If therefore ye have not been faithful in the unrighteous mammon, who will commit to your trust the true riches? ¹² And if ye have not been faithful in that which is another man's, who shall give you that which is your own?**Luke 16:10–12**

As we train ourselves to keep what seem to be insignificant promises, we increase our ability to keep commitments that are of greater importance. When we develop a resistance to quitting in general, the likelihood of quitting in particularly challenging situations (especially those involving our allegiance to the Lord) are greatly diminished.

If our concern in fulfilling promises made to others is of little importance, it's likely we won't be any more concerned with fulfilling other obligations. That's why there are so many that easily give up on financial and relational commitments. When we agree to an appointment, we should always do our best to show up on time. If you say it, follow through with it. If you discover you were too hasty in making a promise, ask permission to be excused of it and explain why. And if you break a promise, admit to it and offer a sincere apology.

While I hold myself accountable to all my promises, I try not to give the appearance that I expect others to be as committed to their word as I try to be to mine. If they let me down, especially if unintentionally, I try to be quick to show understanding and not hold it against them. I too have weaknesses and fail many times. Because God has been patient with me, I've learned I must be patient with others and not put pressure on them to follow through on their promises.

Though I do it infrequently, I remember two occasions where I pressured someone to follow through on a commitment. In 2003

Escaping Your Fallen Nature

my son chose to attend the same Bible School in Saskatoon that I had attended years earlier. When he was accepted at the school his intention was to attend for only one year. On the very day of the deadline for signing up for the post-graduation musical tour, though previously I had tried to persuade him, I phoned one last time to urge him to sign up.

Since I provided most of his support, I suggested that to get maximum output from his only year in Bible School, he needed to go with the musical team on this two-month tour of the churches. Though anxious to return to Hamilton immediately after graduation, but because he realized the team needed him (they told me that he was the school's best guitarist), he agreed to go.

Just prior to going on this tour, after we arrived in Saskatoon to attend his graduation, my son told his Mom and I that he had decided to continue his schooling for at least one and possibly two more years. At the beginning of his third year, as he was registering, suddenly he switched from the three-year to the four-year program.

Since I was providing his support, I told him that if I am to continue, then he must promise me that he will come back to complete his fourth year. To me it would be poor stewardship to put out money for the third year of a four-year degree program and then not require him to come back to do the fourth year and get the degree. After he agreed to keep this promise, I told him, though as I reflect on it now it sounds very harsh, that I intended to hold him to it.

But just before the start of his fourth year, he asked to be released from his promise. But since the circumstances were such that there was no reason that he couldn't fulfill it, and because I wanted him to know the value of following through on promises, I chose not to release him. To not spend the money on the fourth year to complete the degree program would mean that the money spent for the third year was wasted. Again, though my logic was sound, I wonder if possibly it would have been kinder of me to have granted his request.

But much to my son's credit and for which I'm very proud of him, though he could've gone against my advice, he followed through to complete his schooling and earn his degree. I'm not sure that I did the right thing in pressuring him on these two occasions. But I'm confident that he doesn't hold this against me. And I'm also confident that what he learned from me about keeping promises has helped him, as it did for me, in the development of his character and values.

I have also learned that I must be patient with those who don't consider all promises to be of equal importance. I too have broken some promises and feel badly about that. When I realize I haven't followed through on my word, I apologize and make good on it or offer an explanation.

There once was a promise I made that after realizing I had broken it I could do nothing about it. I couldn't fulfill it, I couldn't apologize, and I couldn't make an explanation. It was due to my habit of procrastinating. The broken promise concerned the man who was God's answer to my prayer following my 1973 car accident that I shared in an earlier chapter.

I knew the man who had helped me fix my car wanted me to keep in touch with him to let him know how I had made out. After giving me his address, I promised to write. But after a long while, when I wanted to write, I had forgotten where I had put his address information. I never did provide him with an update. He deserved much better. I still feel badly for breaking that promise.

An excellent foundation on which to build character so we won't quit on the Lord is learning the importance of being faithful to our word. We are especially encouraged to do so when we allow ourselves to be inspired by the example of others including those in the Bible.

Take for instance the story of the Israelites conquering Jericho. In preparation for taking the city, the commander, Joshua, sent

Escaping Your Fallen Nature

out spies. After their presence was discovered, Rahab, one of the residents, took the great risk by hiding them. Soon, Jericho's security forces arrived. But after searching for several days, they were unable to find them (for context see Joshua 2:1–23, 6:1–27).

Believing the Israelites were commisioned by God to destroy the city,Rahab asked the spies to spare her and her family from the attack. They promised to rescue her on the condition that she leave hanging out her window this same scarlet rope that she used to lower them to the ground.

Rahab convinced many of her family to put their trust in the word of these spies. When the Israelite forces arrived not only were they willing to show kindness to Rahab and her family but also to the whole city. They circled the city once a day for six days and marched around it seven times on the seventh day. It's hard to believe that throughout all those marches there were none, except for Rahab,who were humble enough to cry out for mercy.

I drive bus for my church. Six buses travel around the city of Hamilton every Sunday to pick up people who want to come to the church to hear the gospel. The driving of church buses around Hamilton and the marching of the Israelites around Jericho is very similar. The residents of both cities were alerted of the possibility of God's wrath against them and were given an opportunity to respond to His mercy while it was (is) yet available.

As it was for the residents of Jericho, most of the people in Hamilton, when seeing our buses, are unaware that we, as we continuously circle the city, are carrying the message of salvation. If they would only pay attention and come to realize their need, then, like Rahab, they would respond to the mercy that the Lord is presently offering them. To receive God's mercy the family of Rahab were told that they must go to her place. So also, to receive God's mercy, the residents of Hamilton are learning that they must go to the place where they will have a personal encounter with Jesus.

As the Israelites were in the process of conquering the city, it is evident that the Israelite army was aware of the promise made by the spies to Rahab. It's amazing that these spies cared enough for Rahab that they told their commander not to destroy the house with the scarlet rope hanging from its window. They spared Rahab and her family because her leaving out the scarlet rope proved that she was serious about her agreement with them. She had trusted them to keep their word. In showing her mercy, the spies proved there was no such thing as a pledge that had less value than other promises.

In this chapter I have shared on how the Lord was faithful, for which I am very grateful, in helping me to escape my temptation of returning to my habit of quitting. We've also learned that we must not make promises that are empty of meaning. Persevering to fulfill our commitments shows integrity and demonstrates our trustworthiness to do what we said we would do. We confirm that we are escaping our fallen nature when we also are resisting nurturing a defeatist mentality.

CHAPTER 15

RESISTS NURTURING A VICTIM MENTALITY

One of the most prominent characteristics about our fallen nature is our tendency to gripe and complain when things don't go our way. Often, we take offense when we come to realize that others have used their power and position to take advantage of our inexperience and vulnerability.

Earlier, I spoke of a mistake that I made when I purchased a certain product and afterwards tried to get a refund. The company's response to my attempt to get justice was to imply that I am a complainer and that I won't be happy unless I get this refund. It's understandable that they would think this way as that's the reaction of most people who, because they didn't get justice, believe that they are victims. Though I was victimized, and my complaint was treated as not legitimate, I did not yield to the temptation of adopting a victim mentality.

God does not want our happiness to depend on correcting what we perceive are injustices. Because we live in a fallen world, we know that there will never be an end to these many offenses. Until evidence is presented that an outsider can prove as irrefutable, we must allow the offender the presumption of innocence. And if there is proof of wrong doing, though we won't necessarily release them of accountability, we should develop the habit of showing patience and forgiveness.

I know a woman whose mother died while under hospital care and who isconvinced that the attending physician was responsible for her death. Her pursuit of seeking justice occupies almost all her time. Considering that she has no evidence to prove her allegations and that the toll on her mental and spiritual health has destroyed her peace and happiness, since there is nothing to gain by pursuing it, I have encouraged her to drop this offense.

Our life should not revolve around offenses nor on our insistence that we must right every wrong. A good father will discipline his wayward son. But he knows that it is never wise to choose a punishment while he is yet seething over his son's bad behavior. We must never pursue justice because of our anger (unless it's our anger against Satan and his kingdom of darkness). If we are going to hold someone accountable for their actions, we must already have the attitude that we are willing todrop the offense and show a spirit of forgiveness.

One of the most hurtful experiences in our lives and a test of whether we have the born-again new heart is when someone, whom we believe is worthy of our trust, betrays that trust. When that happens, it can be quite a battle to overcome our temptation to harbor and nurture these offenses. Though we may speak it,if we refuse from the depth of our hearts to grant forgiveness,we indicate that we have no real appreciation for God's forgiveness of our sins. If after a long time we continue to hold on to offenses, that is a clue that we may not have the new-born heart after all.

My ability to forgive was put to the test when I worked at a part-time security job in 1994 after becoming acquainted with a fellow guard.During our shift change I sometimes witnessed to him about Jesus. When he seemed ready to commit to Him, I influenced him to come to the churchthatI was attending (the one I spoke of earlier), after which he then agreed to be water baptized.

Escaping Your Fallen Nature

During my friend's baptismal testimony, because he knew that I believed in the Trinity, he declared that those whose baptism was in the titles are not born again. A few nights later, when I took over from him at our security post, he branded me a heretic. Because I believed that we were true genuine friends, I felt betrayed and devastated. Shortly after, I called the prayer line for prayer. Though hurt and resentful for a while, God gave me the inspiration and grace to forgive. Over the next few months I tried but was unsuccessful in restoring our friendship.

While the ability to forgive isn't proof of a new heart (even the ungodly can forgive those they love), a dramatic change of dropping longtime offenses usually indicates a transformation. If we understand the sacrifice of Jesus and have truly experienced His forgiveness for our sins, we will, in time, grow in the ability to forgive others of their offenses against us. Jesus said believers are known by our fruit. We sometimes struggle to not harbor resentment, but the desire to forgive those who have hurt us in the way that Jesus forgave us demonstrates this fruit.

If we have continuously refused to forgive others, then that suggests that we probably don't have Jesus's new nature and have not yet experienced His forgiveness (see Matthew 18:21–35). If we can forgive them of offenses we formerly would have allowed to fester until they consumed us with bitterness (see Hebrews 12:15), that's a good indication that we do know the forgiveness of Jesus and have a new heart. It is our Holy Spirit generated newborn heart, not just our willpower to forget, that causes this change.

> ⁶ But brother goeth to law with brother, and that before the unbelievers. ⁷ Now therefore there is utterly a fault among you, because ye go to law one with another. Why do ye not rather take wrong? why do ye not rather *suffer yourselves to* be defrauded? **1 Corinthians 6:6-7**

If our offense is with a fellow believer and we are thinking of going to court to get justice, the scripture tells us that it is better that we suffer the wrong than to make a public display of our displeasure with one another, thus bringing reproach upon the head of our fellowship, Jesus. It is better for the one party to be defrauded with the hope that one day, because they are family, there will be a satisfactory resolution, followed by a genuine restoration.

> [15] Moreover if thy brother shall trespass against thee, go and tell him his fault between thee and him alone: if he shall hear thee, thou hast gained thy brother. [16] But if he will not hear *thee, then* take with thee one or two more, that in the mouth of two or three witnesses every word may be established. [17] And if he shall neglect to hear them, tell *it* unto the church: but if he neglect to hear the church, let him be unto thee as an heathen man and a publican. **Matthew 18:15-17**

This scripture passage tells us that if one of the parties has refused to hear his fellow believer and makes no attempt to reach a resolution, then, after all the instructions have been followed, the offended party can now treat the one who has offended him as though he is not a believer. I take that to mean that since it is established that he is not a believer, going to court is now an option.

> [35] And when it was day, the magistrates sent the serjeants, saying, Let those men go. [36] And the keeper of the prison told this saying to Paul, The magistrates have sent to let you go: now therefore depart, and go in peace. [37] But Paul said unto them, They have beaten us openly uncondemned,

being Romans, and have cast *us* into prison; and now do they thrust us out privily? nay verily; but let them come themselves and fetch us out. **38** And the serjeants told these words unto the magistrates: and they feared, when they heard that they were Romans. **Acts 16:35-38**

Because every Roman citizen is entitled to a proper trial or hearing before they can be beaten and cast into prison, Paul insisted that these magistrates be made aware of what they have done and that they demonstrate accountability and remorse by personally coming to the prison to release them. Not every injustice requires the kind of accountability that we see Paul demanding of these magistrates. We live in a fallen world and are in contact with corrupt people every day. We must be very discerning as to what injustices are worth pursuing.

> **10** Blessed *are* they which are persecuted for righteousness' sake: for theirs is the kingdom of heaven. **11** Blessed are ye, when *men* shall revile you, and persecute *you*, and shall say all manner of evil against you falsely, for my sake. **12** Rejoice, and be exceeding glad: for great *is* your reward in heaven: for so persecuted they the prophets which were before you. **Matthew 5:10-12**
>
> If ye be reproached for the name of Christ, happy *are ye*; for the spirit of glory and of God resteth upon you... **1 Peter 4:14**

Both Jesus and Peter are saying that there are some injustices that we will just have to accept.

> **12** But I would ye should understand, brethren, that the things *which happened* unto

me have fallen out rather unto the furtherance of the gospel; ¹³ So that my bonds in Christ are manifest in all the palace, and in all other *places*; ¹⁴ And many of the brethren in the Lord, waxing confident by my bonds, are much more bold to speak the word without fear. **Philippians 1:12-14**

In this passage Paul is saying that the injustice of being put in a Roman prison has worked for the furtherance of the gospel and for the inspiration of other servants to overcome their fears. Though there are some injustices that we cannot change and with any amount of wisdom can easily discern is futile even to try, yet there are many injustices that can be changed but at present remain unchanged because we have given in to our fears. Paul said he was confident that what happened to him will embolden the fearful to be that much more fervent in serving the Lord and pushing back the powers of darkness. He knew that this injustice against him eventually would work for the furtherance of the gospel.

When bad things happen to people, unless they have the new nature of Jesus in them and are daily replacing the old nature with their new one, these people will ultimately develop a victim mentality. It is only natural that people will think of themselves as victims when others abuse and take advantage of them. There aren't many people who can be victimized and yet resist the very strong temptation of concluding that they are victims.

Our courts are full of people who are arguing that they need a favorable settlement to make up for the mental anguish that their antagonist or abuser has put them through. It becomes obvious that they will experience no joy or peace until they finally get what they are demanding. They have convinced themselves ever before they have given God's grace a chance to help them get through their difficulty that they are justified in quitting or leaving an unpleasant situation.

But those who refuse to think of themselves as victims will remember that their happiness is not contingent on receiving guarantees against personal abuse. The believer's prioritywill be that of using this process for the furtherance of the gospel. That means we will be the salt of the earth to hold back corruption from flowing out of our fallen natures and that we will be the light of the world to reveal to hurting and abused victims the truth about the power of Jesus to deliver.

> To open their eyes, *and* to turn *them* from darkness to light, and *from* the power of Satan unto God, that they may receive forgiveness of sins, and inheritance among them which are sanctified by faith that is in me. **Acts 26:18**

While we can understand why people who have never been born-again may not be able to cope with injustices and lack, there is no reason why we as born-again believers cannot cope with the many abuses and hardships that others may put us through. There are some situations where there is severe abuse in which it would not be wise to remain. For the sake of their own safety and that of others, they must leave. But when we find ourselves forever thinking of ourselves as victims of someone's injustice and abuse, we have forgotten that God has promised to provide us with the grace that will enable us to escape the evils of their fallen nature.

Rather than seeking justification for leaving situations where we are treated as victims, we should look for sources of inspiration to help us to be patient. There are many examples of people who have proven the faithfulness of God in providing them with grace to help them in their time of trouble. Because we have God's nature in us, even as He is faithful, so also, we can be faithful.

Severe abuse can cause rifts in relationships, but that's never a reason to give up hoping for reconciliation. Though abuse initially makes a person a victim, and if severe enough requires them to leave, he or she needs to be careful not to let their victimization turn into a permanent attitude.

Two stories, one about Dad and Mom and the other about my older brother and me, illustrate the value of resisting this attitude of being a victim.

In the 1960s, a friend told me that his mother, a victim of polio, was unable to breathe. She had to remain in the hospital attached to a breathing machine. I was shocked when he told me his father had chosen to leave his mom because she could no longer be a wife to him. It was the first time I had heard of a Christian couple permanently separating.

In the 1970s, my Dad and Mom also went through marriage problems. According to the lack of tolerance we see today in Christian marriages, Dad could easily have justified leaving Mom by claiming emotional abuse. But separation never occurred to him, not only because he truly meant his vow to stick with Mom through hard times, but because he also genuinely loved her.

I was always impressed with how Dad and Mom resolved their conflict. While Dad showed patient gentleness toward Mom, Mom overcame being a victim of the attacks of the enemy through her continual devotional time with the Lord. Because the fruits of the Spirit flowed through them, my memory of them, which is a great inspiration to me, is never of them as victims, but of Dad's gentleness and of Mom's sweetness.

During my preteen and early teens, there were times when my older brother used me as a punching bag. So bad was my brother's abuse that I developed extreme fear. Often, because Dad worked until after midnight, I didn't go home from school until after Dad came home. In my early teens, I ran away from home five times because of this fear. When I was just fourteen, to escape this abuse I hitchhiked from Winnipeg to Thunder Bay. The police picked me up and forced me to return. A few weeks later, I tried again. I hitchhiked from Winnipeg past Toronto making it all the way to my aunt's in Sarnia, Ontario. I was greatly disappointed when she also sent me back.

In the early 1980s, my wife and I visited Dad and Mom in their Winnipeg apartment. While visiting them, my older brother arrived. He sat down in front of me and apologized for the years of abuse that I had to endure at his hands. He sincerely asked me to forgive him. I had no problem overlooking these abuses. Though I always feared him, I told him I never held these abuses against him. His humility during those few moments was very moving and strengthened my hope that one day we would be reconciled as brothers.

When he died in 2004, I had the privilege of speaking at his funeral. I shared how all my life I wanted to have a relationship with him but couldn't. In the summer he died, it had been my plan to go to Winnipeg and take him out to dinner. Love casts out fear, and it was a great disappointment never to have had the chance to demonstrate I no longer feared him. I was greatly comforted when my younger sister shared that in the months prior to his death, he studied the Bible regularly with her over the phone, thus indicating that he may have surrendered his life to Jesus before he died.

I've shared these stories about Dad and Mom's marriage problems and of my older brother's violence toward me to demonstrate that the hope of victory and reconciliation is stronger than the feeling of victimization. No matter how severe the abuse, our maintaining the hope of a restored relationship is much more beneficial than deliberately nurturing a victim mentality.

Though the abuse in many marriages is so great that the victimized spousesmust leave theirmarriages, the abuse they've endured is not a reason for them to cease hoping for reconciliation. Where one of the parties in a marriage is born again, though there was infidelity, abandonment, or even violence, there is always the hope, because of God's grace, for forgiveness.

Key to overcoming the urge to quit on our vows is that ever before the temptation to quit comes, we already are totally committed to keeping them. That is the premise of a formal marriage ceremony. The minister tells us that there will be good times and bad. Remembering the vows "for worse" and "until death do we part" helps us to cope with our troubles so that we won't quit on one another. That is the reason why we made the vows in the first place; they act as an anchor to prevent us from being blown away when the storms come.

Many believe that adultery is a legitimate reason for divorce. But the passage they use to support this view (see Matthew 19:3–9) reveals that hardness of the heart is the real reason that many victim spouses make no attempt to reconcile. It's the tool that the devil uses to steal, kill, and destroy marriages. While they fight in court to keep possessions or recover stolen assets, they don't realize that the greatest theft against them was the work of the devil to steal their spouse.

There would be far less divorces if victim spouses were to put as much effort into recovering the theft of their spouses as they did in trying to recover the things that they believe their spouses stole from them. When victims, especially if they are believers, remember their vows, then they would overcome feelings of unforgiveness toward their spouse and, instead, (though they would have no guarantee of it) believe for the restoration of their marriages.

James told us we shouldn't make oaths. Rather, our yes should mean yes, and our no should mean no. God Himself set the example that we should make an oath to declare that we have bound ourselves to our word. Marriage, which is often referred to as a covenant relationship because of its permanence, is one such occasion when the making of an oath is proper and necessary.

Wedding rings, like Rahab's scarlet rope, are tokens of faithfulness. The public exchange of vows offers additional protection to help couples know they have bound themselves to their word. Couples are inspired to keep their vows when they remember the community of witnesses before whom they made them. Thesewitnesses will encourage them to believe that they can be faithful.

In this chapter, we have learned that if we are victims of abuse and tempted to quit believing in the possibility of restoration, there are sources of inspiration to help usto not give up. If we have already developed the habit of resisting a defeatist victim mentality, believing instead that our victimization need not be permanent, we will quickly access God's grace to deliver us. This grace is available, especially when we intend to use it for the furtherance of the gospel.

CHAPTER 16

REFUSES TO JUSTIFY QUITTING ON LIFE

But far more dangerous than quitting on the hope of a restored marriage or relationship is the temptation to give up hope of a fulfilled andlong life. Thankfully, the enduring quality of the newborn nature is ever available to help believers overcome the temptation to commit suicide.

How sad that life has become so filled with misery and heartache that every year thousands of people commit suicide. They prefer to be dead than continue without hope that life can improve. While it's tragic that family and friends are devastated, the ultimate tragedy is that suicide victims have cut themselves off from any hope of getting into heaven.

When true believers who have become discouragedcome to fully understand the durability of their born-again natures, they will stop giving any further consideration to taking their lives.

Many despondent believers have asked me about what might happen to them if they went ahead with their thought of committing suicide. They hoped that I would tell them that God would understand that they just couldn't bear their pain any longer. They believed that ending their lives was their only

Escaping Your Fallen Nature

recourse to freedom from the weight and heaviness of their grief and despair.

If you claim you are born again, it is precisely that kind of crisis that will cause your born-again nature to arise and deliver you from the temptation to quit on life. The temptation to take your life is not a sin, nor are any other temptations. But if you claim you're a born-again believer, your present crisis is an occasion to provide evidence that supports your claim. If, however, you go through with your thought of suicide, such a decision and act will demonstrate you had no grounds for claiming you were born again.

We will surrender to many temptations when we reject the grace that God has made available to us. But because of its severity, suicide is the one contemplation that certainly puts to test whether we even have the born-again nature of Jesus. The thought of suicide will produce a loud enough scream to awaken out of hibernation the new nature of every despondent but genuine believer.

Because of the endurance quality of their new nature suicide is the one temptation to which we know that born-again believers will never surrender. If any become discouraged enough to be tempted to quit on life, the spiritual adrenaline of their new nature, which I discussed in a previous chapter, will begin to flow just in time *to escape* this temptation.

Many people justify a victim's decision to take his or her life. Because of severe suffering, victims believe that they are entitled to put an end to their misery. But if they're not born again, the anguish they're presently experiencing is much more tolerable than and preferable to the pain that they would suffer in hell. Suicide is not the only way to escape their misery. By choosing to end their lives they have deliberately rejected the alternative grace that is guaranteed to succeed and that has always been available.

²⁸ Come unto me, all *ye* that labour and are heavy laden, and I will give you rest. ²⁹ Take my yoke upon you, and learn of me; for I am meek and lowly in heart: and ye shall find rest unto your souls. **Matthew 11:28-29**

Some people say they can't take it anymore. Some say God let them down. They often say, "God will not give us more than we can bear." When they believe that God has given them more than they can bear, they feel betrayed. Becausethey believe that God has refused to take away their burdens and that they have reached the maximum of what they can tolerate, many people feel justified in taking their lives.

Whether we are believers or unbelievers, we have no guarantee that we will be free from suffering. Jesus guaranteed, as I quoted earlier from John 16:33, that there will be tribulations and trials simply because we are residents in a fallen and corrupt world. There is no way of avoiding these troubles. The best thing that we can do is to equip ourselves so that we can get through them.

Jesus went on to say that the believer will have special access to a power that will enable us not only to cope with our troubles but to totally overcome them. We can overcome because of the power of Jesus in our new nature – the one that replaced our fallen nature. Therefore, we cannot claim that any continuance of suffering we presently are going through is because God allowed it.

God will not suffer you to be tempted above that ye are able;**1 Corinthians 10:13**

This means that if you are tempted to give up on your troubles, even life itself, you can trust that God will not allow you to go through this temptation totally on your own. He is ever offering you the grace that will enable you not only in bearing

Escaping Your Fallen Nature

what you are going through but also in *escaping* the fallen nature that led you into this temptation.

Though every suicidal person has encountered many factors causing their despondency that is beyond their control we are increasing their anguish if in our attempt to sympathize with them we deliberately withhold the whole truth. Both they and their families need to know that God has, indeed, provided a way for them to escape this temptation.

If after a suicidal person rejects the escape that God made available and we then assure them that if they go ahead and do it anyway that God in His mercy will welcome them into heaven, we have done them a great injustice. To offer them hope that after they've rejected God's mercy on this side there will be an abundance of mercy on the other side is to give them permission to do it.

Despondent people cannot justify the decision to commit suicide by claiming it's their right. They have no more right to take their lives than a pregnant woman has the right to kill her unborn baby. Those who say they are believers cannot claim the right to be counted as members of God's family through the newborn birth and at the same time the right to commit murder. It is inconsistent for believers to convince others that they have yielded their lives to Jesus but then insist on their right to take back the same lives that they supposedly had surrendered.

You may claim that you have assurance that you will make it to heaven because you know that God is loving and very abundant in His grace to forgive. While it's true that God's forgiveness is available, if you decide to take your life, your decision to do it is proof that you have rejected the mercy and grace that would have led to you escaping this temptation.

> Father, forgive them; for they know not what they do. **Luke 23:34**

Those who are considering suicide need to know this heartfelt prayer of Jesus was meant for them. Even as Jesus's murderers did not know that they were rejecting their salvation, so also suicidal people are unaware that they are rejecting God's mercy. For many of these murderers, Jesus's prayer for forgiveness was answered several weeks later when they asked Peter what they must do. So also, it is our prayer that suicidal victims receive Jesus's forgiveness before it is too late.

If you are justifying your right to end your life, realize that not only is your physical life ending but also the formation of the life of Jesus in you is ending. You might think you are already born again because of the pre-salvation grace presently working to form and grow Jesus in you. But if you are unable to endure the troubles that are making you want to end your life, according to the parable of the sower, which wecovered earlier, you have quit before harvesting any fruit. The formation of Christ, since it did not reach full term, was aborted. There never was a newbirth.

To continue contemplating suicide means you're not aware that suicide will eliminate all hope of you making it to heaven. But if you will admit your need for forgiveness, you can right now give all your burdens and hurts to Jesus. Instead of throwing your life away, if you threw it at Jesus, He would catch you. Fully commiting your life over to Him allows the formation of Jesus in you toreach its completion. Your life draining old fallen nature then would be replaced by the life sustaining new nature of Jesus.

In 1979,after learning that my cousin was very despondent over her broken marriage my wife and I went to St. Thomas, Ontario and visited with her. She told us her husband had even turned her children against her. I realizedthat she was in desperate need of help. Very lovingly, we shared what Jesus could do for her if she would cast all her hurts and brokenness on to Him. We assured her that He would heal her crushed heart.

About three months later, I received news from her mom that she had committed suicide by throwing herself in the path of a

Escaping Your Fallen Nature

train. I felt very badly. Ever since then, I have regularly thought about her. In my mind, I often ask her, "Why didn't you take Jesus up on His invitation and cast all your burdens onto Him so that He could give you His peace and rest?"

Perhaps some of you want to excuse a loved one's decision to quit on life because you do not want to believe he or she may have missed heaven. I feel very sorry for those of you who are now grieving over a loved one who made such a terrible decision. But if you insist your loved one went to heaven, you are inadvertently influencing other people, who are looking for an easy escape to heaven, to ignore Jesus's attempt at rescuing them.

Many years ago, I worked as a security guard at a hospital watching over a nine-year-old boy who had been unsuccessful in his attempt to take his life. I was responsible to make sure he didn't make another attempt. During his stay, I found out that 22 psychiatry experts interviewed him to see why he tried to do this at such a young age. On my final shift, I asked him myself as to what motivated him. He said that his grandmother had died a few days earlier and that others had said that she went to heaven. He missed his grandma so much that he figured it out that since it was through death that she went to heaven that that would be the only way he would get there too so that he could see her again. He tried suicide simply because of this misinformation.

If you are wishing your loved one had given you the chance to rescue him or her, you do have another chance. You can inform those people whom you know and whom you believe are despondent and possibly contemplating suicide that there is a much better way to deal with their pain. You can tell them the truth of how they can escape these troubles and temptations when they choose to cast all their hurts and burdens on to Jesus.

Some want to believe that believers who have demonic strongholds in their lives can commit suicide against their will and thus not be accountable. We know, based on thorough study and observation, that demonic powers do indeed influence and even control the thoughts of suicidal people. Many have committed suicide because demons deceived them into believing there was no other way out of their troubles. My heart breaks for them.

However, born-again believers cannot justify suicidal thoughts or behavior due to demonic stimuli. If people are so controlled by evil powers to the extent that they have no ability to prevent suicide, that is evidence that their master is Satan, not Jesus. Demonically influenced behavior in a believer's life can happen only when they give demons permission to operate in their lives.

These demonically inspired habits that continue to be strongholds in our livesare brokenas we put into practice the truths of scripture(Romans 12:2; 2 Corinthians 10:2–5; Ephesians 1:17–19, 6:10–13;).Regardless of how severe the battle against the lies of the enemy, though tempted,the born-again believer cannot justify giving in to the temptation to quit on life.

While quitting on life usually refers to suicide it also means quittingor giving up on living for Jesus. There are many believers whose struggles with habits and addictions are so severe that they too are suicidal. Believing the lie that Jesus has abandoned them they then struggle with the temptation of abandoning Him also.

But it's the ability to endure the temptation to give up on our faith that distinguishes believers from unbelievers. Those who give up in their struggle to live a godly life (and many do) reveal hearts that possibly were never fully committed to Jesus. Because we know, as previously studied, God knows how to deliver the godly out of temptations, believers will never permanently give up on their life in Jesus, but instead will endure to turn their occasional defeats into glorious victories.

Some claim that when we suffer defeat it is evidence of generational curses that were passed on to us from our ancestors, and thus beyond our control. But that's like saying that our old nature is stronger than our new nature. These generational curses (also evidence of our fallen nature) were nullified when we were delivered from our old nature to become new creations in Christ Jesus.

> [10] Now is come salvation, and strength, and the kingdom of our God, and the power of his Christ: for the accuser of our brethren is cast down, which accused them before our God day and night. [11] And they overcame him by the blood of the Lamb, and by the word of their testimony; and they loved not their lives unto the death. **Revelation 12:10-11**

Our strategy in overcoming the flesh and the devil is to declare the defeat of our old nature and to acknowledge, because Jesus and His nature is in us, the conquering power of our born-again new nature. When we confessed Jesus as Lord we demonstrated faith in the work of His shed blood to replace our corrupted hearts with hearts that can endure the threat of death. We can celebrate our deliverance from these generational curses because our testimony of escaping the corruption of our fallen nature has silenced our accuser. We will no longer listen to his lies of condemnation.

What appears to be curses revisiting us are bondages and strongholds in our minds. Rather than needing another round of deliverance, we celebrate the deliverance that the Lord has already given us. We experience the benefits of our deliverance when we renew our minds on His Word and lift Him up in praise. In this way our new nature will be sufficiently stirred up to release from out of our born-again new nature the flow of Holy Spirit living water. This powerful flow will wash away our negative feelings and lift off of us this spirit of heaviness (see Isaiah 61:3).

For most believers, at least in our affluent society where we don't face the threat of losing our freedoms because of our beliefs, the commitment to make Jesus the Lord of our lives was a very long drawn out process. We heard many voices from all directions that tried either to prevent us from making an immediate decision or to influence us to make the wrong decision.

In a courtship, while it may take a long time to evaluate and consider all the information that we have learned about this person, once we have made our decision and have chosen our mate, we do not, when adjustment problems arise, start planning for a separation or divorce. Though our society in the last century or two have tolerated a quick end to marriages, for the most part over previous centuries, marriage was considered permanent and usually ended only through death.

The decision-making process about our relationship with the Lord was made prior to ourcommitment to Him,or during the pre-salvation or pre-birth stage. Once we made our decision, there was no talk about backing out. Jesus said that the person who does look back after making their decision is not fit for the kingdom of God.

This lengthy decision-making process where we seriously consider and evaluate whether we want to be permanently tied to Jesus is the formation of Him in our hearts. But once this formation of Him has been completed to produce the new birth, so also has the decision-making process been completed. Rather than anymore contemplating whether we will recognize the Lordship of Jesus, we will now acknowledge that we are in a relationship that will last forever. When trials come, rather than they becoming a tool by which Satan tempts us to quit or to give up on our life in Jesus (spiritual suicide), they become the occasion that proves that our relationship with Him is secure.

If you are heavyhearted and contemplating giving up on life (either physically or spiritually), you need to draw encouragement from the apostle Paul's example. Because he conquered over his many hardships, he is a powerful inspiration to help us believe that we also are conquerors.

CHAPTER 17

DRAWS INSPIRATION FROM CONQUERORS

Paul had moments when he feared persecution and was tempted to give in to discouragement and possibly even quit being a witness. When he was in Athens he was ridiculed for identifying with the resurrection of Jesus. Then, when he came to Corinth, he was fearful of facing similar opposition. It took a revelation from the Lord to help him overcome his fears and to inspire him to continue preaching boldly.

> [9] Then spake the Lord to Paul in the night by a vision, Be not afraid, but speak, and hold not thy peace: [10] For I am with thee, and no man shall set on thee to hurt thee: for I have much people in this city. **Acts 18:9-10**

He testified that it was this power of the Holy Spirit that enabled him to overcome his fears.

> [1] And I, brethren, when I came to you, came not with excellency of speech or of wisdom, declaring unto you the testimony of God. [2] For

I determined not to know any thing among you, save Jesus Christ, and him crucified. ³ And I was with you in weakness, and in fear, and in much trembling. ⁴ And my speech and my preaching *was* not with enticing words of man's wisdom, but in demonstration of the Spirit and of power: ⁵ That your faith should not stand in the wisdom of men, but in the power of God. **1 Corinthians 2:1-5**

But in other places he faced not only fear and ridicule but many other distressful situations.

> ²³ Are they ministers of Christ? (I speak as a fool) I *am* more; in labours more abundant, in stripes above measure, in prisons more frequent, in deaths oft. ²⁴ Of the Jews five times received I forty *stripes* save one. ²⁵ Thrice was I beaten with rods, once was I stoned, thrice I suffered shipwreck, a night and a day I have been in the deep; ²⁶*In* journeyings often, *in* perils of waters, *in* perils of robbers, *in* perils by *mine own* countrymen, *in* perils by the heathen, *in* perils in the city, *in* perils in the wilderness, *in* perils in the sea, *in* perils among false brethren; ²⁷ In weariness and painfulness, in watchings often, in hunger and thirst, in fastings often, in cold and nakedness. ²⁸ Beside those things that are without, that which cometh upon me daily, the care of all the churches. **2 Corinthians 11:23-28**

Paul spoke of these many agitations against him as a "thorn in the flesh". These distresses were so severe that he considered the temptation of somehow finding a way of avoiding them.

But instead of giving in to this temptation, he turned to God in prayer and asked Him to make it go away. He then gives a brief explanation on how these temptations were resolved.

> ⁷ And lest I should be exalted above measure through the abundance of the revelations, there was given to me a thorn in the flesh, the messenger of Satan to buffet me, lest I should be exalted above measure. ⁸ For this thing I besought the Lord thrice, that it might depart from me. ⁹ And he said unto me, My grace is sufficient for thee: for my strength is made perfect in weakness. Most gladly therefore will I rather glory in my infirmities, that the power of Christ may rest upon me. ¹⁰ Therefore I take pleasure in infirmities, in reproaches, in necessities, in persecutions, in distresses for Christ's sake: for when I am weak, then am I strong. **2 Corinthians 12:7-10**

Paul referred to this thorn as infirmities, reproaches, necessities, persecutions and stresses.

If any of us had to face the sufferings that Paul went through, wewould have, even if we didn't deny our faith, given in to the temptation at least to complain. We would have been asking earnest questions about God's love and care for us. Like Job, though we wouldn't have cursedGod, we probably would have been tempted to curse the day we were born.

I knew a guy at a family camp in my early teens who made a great impression on me because of his strong dedication to the Lord. He was very inspirational to all of us who were struggling in our walk with the Lord. Just the thought of him doing so much good to help me continued to inspire me years later. I remember thinking that he was the godliest young person that I ever knew.

But then when I was working at a job delivering telegrams, I had to deliver a telegram at a Liberal political convention at a downtown Winnipeg hotel. After meeting this same fellow in the hotel lobby, rather than affirming my compliment of him and how his godly example years earlier had greatly influenced me, he said that those years when he served the Lord in his youth was a mistake and that he had been deceived. He said he is enlightened and now knows that there is no such thing as a God of love and justice, implying that God had let him down.

For some, such a revelation would have caused them discouragement and the temptation to also give up on the Lord. It does happen. Many followers of preachers and evangelists who have fallen morally became so disillusioned that they decided that if that's Christianity, then they didn't want any part of it. Though this manhad been a great example and inspiration to me and caused me some disappointment, his betrayal of God had no effect on me to also turn against Him.

Thankfully, we have the example of the apostle Paul who proved that going through the worst of troubles cannot cause the person who is truly committed to the Lord to turn away from Him. There is no evidence that Paul lived a defeated life after committing his life to Jesus. After he met Jesus on the road to Damascus and his prayer for deliverance from the old nature was finally answered,he then consistently lived a victorious life.

> [19] Whereupon, O king Agrippa, I was not disobedient unto the heavenly vision: [20] But shewed first unto them of Damascus, and at Jerusalem, and throughout all the coasts of Judaea, and *then* to the Gentiles, that they should repent and turn to God, and do works meet for repentance. [22] Having therefore obtained help of God, I continue unto this day, witnessing both to small and great, saying none other things than

those which the prophets and Moses did say should come: **Acts 26:19-20,22**

But considering all the sufferings the Lord required of him, it should come as no surprise that he like the rest of us was tempted to complain and seek relief. In asking the Lord that his thorn in the flesh depart from him, Paulwantedthe Lord to lessen his sufferings(see Acts 9:15,16).Buthe learnedthat when there issevere opposition and a temptation to withdraw due to fear,the Lord is faithful to provide the grace that would enable a believer to endure and to conquer.

There is no better example than the apostle Paul of a believer appropriating God's grace to resistthe temptation to let up, even slightly, of living for the Lord. Paul obeyed the command of the Lord who said to us that when we go through severe tribulations we must choose to be of good cheer and to refuse to let our hearts be troubled (see John 14:1; 16:33).

> [11]Persecutions, afflictions, which came unto me at Antioch, at Iconium, at Lystra; what persecutions I endured: but out of *them* all the Lord delivered me. [12] Yea, and all that will live godly in Christ Jesus shall suffer persecution. **2 Timothy 3:11-12**

Because His faith in God's strengthening power had been built up, when he was in Ephesus and was about to go into very dangerous territory he was confident that God's power would once again sustain him. His remarks to these believers at Ephesus area great encouragement to us.

> [19] Serving the Lord with all humility of mind, and with many tears, and temptations, which befell me by the lying in wait of the Jews:

> ²² And now, behold, I go bound in the spirit unto Jerusalem, not knowing the things that shall befall me there: ²³ Save that the Holy Ghost witnesseth in every city, saying that bonds and afflictions abide me. ²⁴ But none of these things move me, neither count I my life dear unto myself, so that I might finish my course with joy, and the ministry, which I have received of the Lord Jesus, to testify the gospel of the grace of God. **Acts 20:19, 22-24**

According to Strong's Dictionary, the word temptations in verse 19 means "a putting to proof." In defeating his temptations, Paul proved the power of his newborn nature. With every crisis he faced, when the temptation arose to give in to discouragement, Paul found that God's grace was more than adequate. Hesaid he gloried in his infirmities as it was in this state that theHoly Spirit living water within his new nature sprung up to create a powerfulflow of strength.

Some people remind us about the struggles Paul went through as we read in Romans 7.

> ¹⁸ For I know that in me (that is, in my flesh,) dwelleth no good thing: for to will is present with me; but *how* to perform that which is good I find not. ¹⁹ For the good that I would I do not: but the evil which I would not, that I do. **Romans 7:18-19**

They believe this description of Paul's struggles indicates that born-again believers will have similar struggles in trying to please God. They believe Paul's battles are corroboration of their own inability to achievevictory in their clashes with fleshly inclinations. They seem comfortable with defeat and cite Paul's failure to overcome defeat in his life as justification for defeat in their own lives. The fact some of us struggled to get victory in the months after we came to the Lord doesn't mean Paul experienced these same conflicts after his conversion.

The frustrations Paul described grew from his attempts to please God when, as he admitted later, he was the Pharisee of Pharisees. In this Romans 7 passage, Paul was describing the old nature in him and how he tried to bring it in line with the will and commandments of God to win His approval. But he discovered it was impossible to please God in his flesh. As hard as he tried in his unregenerate state to do so, he had to admit failure. Because of these constant defeats, he became very frustrated and finally prayed for deliverance.

> [24] O wretched man that I am! who shall deliver me from the body of this death? [25]I thank God through Jesus Christ.**Romans 7:24, 25**

Though Paul acknowledged in many passages the conflicts believers have with the flesh, no scriptures indicate he struggled to overcome the flesh the way we often struggle. On the contrary, we see in him the same fervor while he was chasing believers thinking that they were his enemies, demonstrated later against his newly revealed enemies, the flesh, the world, and the devil.

None of these battles were as he described in Romans 7. In all his skirmishes following his conversion, he continually gave testimony of the sufficiency of God's grace. Through this grace he quickly overturned any of the defeats that he did suffer into victory.

Those who cite Romans 7 as evidence that Paul lived a defeated life following his conversion don't realize that he experienced these defeats ever before he met Jesus on the road to Damascus. In view of what I've taught in previous chapters about self-examination, it probably would be a good thing for those who are struggling to consider the possibility that the defeats that they are experiencing are evidence that possibly they donot yet have the newborn nature in them after all.If their struggles are likewhat Paul went through,perhaps they will become as frustrated with their defeats as Paul was with his and will pray for deliverance with the hope that they will meet Jesus.

Paul's purpose in sharing these truths wasto inform his readers that they cannot expect to please God through human effort, and that deliverancecan comeonly when they've surrendered to Jesus. He explained that it was his frustrations with failing to measure up to God's high standards that had led him to pray and seek for deliverance. When God saw his heart, He answered his prayer for *escaping his fallen nature* by sending Jesus to meet him on his way to Damascus.

The apostle Paul did not struggle to overcome fleshly tendencies in the same way most of us struggle. Though every day he battled the flesh, he understood better than anyone the power of his born-again new nature. It was because he had a full grasp of this truth that he claimed that he was more successful than all his peers in overcoming the inclinations of the flesh.

> But by the grace of God I am what I am: and his grace which *was bestowed* upon me was not in vain; but I laboured more abundantly than they all: yet not I, but the grace of God which was with me. **1 Corinthians 15:10**

Earlier, we studied the temptations of the Hebrew believers to give in to discouragement and to turn away from Jesus. The writer of the letter to the Hebrews said that these Hebrew believers ought to already have been convinced that there was no one better than Jesus to help them with their temptations. Because of the many lessons and pointers that they learned through the sacrificial system, rather than being as babies in their understanding about

Escaping Your Fallen Nature

Jesus they ought to have had such a grasp of these truths that they now would be teachers (see Hebrews 5:11-14).

Paul is the perfect example, because of his previous training, of fully comprehending all the material that this Hebrews writer was teaching. He immediately understood that Jesus was the one to whom the sacrificial system pointed. He did not let any of this pre-salvation grace that he grew up on go to waste. Once his focus was turned to Jesus everything that he previously struggled with now fell into place. He did not need to continue in the baby stage pre-salvation former raingrace of the old testament sacrificial system that many of the Hebrew readers were still languishing in.

Paul got it and is inspiring us to "get it" as well. The whole point of Paul's teachings in many of his letters was to inspire us to believe that our new-born nature, because it is born of the Spirit, will prevail over all our fleshly desires. The grace that delivered Paul from his old nature and was then effectual to keep him free is the same grace that enables us to maintain our deliverance also.

Though he didn't detail how he met Jesus, he assured the believers in Rome that Jesus had forever changed his life and made him into more than a conqueror. It was to his experience of meeting Jesus on the Damascus road and his committing to Him when Ananias came to pray for himthat Paul was referring when he thanked Jesus for deliverance.

With a heart of thanksgiving, he confidently and boldly claimed that nothing, not even the worst of temptations, would ever separate him from God and His love. He boldly claimed there was no crisis regardless of its severity that could destroy his relationship with the Lord.

> [35] Who shall separate us from the love of Christ? *shall* tribulation, or distress, or persecution, or famine, or nakedness, or peril, or sword? [36] As it is written, For thy sake we are killed all the day long; we are accounted as sheep

> for the slaughter. ³⁷ Nay, in all these things we are more than conquerors through him that loved us. ³⁸ For I am persuaded, that neither death, nor life, nor angels, nor principalities, nor powers, nor things present, nor things to come, ³⁹ Nor height, nor depth, nor any other creature, shall be able to separate us from the love of God, which is in Christ Jesus our Lord. **Romans 8:35-39**

This statement also showed Paul's extraordinary confidence in the durability of his born-again new nature. He knew the sufferings and attacks against him could not make him contemplate letting up on serving Jesus. Such confidence was not his willpower to obey as described in Romans 7 but was the power of the Holy Spirit new nature of Jesus in him as he described in Romans 8.

Because he knew this nature was incapable of quitting on God, he had assurance of eternal life. Just as nothing could cause him to lose his salvation, nothing in this world could take away his assurance either. He had this assurance because the temptations he knew that Jesus had endured and conquered had proven the invincibility of this new Jesus nature that now was in his own heart.

> But I keep under my body, and bring *it* into subjection: lest that by any means, when I have preached to others, I myself should be a castaway.
> **1 Corinthians 9:27**

According to *Strong's*, this word translated as "castaway," which means "rejected" in several other passages, is translated "reprobate." Paul said endurance proves the quality of one's character. To suggest that he might become a castaway if he didn't endure is an oxymoron or contradiction.

Paul was able to bring his body into subjection and withstand hardships all his life because of the enduring quality of the born-again, new nature of Jesus in his heart. It was true that he would be a castaway if he had been unable to endure. Those who do not have this ability to endure, which means they don't have Jesus in them, indeed become castaways. However, with Paul, there was no possibility whatsoever that the Jesus diamond in him could be broken or that he couldn't endure.

> [17] For our light affliction, which is but for a moment, worketh for us a far more exceeding *and* eternal weight of glory; [18] While we look not at the things which are seen, but at the things which are not seen: **2 Corinthians 4:17-18**

Paul persevered through his troubles because his attention was on the eternal. He said that all the sufferings that he went through were not worthy of being compared to the glory that would be revealed to him when he got to heaven (see Romans 8:17,18). Just before he died, Paul wrote:

> [6] For I am now ready to be offered, and the time of my departure is at hand. [7] I have fought a good fight, I have finished *my* course, I have kept the faith: **2 Timothy 4:6-7**

In this chapter, we have learned that the tone of Paul's teaching is that victory, not defeat, should be the expectation of all believers. Though we sometimes refer to Paul's description of his struggles against the flesh as justification for our defeats and failures, we often tend to dismiss his example of conquering the flesh as being beyond the normal Christian's reach. Though there will be occasional defeats, Paul has inspired us to believe that we have already escaped the corruption of our fallen nature and that God's grace is adequate to help us defeat all our temptations.

In the next few chapters, we are further inspired as we learn about the conquering nature of Jesus. We will discover that it's this new nature of Jesus in us that gives us the confidence that we too are conquerors. As we focus on the perfect nature of Jesus, realizing that His nature is now ours, we will increase in our resolve in *escaping our fallen nature.*

PART III

PROOFS THAT JESUS IS YOUR ESCAPE

CHAPTER 18

DEMONSTRATED SUPERIOR NATURE

Our hope of Jesus replacing our corrupt hearts with new ones depends totally on the nature of His own heart that He embodied when He lived on earth. We have salvation and the assurance of overcoming any threat of losing it simply because we know that our new nature (Jesus Himself) that replaced our old one proved to be unconquerable. Jesus's victory over temptation is our proof that our new nature is superior to the corrupt nature we inherited from Adam.

If there comes a time when we are tempted to quit on the Lord, these revelations that we have learned about Jesus will inspire us to remain faithful even as He was faithful.

> For as by one man's disobedience many were made sinners, so by the obedience of one shall many be made righteous. **Romans 5:19**
>
> ⁴⁵ And so it is written, The first man Adam was made a living soul; the last Adam *was made* a quickening spirit… ⁴⁷ The first man *is* of the earth, earthy: the second man *is* the Lord from heaven… ⁴⁹ And as we have borne the image of

the earthy, we shall also bear the image of the heavenly. **1 Corinthians 15:45-49**

Paul contrasted the image of the earthy with the image of the heavenly. When he said we bear the image of the heavenly, he spoke of the new nature in us and affirmed that it bore the image of Jesus:

> And have put on the new man, which is renewed in knowledge after the image of him that created him. **Colossians 3:10**

The nature Jesus displayed while on earth was as different from Adam's original nature as our new nature is different from our original or old nature. The nature of Jesus is precisely the same as thenew man we put on when we were born again. This Corinthians passage makes it clear that the human nature of Jesus was not the same as the pre-fall human nature of Adam. If the nature of Jesus and the nature of Adam before he fell were the same, our new nature, since it is the same as Jesus's, would be the same as Adam's pre-fall nature. Therefore, being restored to Adam's original nature would have been adequate for entering heaven. However, we know that Adam'spre-fallnature was susceptible to sinning.

Many believe Jesus was vulnerable to sinning also. Since our born-again nature is the same as that of Jesus's, our new nature would also have the potential to sin.Knowing about Adam's potential to sin, it brings us no comfort to learn God restored us to Adam's pre-fall nature. But by Paul informing us that we bear the image of the heavenly and not of the earthly, we are comforted to know that our born-again new nature is not the same as Adam's original pre-fall nature.

> Forasmuch as he is the image and glory of God.**1 Corinthians 11:7**

Escaping Your Fallen Nature

Though Adam was the glory of God, his glory was far different from that of Jesus.

> The Word was made flesh, and dwelt among us, and we beheld his glory, the glory as of the only begotten of the Father,) full of grace and truth. **John 1:14**
>
> Being the brightness of his glory, and express image of his person. **Hebrews 1:3**

Many believe that Jesus took on Adam's pre-fall nature to become the second Adam and that His victory over temptation was in no way aided by His divinity. Romans 5 contrasts Jesus's obedience with Adam's disobedience and seems to support the view that His victory was through His human nature. But if this were true, He would have had no more probability of overcoming temptation, other than having a will more determined to obey God, than Adam had.

Though it may not be popular, I am convinced it was the divine nature of Jesus as the second Adam that set Him apart from the first Adam. His obedience was dependent on the combination of His divine nature with His human nature. He was the God-Man. The reason Jesus didn't give in to temptation was that He was divine. God sent Him to be the second Adam because there was no one else who could hold out against the temptation to sin.

In the Garden of Gethsemane, Jesus indicated that if there were another way to accomplish God's plan then the cup that was full of the sins of the world would pass. Adam's surrender to his human nature was proof that there was no other way. While Adam sinned because it was his nature, Jesus resisted sin because as the Son of God there was no potential in Him to sin. Jesus outlasted Adam simply because His nature was far superior to Adam's.

> Adam was not deceived, but the woman being deceived was in the transgression. **1 Timothy 2:14**

Adam knew that the fruit of the tree that was offered to him by his wife was forbidden. When he gave in to the temptation to eat it, he displayed the true character and nature of his heart. He was not deceived but deliberately rebelled against God.

Though Adam could hold out for a while from giving in to temptation to go his own way, he had no possibility of holding out forever. As the enticement to do his own thing increased in his heart, he was unable to resist and finally wilted under its full weight.

Even if Adam had lived all these thousands of years and had not yet yielded to temptation, each of us would have had Adam's potential to sin. Adam was not able to hold out indefinitely because he, unlike Jesus, had a breaking point. But this breaking point was not because of a fallen nature but because of his originally created pre-fall human nature. After all, he was "earthy".

> Thou wast perfect in thy ways from the day that thou wast created, till iniquity was found in thee. **Ezekiel 28:15**

This verse is referring to Lucifer. If Adam had been created perfect, where did his inclination toward evil come from? Was it found in him in the same way it was found in Lucifer? Or was the potential and desire to go his own way always in his heart?

Those who believe Jesus had the potential to sin should therefore have no difficulty in agreeing with me that Adam also had the potential to sin. And yet many believe that Adam did not in his pre-fall state have that potential.

During the future reign of Jesus on earth, no one will commit sin. That's because Satan won't be around to tempt anyone. But when he is subsequently released for a short season, people will again have the potential to sin. Until Lucifer arrived, there was no occasion for Adam to manifest the inclination in his heart to sin. But the enticement Lucifer used through Eve was the event that drew out of Adam's heart the desire to be independent of God.

Since God gave Adam a will, he had the ability to choose. Adam probably would have claimed he would forever choose to follow the ways of the Lord. But was his heart such that he could follow through with that claim? Only a test could determine what was truly in his heart!

Prior to the test, God made the prediction that Adam would choose to go his own way:

> But of the tree of the knowledge of good and evil, thou shalt not eat of it: for in the day that thou eatest thereof thou shalt surely die. **Genesis 2:17**

Many would argue that God made this statement due to His foreknowledge. But God said this because He knew Adam's heart. Even before he sinned, Adam gave indication of a desire to be independent from God. His giving Eve no argument after she offered him the forbidden fruit but before eating it is strong evidence that it was already in his heart to defy God's command.

Though he could have partaken of the fruit of the Tree of Life, it seems his curiosity about the forbidden tree had to be satisfied first. Like a sign saying, "Wet Paint," he felt compelled to check out this forbidden tree. I don't know if he planned to take the forbidden fruit some day on his own, but when the opportunity came, he couldn't resist using his wife to test the "waters."

Adam saw her as an opportunity to get free from his obligations to God. He used his wife the same way a king uses an official wine taster to test for any poison. When Adam observed that Eve didn't die after she ate the fruit, he reasoned he wouldn't either.

I think every young person faces the same temptation that Adam faced. When I was in my mid-teens, observing that other young people were rebelling against parental authority, I decided to do the same. To get free from their authority I deliberately disobeyed some of their instructions and insisted on doing things my own way. Then, to demonstrate that I no longer needed to depend on their resources or help, I moved out to live on my own. I figured that since I am my own boss I could now enjoy life without restraints.

When I took an apartment in downtown Winnipeg it wasn't very long before I realized what life is really about. On my very first day, a Monday, a young man in a neighboring apartment took a liking to me and said that he would set me up with one of his girlfriends for that Friday. He gave me instructions on how to prepare a girl for sex. He said that as soon as I meet her at the restaurant I should kiss her. I'll say more in a later chapter on how the Lord delivered me from this temptation.

Certainly, God wants all young people to grow up and eventually to live independently from their parents. But He doesn't want us to leave with an attitude of rebellion and disobedience. When we rebel against our God-given authority, be it parents or bosses, we open ourselves up to all kinds of devastating consequences that could very well destroy our lives.

I've heard of young people who after living all their lives under the strict moral authority of their parents, when they finally broke free, threw all caution to the wind and followed without any hesitation the dictates of their flesh, that is, their fallen nature. There was one young man who had all his life lived within the high standards of his church who, after accepting an invitation to go to a drinking party, drank so much that he died. So sad! Apparently, he was on a certain medication that when combined with alcohol will cause his system, because it can't handle it, to shut down.

When we follow the urgings of our old nature we will always risk experiencing negative consequences, especially when our decision is contrary to what we already know is right. Because Adam, unlike his wife, was not deceived, therefore he partook of the fruit knowing full well that this was an act of rebellion. The fact that Adam disobeyed is proof that he already had in his heart during the temptation stage prior to sinning the potential to sin.

On the other hand, the temptations Satan put before Jesus at the end of His forty-day fast to thwart His Father's plan had no appeal to Him. Because of His holy nature, He knew it would be a great hardship to take on the sins of the world. Though He wanted to run away, His loving nature gave Him the ability to endure this temptation. Such was His nature that no matter how heavy the temptation to bypass the stench and ugliness of our sins, He would have resisted it forever.

> Then said Jesus unto Peter, Put up thy sword into the sheath: the cup which my Father hath given me, shall I not drink it? **John 18:11**

When Jesus resisted the temptation to bypass this cup, He demonstrated the character of His heart. He deliberately chose to obey because to do otherwise was not in His nature. His temptation didn't merely demonstrate that He had the willpower and determination never to give in to it, but it also proved that He was of a different substance, that He was God in the flesh. That doesn't mean He wasn't wholly human. Having normal appetites and emotions, He was subject to the same infirmities or weaknesses that we all go through.

> Who can have compassion on the ignorant, and on them that are out of the way; for that he himself also is compassed with infirmity. **Hebrews 5:2**

If we say it was possible for Jesus to sin, we would have to conclude that He, like Adam, was inclined to sin. Since He didn't already have this propensity to sin, where did this possibility of sinning come from? Since it was not in His heart, there never was a possibility of Him sinning.

Some would say He took on the potential to sin so He would be like us in every respect. If that were true, we would have to wonder why Paul distinguished Jesus's God-Man nature from Adam's pre-fall nature. Paul also said Adam was a living soul while Jesus was a quickening spirit. He wanted us to know that the nature of Jesus was always superior to Adam's.

Some believe that God rewarded Jesus for His obedience by changing His earthly nature with a potential to sin to a heavenly nature without that potential (see Philippians 2:9). They seem to imply that the new nature that God gave to each of us is after the nature of a heavenly Jesus but not after the nature of the earthly Jesus. But Jesus's obedience is proof that He had no potential to sin (which I also explain in a later chapter). And of course, we must remember this scripture:

> Jesus Christ the same yesterday, and to day, and for ever. **Hebrews 13:8**

Though Adam always had the potential to sin, he was considered perfect because he had not yet corrupted himself with sin. It was the possibility of Adam committing sin that made him less than perfect. Since he was never perfect it was not from perfection that he fell but from innocence.

Whereas Adam was not yet corrupted before he sinned, we are evil from the moment of our birth because we are his descendants. Because we were in Adam, his fall was the fall of the human race. Thus, a second Adam was needed. And Paul called Jesus the last Adam because, having the divine nature as well as the human, he knew that Jesus would not fail. He knew that there would never be a need for another Adam.

Thus far, we have compared the natures of the two Adams. We have learned that whereas the first Adam failed because of his imperfect nature, the last Adam succeeded because He not only was the Son of Man, He was also the Son of God.

Jesus couldn't sin regardless how strong the temptation since He was God's Son:

> But when the fulness of the time was come, God sent forth his Son, made of a woman, made under the law. **Galatians 4:4**
>
> ⁶ Who, being in the form of God, thought it not robbery to be equal with God: ⁷ But made himself of no reputation, and took upon him the form of a servant, and was made in the likeness of men. **Philippians 2:6–7**

We are humble when we acknowledge that outside the resources that God provides us we are nothing and have nothing. Jesus's act of making Himself of no reputation and hiding His divinity includes this kind of humility, but it was much more than that. Jesus did not manifest the fullness of God that was always within Him but instead put Himself under many limitations.

Though Jesus was God, during His growing-up years, He never once tried to demonstrate who He was. When He visited the temple at age twelve, He indicated a special connection with His Father. When He told His mother that He had to be "about His Father's business," He implied that He believed His mother already knew. This verifies that His mother must have told Him the circumstances of His birth, but He said nothing about it to anyone else. Until He began His ministry, the people with whom He grew up had no idea that He was anybody special.

The people of Nazareth were shocked and offended when Jesus referred to Himself as being the fulfillment of scripture that He quoted from Isaiah (see Luke 4:14–30). Until the day of this revelation, Jesus conducted His life as any other citizen of Nazareth. He had made no revelation or reputation about His divine nature. It appears that the people of Nazareth had not yet learned of the fame Jesus had already begun to draw just weeks or days earlier. The divinity in Him, other than His holy and righteous living, had no effect on how people formed their opinion of Him.

While Jesus emptied Himself andobscured His divinity,we should not interpret that to mean He ceased to be divine in His nature, the very essence of His being. This emptying was to last only until the day of His revelation. Once John the Baptist declared Him the Lamb of God who takes away the sin of the world (see John 1:35), His divinitywas no longer obscured.

But when Jesus claimed fulfillment of the passage that He quoted in Isaiah, no longer could people claim they didn't know He was God. If the emptying of His divinity continued past this revelation, how could He fault people for not recognizing Him as the Son of God? Though Jesus's flesh veiled most of His divinity, the mystery of Him had been declared and partially manifested.

Sincein John 6, He made it clear that He was the bread that came down from heaven, no longer was Jesus without reputation concerning His divine nature and origin.Though God revealed that Jesus was the Christ, the Son of God, it was the manifestation of His divinitythat led Peter to this confession(see Matthew 16:13–20). Jesus showed enough of His divinity that anybody who was sincerely interested in discovering who He was would have come to the same conclusion.

Jesus expected people to decide if He wasGod's Son. Some people don't understand how He could be God and the Son of God at the same time. When He claimed to be the Son of God (see John 10:24–38), His enemies had no difficulty believing Him to be saying He was claiming to be God. That is why they accused

Him of blasphemy. Whenever Jesus said "Father" in referring to His relationship with God, He was claiming to be the Son of God. And when He declared that He and His Father were one, His enemies became so provoked that they wanted to kill Him.

To make the assertion that He was the Son of God was to claim that He was God. Since there is no possibility that God could sin, Jesus's claim to be God's Son was synonymous with declaring, because of His nature, that there was within His heart no potential of committing sin:

> Which of you convinceth me of sin? And if I say the truth, why do ye not believe me?**John 8:46**
>
> Thou hast loved righteousness, and hated iniquity; therefore God, even thy God, hath anointed thee with the oil of gladness above thy fellows.**Hebrews 1:9**

Just making this claim alone is enough to convince us that Jesus's nature is entirely different from Adam's. Though He experienced every other limitation of the human condition, He was not limited in His relationship with His Father. His soul was perfectly righteous and was without any hint of corruption. Never was there a possibility of sin coming between Him and His Father until just prior to His arrest when He voluntarily took upon Himself all the sins of the world.

If, as many claim, there was a possibility of Jesus sinning, He would have known about that potential. Jesus had not yet lived His whole life to prove that He had the fortitude to resist every temptation. Therefore, it would have been presumptuous of Him to make such a claim. Rather, He would have let the tests of His life demonstrate whether He could resist every sin. If sinning were possible, Jesus knew there just might be the possibility of not resisting the most severe temptation yet to come, that of refusing to take on the sins of the world.

> Let him that thinketh he standeth take heed lest he fall. **1 Corinthians 10:12**

Only those who have the potential of committing sin, which is all of us, need to take heed to this warning. Jesus did not pay heed to this warning because He not only thought he could stand but knew with a 100% certainty that He would never fall. If He believed there was the potential of falling, then He wouldn't have claimed to be God's Son until He had overcome all His temptations.

Jesus'ssonship is proof that He could never have sinned.Of course, that would verify, as I taught in an earlier chapter, that John's claim that he who was born of God, referring to our new born-from-above nature, cannot sin (see 1 John 3:9; 5:5). But some people take John's statement to mean that our new nature cannot sin habitually. But the part of us that commits sins is not our new spirit man but the soul of our old natural man. Paul said that the Holy Spirit sealed this new spirit man and that itcould never be corrupted by the old nature (see Ephesians 1:13).

Thomas doubted the resurrection of Jesus until he saw His wounds. Likewise, many need additional evidence beyond Jesus's claim before believing that their new nature has no possibility of sinning. How can they believe it? Since they maintain that there was the possibility that Jesus could give in to temptation, it stands to reason that they will insist that our new nature can sin also, albeit not habitually.

Rather than being an occasion to see if He could sin, Jesus's temptations were the tests of His character and nature to prove that He could not sin. When Jesus came through severe testing, He proved that He had a nature that could not possibly have given in to the temptation to sin. It proved that He was indeed, as He had claimed, the Son of God.

The suggestion that the righteousness of Jesus's divine natureenabled Him to escape the temptation to sin,many will argue, makes Him less than 100 percent human. But that doesn't make sense considering that they have acknowledged that Jesus didn't have an earthly father. We know that the conception of Jesus was from Mary's seed and that He did not require a man's seed. His virgin conception convinces us that He was unique in His humanity and therefore proofsome have misinterpreted the scriptures suggestingthat He was no different from Adam (Hebrews 2:14-18).

I'm not sure if science can confirm it, but it seems that our tendency to sin is passed on only through the seed of our fathers, not of our mothers. Though Jesus was a descendant of Adam and thus fully human, He had no susceptibility to sin as had Adam because He didn't have an earthly father.Jesus was conceived of a virgin woman by the power of the Holy Spiritnot only to bypass Adam's guilt but also to sidestep Adam's sin nature, which carried with it the potential to sin.

Jesus,the incorruptible seed of the Word of God, came down from heaven to merge with Mary's seed and became fully human. Because He had successfully avoidedthe corrupted nature of Adam's seed, He was "quickened unto life" by the Holy Spirit. Though He became the last Adam and fully took on Adam's humanity, He relinquished nothing of His divine nature. Though He voluntarily put Himself under many limitations, he continued to be the Son of God.

To not insult God's intelligence, many argue that Adam was perfect and had no potential to sin, at least not before his fall. If they were to admit that Adam already had that inclination, it would reflect on God's creativity as if He had failed in His attempt to make a perfect human being. Yet at the same time, they claim that the perfect Son of God,Jesus, did have the potential to sin and to give in to temptation.

But if He had this potential, He would not have been the Son of God. Neither would He have claimed He had the power to forgive people of their sins until after He had defeated every one of His temptations. Thankfully, because Jesus had no inclination whatsoever to disobey His Father, He obeyed His Father. As a result, though we had inherited guilt and condemnation from Adam, we now have inherited from Jesus His righteousness and His eternal life (see Romans 5:12–21).

In this chapter, we have come to understand that the nature of Jesus was a combination of His humanity with His divinity and that He revealed His identity only when the time was right. Because of what we've learned about Him, we now should have no difficulty in interpreting His claim of Sonship as proof of having no potential to commit sin. We have also learned that while many have defended the intelligence of God, at the same time they have insulted the integrity of Jesus. The scriptures are full of evidence that proves that He had no potential whatsoever of going back on His Word.

CHAPTER 19

VALIDATED HIS TRUSTWORTHINESS

Ever before Jesus came into the world, He made a commitment to do the will of the Father and fulfill the purpose for which the Father had sent Him. Included in that promise was not to quit on His Father or on the people He came to save.

I used to think it was in the Garden of Gethsemane after enduring that terrible hour of agonizing prayer that Jesus settled it once and for all that there would be no turning back. But I now know it was in heaven that He had made up His mind:

> Who verily was foreordained before the foundation of the world, but was manifest in these last times for you. **1 Peter 1:20**
> The Lamb slain from the foundation of the world.**Revelation 13:8**

God made His plans for Jesus before the foundation of the world. Jesus made statements indicating that nothing would prevent them from being fulfilled. To determine if He could have surrendered to the temptation to be a quitter, we need to know more about His commitment.

Scripture tells us that there could never have been even a single moment that Jesus was tempted to go contrary to His

Father's will. From it, we learn a lot about the mind-set of Jesus and His Father.

> Then said I, Lo, I come ... to do thy will, O God.**Hebrews 10:7**
>
> And he said unto them, How is it that ye sought me? wist ye not that I must be about my Father's business?**Luke 2:49**
>
> Jesus saith unto them, My meat is to do the will of him that sent me, and to finish his work. **John 4:34**
>
> I say unto you, The Son can do nothing of himself, but what he seeth the Father do: for what things soever he doeth, these also doeth the Son likewise.**John 5:19**
>
> I can of mine ownself do nothing: as I hear, I judge: and my judgment is just; because I seek not mineown will, but the will of the Father which hath sent me.**John 5:30**
>
> I have finished the work which thou gavest me to do.**John 17:4**
>
> And he went a little further, and fell on his face, and prayed, saying, O my Father, if it be possible, let this cup pass from me: nevertheless not as I will, but as thou wilt.**Matthew 26:39**

It's one thing for people to suggest that Satan will try to stop God's plan; indeed, he does as we see from these scriptures:

> Then was Jesus led up of the Spirit into the wilderness to be tempted of the devil. **Matthew 4:1**
>
> But Jesus perceived their wickedness, and said, Why tempt ye me?**Matthew 22:18**

This they said, tempting him, that they might have to accuse him.**John 8:6**

But it's quite another thing to suggest that Jesus may have considered, from His own free will, of backing out at the last minute and upsetting God's plan for the salvation of all humanity.

When Jesus's enemies, including Satan, tempted Him, He was not truly tempted within Himself. The Bible confirms Jesus experienced temptation. However, none of these enticements of the devil found anything in Him that would respond with an awakened desire for it. Though a temptation to the rest of us, for Jesus, it was never a temptation to go contrary to the assignment His Father had given to Him. We know that Jesus would never have betrayed His Father's trust.

In our relationships with people, however, we have learned through tragic experiences that many are not worthy of our trust. But thankfully, some of us know of at least one person who, if circumstances required it, would prove his or her trustworthiness by even risking his or her life.

There has never been an occasion where I actually risked my life to save the life of someone else. But right now, I am recalling a situation where I would have risked my life to make up for some very foolish mistakes that I had made that potentially put the life of a loved one at risk.

When my younger sister and I went to Europe back in 1976 I had to convince our parents that since she was just 17 years old and very pretty I would protect her from any man who might show an interest in her. For the most part I was very protective. Because I had promised my Bible school teacher that I would look up a nephew of his in a refugee camp outside of Vienna, Austria, I left my sister on her own at the Vienna train station making her promise me that while I was gone to the camp, which I knew would be for most of the day, she would not allow any young man to persuade her to leave the train station with him. Thankfully, when I returned, she had resisted the guys who had shown an interest in her.

And there were two other occasions where we were apart for most of the day as well. At the time, I was convinced my sister was very street wise and that I could trust her to be on her own. On the one occasion, not realizing the train station had an early closing time, my sister was forced to leave the station and go out on to the street. When I got back to the train station, she told me that other tourists had allowed her to stay with them. Thankfully, they proved to be trustworthy.

But if on any of these occasions I had come back and had not found my sister where we had agreed to meet I would have been torn with grief. I would have done anything to find her. I could not possibly have returned to Canada and then tell my parents that it was through my foolishness that I lost her. I would have at least tried to prove my trustworthiness to my parents by taking full responsibility of my mistake. In searching for her, I would have taken risks, even to sacrifice my life if necessary. I thank God that it wasn't necessary to make up for my original untrustworthiness.

Surely, after reading the above scriptures about Jesus's commitment, we are now convinced that Jesus is fully worthy of our trust. Though He said He would lay down His life for us(see John 10:15), some think that until He carried out His sacrifice, we couldn't be absolutely sure that He wouldn't back out at the last minute. To suggest that He might not have enough of a commitment to carry out the plan that His Father gave Him is to malign His good character and integrity.

If we don't fully trust Jesus, we are projecting onto Him, because we know that He was fully human, the weaknesses that plague all humanity. Indeed, Jesus had weaknesses. But there is no evidence that the scriptures referring to His limitations meant that He might have been weak in being faithful to His Word. His claim that He was the Son of God and His track record of fulfilling all His commitments is more than enough evidence to convince us that He is worthy of our trust.

One of the reasons we can be confident that Jesus would not go back on His Word is that we would expect Him to be no less faithful in keeping His commitments than Abraham and others were in keeping their commitments: "And truly, if they had been mindful of that country from whence they came out, they might have had opportunity to have returned" (Hebrews 11:15).

Abraham was so committed never to return to the old country that for more than a hundred years, he did not allow thoughts of returning to occupy his mind. If Abraham had been mindful of the country that he had left, then he would have been open to the temptation to return. But scripture says he allowed himself no such opportunity to even contemplate disobeying the Lord's command.

We know that Jesus' nature is far superior to Abraham's. And since Abraham did not allow thoughts of returning to his home country to tempt him, we know that Jesus wouldn't have allowed such thoughts of quitting to occupy His mind either. We should expect Jesus to be more faithful in keeping commitments than Abraham (Hebrews 3 compares Jesus's faithfulness with Moses).

Earlier in this study, I wrote about the necessity of examination and testing to determine if we have a born-again new nature. Well, Jesus also submitted to examination and testing. It was the practice of the Jewish religion every year that the high priest select a lamb from the flocks that became the sacrifice for their yearly celebration of the Passover feast. After the selection, the priest took four days of examining it before presenting it for sacrifice.

The examination of the lamb ensured it was without spot or blemish. Once it was thoroughly examined, the high priest declared it to be the Lamb of God who took away the sins of their nation for another year. This Passover lamb pointed to the sacrifice that would take away the sins not of one nation but of the whole world and not for one year but forever.

Since Jesus was this Lamb of God, He also needed to be thoroughly examined. He submitted to this examination through His trials just before His crucifixion. At the end of it, Pilate, who was the governor, rendered a verdict of "I find no fault in him" (see John 19:4). No blemishes were found in Jesus, not even the potential to do wrong. He was the perfect sacrifice.

> ⁷ Who in the days of his flesh, when he had offered up prayers and supplications with strong crying and tears unto him that was able to save him from death, and was heard in that he feared; ⁸ Though he were a Son, yet learned he obedience by the things which he suffered; ⁹ And being made perfect, he became the author of eternal salvation unto all them that obey him; **Hebrews 5:7-9**

When we read or hear the phrase "yet learned he obedience by the things which he suffered," I think many of us believe He learned to obey in the same way our children learned to obey. But that isn't true. Most parents can tell us how their children learned to obey. Perhaps it was through denying them a particular privilege or even giving them a spanking. We disciplined and trained them to help them respect our authority and obey our commands. When trying to decide whether to obey, they remembered previous experiences. They did not relish the idea of suffering further punishment. Finally, our child, we were happy to discover, had learned obedience.

I think it was when I was in grade five or six that a severe act of discipline from my classroom teacher taught me the importance of obedience, not even to play with the temptation to disobey. During an afternoon fun time the teacher sent the class to the ball diamond where we all played some baseball. Most of us, while waiting our turn to come to bat for our team, sat on the third

Escaping Your Fallen Nature

base side of the field on the gravelly grass. As kids would naturally want to do, in past games many of us were known to pick up small stones and toss them a short distance just for the fun of it. We didnot think there was any danger of hitting anyone.

But our teacher, being safety conscious and knowing that in previous games some of us had the habit of throwing stones, ordered us not to throw stones. When our fun time was over, and we came back into the school our teacher, who had remained in the classroom, asked who of us had picked up stones. Four of us confessed. As a punishment our teacher gave each of us a very hard strapping on the palms of our hands.

I could have argued that he was unjust to include me to be punished. He had originally ordered us not to throw stones. But in his questioning of us he asked who of us had picked up stones. While the other boys had indeed thrown stones, I went no further than to simply pick them up after which I put them down. While punishing the others and rightly so, for throwing stones, he punished me, though my action didnot contradict his original order, for merely picking them up.

Picking up the stones could be interpreted as a temptation to throw them. Though I obeyed the actual order, I had been punished for simply having the temptation. While the Bible says it is not a sin to be tempted, neither is it wise to even play with temptation. The lesson I learned that afternoon was that it's not only important to obey orders but equally as important not even to play with the temptation to disobey. The strapping I received reinforced the importance of that lesson.

In saying that Jesus learned obedience, this scripture passage seems to imply that He learned to obey in the midst of a temptation to disobey. What it means, however, is that for the very first time Jesus became acquainted with the sufferings that would come with obedience. His prayers and strong crying when in the Garden of Gethsemane were not a plea to His Father to exempt Him from physical pain, but rather a reaction to the weight of the sins of the whole world being laid on His holy and righteous soul.

Though He was the Son of God and thus entitled to His Father's favor, He learned through these experiences that His connection with His Father had not releasedHim from His sufferings. He obeyednot because He was better instructed, stronger willed, or feared punishmentbut because it was His nature, as the God-Man, to always obey.

Jesus's perfection and ability to obey were never in doubt. His obedience originated from His nature. "Being made perfect" meant that the ability to finish the work that His Father had given to Himwas within Him all along, thus corroborating His claim as being the Son of God.

I can imagine it was with much emotion that Jesus yelled on the cross, "It is finished" (see John 19:30). And it was because of this completion that the writer of Hebrews not only declared Him the author of our salvationbut also the finisher of our faith (see Hebrews 12:2).

Since we know that our born-from-above nature has no potential to sin (see 1 John 3:9), how much more then should we be convinced that the very nature from which our born-againnature has proceeded also could not sin?Since we know that God made our new nature after the image of Jesus, we can conclude, therefore, that there was no potential for Jesus to sin either.

If we believe Jesus could have been tricked into sinning, we need to ask whether God could sin also. If Jesus could quit prior to the cross, could God also quit on us? What if God decided He no longer wanted the company of the people in heaven? Could He cast them into hell? We say that's impossible because of this scripture:

> That by two immutable things, in which *it was* impossible for God to lie. **Hebrews 6:18**

Escaping Your Fallen Nature

I realize no scripture says exactly that it was impossible for Jesus to sin. However, can we not conclude based on the overwhelming evidence that even as "it was impossible for God to lie," so also it was impossible for Jesus to sin? Should we not be convinced that Jesus before His testing was likely to be as faithful to His Word as we would expect His Father to be to His? Jesus gave evidence proving to us that there was no possibility that He would quit and surrender His integrity.

We too will be tested as to our integrity. Mine was tested when I got a job driving a truck in Toronto in 1989. Though I already had experience driving school buses during my years in western Canada, I needed to be tested in my ability to drive a truck. Surprisingly, the boss hired me without requiring me to drive for several blocks to test my driving skills. He decided I was a good driver simply because I demonstrated that I could back the truck into a narrow parking space between two other trucks and do so without hitting the fence. I was very grateful and much beholden to him that he gave me this job.

Because I was beholden to my boss I could very well have been tempted to go contrary to my integrity when, after he assigned me to drive all day delivering products for a client all around Toronto, he asked me to cheat by turning in a false report. Since the truck was equipped with a radio, my boss asked me that rather than returning to the client after a delivery I would make a pickup and delivery specifically for him. He wanted me to chalk up this extra hour that it had taken me to get back to the client as time that the client would have to cover.

At the end of the day, I would turn in a time sheet of my hours that my boss wanted me to ask the client to sign. This signed time sheet would be the basis for billing the client. But since I knew one hour of my time had been spent making that pickup and delivery for my boss, I deducted that 1-hour lunch break time so that the client would not have to pay for it. I explained to my boss that if I did not deduct that hour then I would be lying to the client about my time. My boss was very angry with me for not getting the client to sign for the whole time.

Surprised that he didn't immediately let me go, he kept me on and allowed me to continue driving every day. But because he was continually angry, after two weeks of tension I told him that the only way that this tension and conflict could be resolved is that he needed to hire someone else who would do it his way, after which I then thanked him for the opportunity and left.

Because I was beholden to him for hiring me it did occur to me that by not doing it his way I was not showing him much appreciation. But I had to be honest. Though I wanted to please him, but because I had a built-in character of honesty and integrity, though Satan used my boss to try to tempt me, I did not for one moment consider doing what he asked.

And yet, as I explained back in chapter one, years later I did consider and partially gave into the temptation to withhold important information about that request for a refund. It just goes to show how important it is that we always be on guard to watch for the evil ways of our fallen nature.

Like the experience I described above, I know of a professional lady who demonstrated the integrity of her heart when she refused to go along with the worldly tactic of booking clients for more sessions than necessary. Instead of the usual number that others in her field may book, she scheduled only what she believed that her clients needed, thus saving them from unnecessary costs.

The determination of believers to be people of integrity is not only due to Jesus's inspiring example of faithfulness but also because of our new nature. Any time the devil throws a temptation at us we already have the grace and weaponry to resist and fight off his enticements. The power to overcome Satan comes from the fruit of the Spirit springing up and flowing from out of our newly transformed hearts.

Some believe that Jesus could boldly claim the success of His mission because He, from His studies of the Old Testament

Escaping Your Fallen Nature

scriptures,would have already known the outcome.Certainly, it is true Jesus knew the scriptures and that His knowledge of them had the potential of bolstering His courage to endure sufferings.

But we must ask what most influenced His decision to remain faithful: His integrity never to quit regardless of how powerful the temptation? or His learning the prophecy informing Him that He would endure this temptation? But that's like asking: Did Judas betray Jesus because the prophetic scriptures said he would? Or did the scriptures prophesy his betrayal because in looking into the future, it could be perceived it was already in his heart to betray the Lord?

The prophet wrote of Judas's betrayal of Jesus because God revealed to him what He knew would be Judas's decision when this thought reached his heart. If Judas hadtruly loved Jesus, there would never have been a prophecy predicting his betrayal.

Likewise, God revealed to the prophets the integrity that was already in Jesus's heart. If Jesus had the potential to sin, then the prophecies of His integrity would never have been written.Jesus didn't declare that He would finish His work because He had read it in the scriptures. Rather, once He learned of His Father's will, due to His integrity, He never doubted that He would fulfil it.

In this chapter, we have come to appreciate Jesus and grow in our trust of Him because upon examination there was found in Him no blemishes, not even the potential to sin. There's plenty of evidence of His perfect integrity. We will continue to grow in our appreciation of Him as we now study the incredible uniqueness of His temptation.

CHAPTER 20

REPULSED AT THE STENCH OF SIN

No one ever hated sin as much as Jesus hated it. And yet, though He lived with people whose hearts were filled with wickedness and deceit, He became known as a friend of sinners. Jesus was able to tolerate the disgrace of sin and its very presence because of His determination to redeem us. He so loved sinners that He not only decided that He would endure the suffering and the shame of the cross but also made no attempt to defend Himself when falsely accused. His commitment never to turn away from sin until it was fully dealt with was the reason He didn't protest.

> He was oppressed, and he was afflicted, yet he opened not his mouth: he is brought as a lamb to the slaughter, and as a sheep before her shearers is dumb, so he openeth not his mouth. **Isaiah 53:7**

Though Jesus did not defend Himself from these false accusations, there was yet another very significant reason for the prophet to make this statement. Jesus's decision not to open His mouth was His way of defeating the only temptation that truly had an appeal to Him.

When we're going through severe suffering and want to open our mouths, what do we expect to come from out of it? Probably, our first and only word would be "Help!" Jesus said there were many legions of angels waiting for His call. If He had opened His mouth, it would have been to summon those angels to come and rescue Him.

I am sure all the angels of heaven had their hands on their swords waiting for His signal. They would have been flashing billboard-size signs in front of Him saying that the people for whom He was about to die weren't worth it. Some of them already had their trumpets at their lips anxious to blast out the charge signal.

Though Jesus did speak throughout His trials and sufferings, the point made by the prophet was that He would not give in to the temptation to call on the angels to deliver Him. He knew that they were waiting for His signal. But He considered this temptation only because of the extreme ugliness and weight of the sins of the world on His soul which began to be placed on Him during His time of prayer in the Garden of Gethsemane. Even in the garden, though the angels ministered to Him, He stedfastly resisted any suggestion that they might have made to reconsider His decision.

Jesus's temptation was incredibly unique. Whereas our temptation is to surrender to the appeal of sin and embrace it, Jesus's temptation was to resist sin from enveloping Him and to run far from it. Though it was His nature to repel sin, He not only received all our sins but became sin so that the whole world could be set free from sin. Because it wasn't possible for Jesus to renege on His Word, He ignored the pleas of these angels and opened not His mouth.

Though Jesus rebuked Peter for suggesting that He not go all the way to the cross (see Mark 8:33), it was these angels from whence came His only true temptation. Instead of giving in to this temptation, He allowed sin to completely saturate His being, so you and I would become the very righteousness of God. He boldly announced that once He became sin, He would draw on to Himself all judgment for these sins, like a lightning rod would draw lightening.

> ³¹ Now is the judgment of this world: now shall the prince of this world be cast out. ³² And I, if I be lifted up from the earth, will draw all *men* unto me. ³³ This he said, signifying what death he should die. **John 12:31-33**

In the KJV, the word *men* is in italics because it was not in the original text. This means the translators inserted this word because to them, that was the best word to make sense of what they believed Jesus was saying. However, the context of this passage shows that rather than drawing "all *men*", the translators should have said He would "draw all *judgment*" on to Himself.

To more fully appreciate our new birth, our being set free from the judgment of our sins, and, our walk in the freedom of the Spirit, we need to understand what Jesus went through.

> ⁸ And the LORD said unto Moses, Make thee a fiery serpent, and set it upon a pole: and it shall come to pass, that every one that is bitten, when he looketh upon it, shall live. ⁹ And Moses made a serpent of brass, and put it upon a pole, and it came to pass, that if a serpent had bitten any man, when he beheld the serpent of brass, he lived. **Numbers 21:8-9**
>
> ¹⁴ And as Moses lifted up the serpent in the wilderness, even so must the Son of man be lifted up: ¹⁵ That whosoever believeth in him should not perish, but have eternal life. **John 3:14-15**

Jesus said that His being lifted up on the cross was like that of the serpent lifted up by Moses. Since the people of Israel complained to the Lord for bringing them into the wilderness, God sent fiery serpents to punish them. This brass pole that represented these poisonous snakes that had bitten them also signified their rebellion and sin.

Yet Moses said that if they wanted to be healed, they had to look at this brass snake. Because the snake was not only the cause of their pain but also a reminder of their rebellion, it's not at all surprising that many of them refused to look to it for their healing. Only those who would admit to their rebellion were willing to look.

> [23] For if any be a hearer of the word, and not a doer, he is like unto a man beholding his natural face in a glass: [24] For he beholdeth himself, and goeth his way, and straightway forgetteth what manner of man he was. [25] But whoso looketh into the perfect law of liberty, and continueth *therein*, he being not a forgetful hearer, but a doer of the work, this man shall be blessed in his deed. **James 1:23-25**

Like this brass snake representing rebellion, Jesus, in being lifted up, represented the corrupt nature of humanity. With James describing the law as like a mirror to show us our uncleanness, so also our looking on the uplifted cross of Jesus is a reflection to show us our filthiness. And even when we look at the law, though it is perfect, it appears to make us unclean, so also Jesus, when we look at Him on the cross, makes us appear unclean. But Jesus does not make us unclean any more than a mirror makes us unclean.

> If I had not come and spoken unto them, they had not had sin: but now they have no cloke for their sin. **John 15:22**

> Was then that which is good made death unto me? God forbid. **Romans 7:13**

Jesus was saying that if we had not heard His voice and seen Him on the cross, we would have had no awareness of our sin. When we look at Him, rather than seeing Him as beautiful, we need to see Him representing our rebellion, like the snake on the pole, as a condemned and cursed criminal. Because He was "guilty" He made no defense when He was accused. Having taken upon Himself all our sins and diseases we need to see Him as repulsive and ugly. The abuse that His enemies put on Him was so disfiguring it's not inaccurate to say of Him that He was "ugly as sin".

> As many were astonied at thee; his visage was so marred more than any man, and his form more than the sons of men. **Isaiah 52:14**
>
> But I am a worm; a reproach of men, and despised of the people. **Psalm 22:6**
>
> He hath made him to be sin for us, who knew no sin; that we might be made the righteousness of God in him. **2 Corinthians 5:21**
>
> Christ hath redeemed us from the curse of the law, being made a curse for us: for it is written, Cursed is every one that hangeth on a tree. **Galatians 3:13**

When I was in Bible College we students went to the Lutheran Seminary at the University of Saskatchewan in Saskatoon to make use of their video equipment. A fellow student made a very astute observation of a cross with the figure of Jesus on it. A few days later he spoke in Chapel and shared with us his impression of this cross. Many other crosses and pictures of crosses with Jesus on it portray Him as somewhat pleasant to look at. But this particular cross, my fellow student observed, was the ugliest he had ever

Escaping Your Fallen Nature

seen. His point in sharing these truths about the ugliness of Jesus was that Jesus truly became sin for us. And it is only natural to expect that as ugly as we know sin to be, Jesus was equally as ugly.

It's when we personally identify the ugliness and curse of Jesus with our corrupt hearts, knowing it was our sins that nailed Him to the cross, that His payment is applied to our account. When we believe it was the shedding of His blood that washed away the curse and ugliness of our hearts, it is only then that we will know that Jesus has forgiven us and cleansed us of our sins.

Though believing Jesus died for their sins, many are offended when they learn that He could not have paid for their sins unless He was lifted up to die a bloody death (see 1 Corinthians 1:23). I have heard of young women who wanted to become nurses who, when encountering it for the first time, just couldn't stomach looking at the blood from people's wounds. I have also noticed how TV news, before showing disturbing scenes, warn audiences of content. They know that some people are very squeamish when seeing others suffer.

Our society is very sensitive to acts of violence. Many are easily offended when some of us refuse to agree with their disruptive views against spanking, capital punishment, slaughtering of animals, and the use of firearms (yet they don't object to killing unborn babies). Some won't sing hymns about the blood of Jesus because of the offensive violence it conjures up in their minds.

Depending on the condition of our hearts, envisioning Jesus in His violent bleeding condition stimulates either offense or humility. If we take offense with the violence toward Jesus, thinking of Him as a martyr, we show that we have not understood the horribleness and gravity of our sins. But it's only when we agree that He literally became sin and that His voluntarily laying down His life to shed His blood was necessary to wash away our sins that we have shown genuine repentance and faith.

> [1]Wherefore seeing we also are compassed about with so great a cloud of witnesses, let us lay aside every weight, and the sin which doth so easily beset *us*, and let us run with patience the race that is set before us, [2] Looking unto Jesus the author and finisher of *our* faith; who for the joy that was set before him endured the cross, despising the shame, and is set down at the right hand of the throne of God. [3] For consider him that endured such contradiction of sinners against himself, lest ye be wearied and faint in your minds. [4] Ye have not yet resisted unto blood, striving against sin. **Hebrews 12:1-4**

"Besetting sin" refers to the sin in our lives that we struggle most to overcome. The Hebrew people struggled most with quitting on Jesus and going back to their former religion because of the offense of the cross. They had a hard time understanding how the violent execution of a "guilty criminal" could save their souls. To inspire them to victory, the writer directed them to focus on Jesus and on how He overcame the offensiveness of the cross. He showed them that because Jesus overcame the temptation to quit He was qualified to help them get through their temptations also.

This passage tells us that far from struggling with it, Jesus endured the cross and overcame its shame with an attitude of joy. Though the cross symbolized a curse, He despised the shame that came with it by giving all His attention to what the cross would accomplish. Jesus considered the disgrace of the cross to be of no significance. The temptations of complaining and attaching blame, those that prevented the Israelites from entering the promised land, never entered his mind. Like Jesus, it is very important that we also, in times of hardship, resist complaining and remain joyful.

> [11] Blessed are ye, when *men* shall revile you, and persecute *you*, and shall say all manner of evil against you falsely, for my sake. [12] Rejoice, and be exceeding glad. **Matthew 5:11–12**

In my first year at the Bible college, I worked every weekend as a security guard at the reception desk at University Hospital. I spoke on spiritual things to many who had accompanied patients to the emergency room while they were in the waiting room. I tried to be tactful in my witnessing, but some of the staff complained to the hospital administration.

My boss told me the security company was on the verge of losing its contract with the hospital because of me. I immediately agreed not to go back. Since the company had no other Friday and Saturday night shifts to offer, I was without a job. Though I knew there could very well be a reaction to my zeal, I figured I was doing the Lord's work by trying to be a good witness. I did not consider the possible consequences because I believed that winning someone to the Lord was well worth the risk.

Though it was nothing compared to what happens in many other countries, the opposition I experienced and the subsequent dismissal from my job was a form of persecution. Since it almost cost the company its contract, consideration for protocol was more important. Not being careful cost me future opportunities to be a witness to others and cost me financially. Thankfully, though it was the middle of the term, I had already earned enough, but just barely, to make it to the end of the year.

At the beginning of my second year, though I had already earned some of the fees, I needed a job to cover the remainder. I applied at a nearby service station for a job pumping gasoline. At the first they told me that they didn't need anyone. A few days later, I spotted the manager when he came to the school to post a job opportunity on the bulletin board for a weekend night attendant. I immediately told him I was available, and he hired me on the spot.

I worked at that job every Friday and Saturday night from eleven in the evening to seven the next morning for over two years. At the end of my schooling, my manager came to my graduation and proudly, like a father, bragged to some of the other students that he was the one who had put me through Bible school. After graduating, the manager promoted me from part time to full time. I worked there from the end of April to the end of August and earned enough money for me and my younger sister to go on a six-week tour of Europe.

Though I had blown it with my hospital job, the Lord was very kind to me. I had been careless, but rather than leaving me to reap what I had sown, the Lord helped me to recover. His mercy more than made up for my mistake. This incident tested my attitude. Would I blame the hospital staff, claim I was a victim of injustice, or blame the Lord for supposedly not taking good care of me? Or would I regain my focus and *escape* these negative feelings?

After losing the security job, I was very disappointed and was tempted to be discouraged. But it was my confidence that the Lord would provide for me, since I was only attending school to please Him, that helped me turn my disppointment (as Jesus did of His sufferings) into joyful optimism. I knew that many people had it far worse, so I refused to dwell on the consequences of my mistake, and instead, trusted the Lord to show me favor. He did that when He opened up for me that service station job.

Until that very moment in the Garden of Gethsemane when for the first time Jesus, in real time, felt the sins of the world, His whole focus was on the finishing of His work. His finished work would grant rest and peace for ever more to those who would look to Him for salvation. It was because His focus was on the effort to redeem believers that He endured the contradiction of sinners and their sinfulness against Himself. Though He was a man of sorrows and acquainted with grief (see Isaiah 53:3), Jesus always maintained an attitude of joy.

Jesus did not mean to give the impression that the cross was so emotionally disturbing that He was tempted, as we are inclined to think, to find a way out of finishing His work (see Matthew 26:37–42). We must not read into Jesus's words about His own will as a temptation to oppose His Father's will. He willed to do only the Father's will:

> My meat is to do the will of him that sent me, and to finish his work. **John 4:34**
> I do always those things that please him. **John 8:29**

Jesus simply stated that He would not go along with a plan different from the original unless His Father willed another plan. When He said, "With God all things are possible" (see Matthew 19:26), He didn't imply it was possible for God to find a way to release Him from going to the cross. He would not have left heaven if He hadn't already known the sacrifice of Himself was the only way of saving sinners from going to hell.

Jesus maintained that anything God willed for Him He would accomplish. Nothing could have prevented Him from fulfilling what He had set His mind to do. Never once did He consider such a thought. He always made His emotions subject to His heart and will and the will of His Father. We have no reason to believe that He was tempted to renege on His promise because of His strong emotions. It was as impossible for Him to back out from going to the cross as it was for His Father to back out from sending Him to rescue sinners.

There was a reason Jesus became emotional when He was in the Garden of Gethsemane. Though He was aware of all the sins of the world, for the first time, He was beginning to feel the weight of them on His soul. His emotionally charged soul prompted Him to react with, "If it be possible, let this cup pass from me" (Matthew 26:39). His words conveyed the impact that these sins had on His pure and holy soul. His request expressed what His undefiled heart, nauseated by sin, wanted. Two stories in the Old Testament illustrate His emotional revulsion toward sin.

There is the story of a servant-slave named Joseph in Genesis 39:1–23. He faced a very powerful temptation to commit sin with his master's wife. Because he had kept his heart pure before the Lord, when presented with this temptation, he considered how offended his heavenly Master would have been. He knew that if he gave any time to contemplate it, this enticement might wear down his resolve to remain pure. His only solution was to run.

Then there is the story of King David in 2 Samuel 11:1–27. While relaxing on the rooftop of his palace, he spotted a beautiful woman. Though he knew it was wrong, unlike the decisiveness of Joseph, he took a long, lingering look that weakened him. He ordered a servant to bring the woman, Bathsheba, to the palace, where David then committed adultery with her. Later, David was sharply reproved by the prophet Nathan.

Jesus was so repulsed by the sins of the world about to be laid on Him that His first reaction, like that of Joseph, was to run. It was running away from the ugliness and stink of sin, not quitting on His Father's plan, that was the one temptation that Jesus faced. His reaction of repelling these sins of the world from enveloping His pure soul, like water repelling oil, should not be a surprise.

As God, Jesus inspired Joseph to flee from the seductive behavior of his master's wife. He also reproved David via Nathan for not running from the temptation to lust for the wife of his neighbor. If it were possible, as many claim, for Jesus to renege on His commitment to meet our needs, then He would have refused to take on the sins of the world. Who would have blamed Him if He had decided to break His promise at that point when He was literally about to become sin? But we are all eternally grateful that reneging on His commitment was never possible.

Escaping Your Fallen Nature

When Jesus refused to open His mouth to protest the false charges, He became a cursed criminal deserving of punishment. But when He refused to open His mouth and chose not to call on the angels for deliverance, He escaped the only temptation that had a strong appeal. But He did this for your sake so that the possibility of *Escaping Your Fallen Nature Entangling Your Life and Blocking Your Way* could become a present-day reality. This was the only way that you could receive His perfect sinless nature and become the righteousness of God.

In this chapter, I have shown that the temptation Jesus faced was not that of surrendering to sin because of its appeal but the temptation to refuse sin because of its filthy repulsiveness. His act of surrendering to sin was not that of committing sin but becoming sin. Because His temptation was unique, none of us can claim that His temptation was in any way like ours.

CHAPTER 21

IDENTIFIED WITH YOUR INFIRMITIES

Though Jesus proved the impossibility of sinning when the severest temptation couldn't persuade Him to open His mouth, some people still believe that Jesus could have sinned.

> For we have not an high priest which cannot be touched with the feeling of our infirmities; but was in all points tempted like as *we are*, yet without sin. **Hebrews 4:15**

Many times, I've heard it said that the temptations that we face Jesus also faced. We've been told it is knowing He endured these same temptations that we face every day that convinces us that He understands our struggles. But the temptations Jesus faced were not at all like the temptations that are common to us. It's the intensity of our temptations, not the individual thousands that we go through, with which Jesus identifies and is touched with the feeling of our infirmities.

I have heard people say that "in all points tempted like as we are" means Jesus faced every temptation we have faced. We believe this because Jesus was fully human. We know that we have been tempted to steal, be envious or covetous of the belongings of others, to lie, to murder, and to commit fornication or adultery. Since the scripture says Jesus was tempted in all points like as we are tempted, we therefore believe that He must have experienced all these temptations also.

James said that sins cannot be committed outwardly until they've been committed inwardly:

> [14] But every man is tempted, when he is drawn away of his own lust, and enticed. [15] Then when lust hath conceived, it bringeth forth sin: and sin, when it is finished, bringeth forth death. **James 1:14–15**

These sins originate from the heart, which Jesus verified:

> [19]For out of the heart proceed evil thoughts, murders, adulteries, fornications, thefts, false witness, blasphemies: [20]These are the things which defile a man. **Matthew 15:19–20**

For Jesus to be tempted to commit murder or fornication, He first would have had to have hate and lust in His heart. Satan may very well have put the thought in His mind to be angry with someone or to desire a woman, but the temptation from without does not mean He was tempted from within. Since only those in the flesh are tempted, Jesus would have to have been in the flesh.

> So then they that are in the flesh cannot please God. **Romans 8:8**

Because we know Jesus always did what pleased His Father, He was never "in the flesh." The sins common to us never appealed to Him. The temptations of the lust of the flesh, the lust of the eyes, or the pride of life (see 1 John 2:16) that Satan tempted Him with had no effect on Him.

During these temptations, Jesus's mind was full of God's Word. Since He immediately blocked these imaginations from His mind, these temptations of His flesh, soul, and spirit had no chance of taking up residence in His heart. In a later chapter, I explain in detail how He defeated the first of these three temptations in the wilderness, that of refusing to change stones into bread.

Because of Jesus's unique nature, He never neglected to spend time with His Father. Yes, He was strengthened by His relationship with His Father, but because He was born of the Holy Spirit, He was already God's Son with the divine nature in Him. Therefore, He had the ability to make His relationship with His heavenly Father His priority. Jesus spent not even one moment contemplating any of the temptations common to us. He was always fully conscious of the presence of His Father and ever mindful of the scriptures that He had committed to memory.

With one exception, none of the temptations people normally attribute to Him ever appealed to Him. This one exception, which I covered earlier, was the temptation not to endure the full weight of the world's sins laid on Him. Because Jesus always was in communion with His Father He never made opportunity for His fleshly appetites and emotions to draw and entice Him. Since Jesus never made provision for the desires of His flesh to tempt Him, therefore He never struggled, as we do, to keep them under control.

It's a mistake about the meaning of temptation to believe that Jesus's temptation was that of appealing to His fleshly appetites to draw Him into sin. His temptation was the occasion to prove that the appeal to indulge the flesh, natural to us all, was foreign to Him. His fleshly appetites were always subject to His will. Nothing in His nature found these excesses of the flesh tempting.

Due to Jesus's emotions and natural drives, He would have considered women attractive and desirable, but we can be confident He never went beyond appreciating a woman's beauty.

Escaping Your Fallen Nature

As God, He inspired Job to make a pact with his eyes not to lust for women (see Job 31:1). If Job knew how to avoid the temptation to lust, never mind entertain it, certainly, Jesus also knew.

If the intemperance of the flesh was appealing to Jesus and caused Him to be tempted to lust, how could He say He always pleased His Father? The fact He was given the Spirit without measure is proof He couldn't have allowed His appetites and emotions to tempt Him. One of the fruits of the Spirit, temperance, helps us to avoid thoughts of temptation. Because Jesus was filled with the Spirit even in His mother's womb, we conclude that He always had His emotions and drives under the control of the Spirit.

To prove that He was fully human some argue that Jesus had to have had inclinations toward sexual lust, alcoholic drinking, and attitudes of anger and unforgiveness. But I can give examples to prove that He had no inclinations at all toward illicitly fulfilling the natural desires of His flesh.

In an earlier chapter I shared about our natural tendency to rebel against authority. When I was 17, because of my rebellious attitude, I moved out of my parents' home into an apartment in downtown Winnipeg. As mentioned earlier, a neighboring tenant on that Monday, after telling me his stories of picking up women, set me up with a date with one of his girlfriends for that Friday.

During that week I met two people who were connected to this neighbor. The man warned me that to have sex with someone that I don't love and who is not my spouse would leave me with a horrible empty feeling. The other person, a woman, told me that to engage in sex before I was 18 would get me into trouble with the law. Though they did not tell me to back out, I felt as though these two people were sent to me by the Lord as a way of helping me to overcome my temptation.

All that week I thought about this temptation. Though this enticement corrupted my mind, the Holy Spirit, through the comments of these 2 people, reminded me of my parental and pastoral training. I have always believed, as I shared in a previous chapter, that when we make promises for appointments, we should do our best to keep them. But when Friday evening came, I decided not to show up. Because I was among the ungodly I also decided that to avoid further temptation I needed to leave. The next day I packed my things and returned home.

I'm not saying I could never have given into that temptation. But if I had let my guard down and ignored this Holy Spirit conviction, then Satan would have exploited my natural drives. My temptation was not so great that I was tempted actually to do it. Though there was the potential for me to give in later, at that moment, the temptation from without did not find anything within capable of awakening to its appeal; the Holy Spirit's conviction in me was just too strong to ignore.

If I was already born again, then it was God's faithfulness to draw from out of my dormant (backslidden) new nature sufficient post-salvation grace to deliver me from my fallen nature. But if I was not yet born again, then it was God's pre-salvation grace (that earlier had started the formation of Jesus) that sustained me through this temptation. In either scenario, though I had lusted, it was God's grace that blocked the temptation from moving into the next stage. Therefore, I know that Jesus, who never once made provision for the lust of the flesh (see Romans 13:14), could never have reached that point, either, of actually being tempted to commit fornication.

Many, when they go to a bar or a wedding, will be tempted to get into the mood and join with revelers to drink. Though attending many weddings at which alcohol was served, because alcohol has never been a temptation I've never had any difficulty in turning away from anything alcoholic. Though I've been tempted from without by others, I've never been tempted from within by my own corrupt natural nature to drink.

Some think that when Jesus attended the wedding in Cana He was tempted to drink. Because others were drinking and becoming intoxicated, the atmosphere to drink was never more

Escaping Your Fallen Nature

favorable. Though this type of temptation was all around Jesus, I maintain He was not tempted. I know this because if I with a sinful nature have never been tempted by alcohol, Jesus could never have been tempted with drinking anything alcoholic either. While many people would argue that there isn't anything wrong with drinking moderately, for Jesus, however, it would have been wrong (a few years ago I wrote a study explaining why, but, since it is a totally new topic, I cannot share it here).

In John 2, we read of Jesus's outburst of anger in the temple. Many would say that this outburst was evidence of a predisposition to sin. If that were a true temptation, we all agree that He overcame it. But, His outburst was more of a proof of His divinity rather than His humanity. There has always been in the divine nature of God the possibility of people provoking Him to anger through their rebellion and sin.

One of the temptations we all have is to remain angry and withhold forgiveness from those who have hurt us. If Jesus were tempted in all areas as we are, we would have to conclude that He was tempted to remain angry, to hold back forgiveness, and even to seek revenge on those who had rejected Him.

In an earlier chapter, I shared how I went through abuse from my brother. I could have gotten bitter, but I never did. Though my brother came to me to ask for my forgiveness, there was never any time that I was unforgiving toward him. Since even with my sinful nature, I was never tempted to hold back forgiveness from family members or seek revenge, I know Jesus could never have been tempted to be unforgiving either.

Furthermore, even at those times when I did harbor bitterness and refused to forgive, never once did those attitudes, though the potential was there, tempt me to commit murder. And if I in my sinful nature wasn't tempted to kill someone, Jesus, though many gave Him reason to be angry, could never have wanted to murder anyone either.

What about the people who have committed horrific crimes against God and humanity? Is the new convert who may be tempted to commit such offenses persuaded of Jesus's care because he is convinced Jesus too was tempted to commit these same wrongdoings? Is the believer who has cursed and blasphemed God for his troubles but is trying to stop blaming Him comforted to know that Jesus also was tempted to curse and cast blame on to His Father?

Consider all the love Jesus demonstrated toward children in gathering them around so that He could show them His care. Consider also His harsh remarks about those who dared offend any of them. Surely, there aren't any who believe that Jesus may have ever considered abusing a child. But some people think they cannot draw encouragement from Jesus until they remind themselves that He went through the same temptations common to society.

These are only a few examples of the temptations that we regularly face. What about the thousands of other temptations people all over the world deal with? Did Jesus experience a drawing and magnetism toward every one of them? Of course He didn't! If the temptations that Jesus faced were not the ones that are familiar to us all, how then can His victory over temptation be a source of inspiration and comfort?

> For we have not an high priest which cannot be touched with the feeling of our infirmities…
> **Hebrews 4:15**

The context of this scripture passage has to do with Jesus sympathizing and identifying with the struggles that we experience in our battles with temptation. This passage seems to say that since Jesus experienced the same struggles that we go through, we can believe that He feels for our infirmities and understands our struggles.

But the reason He feels for our struggles is not because He faced the same temptations. He feels for us because the weight

Escaping Your Fallen Nature

we feel when we experience temptation is the same weight He felt from His unique temptation. Yet His temptation was more severe. It is therefore not imperative that Jesus had to have struggled with the same temptationsthat wehave struggled with in orderthat we would feel His compassion for us.

> Ye have not yet resisted unto blood, striving against sin. **Hebrews 12:4**

The writer of Hebrews is telling us that the way to be free from being wearied and faint in our minds over our disappointments is to remember the extreme intensity of the temptation that Jesus faced. When the writer reminded his readers that they had not yet resisted unto blood, he was verifying his statement about the intensity of the temptation that Jesus went through in the Garden of Gethsemane.

Usually, people think this phrase "resisted unto blood" is referring to Jesus's sufferings on the cross. But that does not set Jesus apart if we consider the multitudes of people who have died for loved ones without flinching. So intense was His temptation that during His prayer the weight of the world's sins coming upon Him caused Him to sweat drops of blood:

> And being in an agony he prayed more earnestly: and his sweat was as it were great drops of blood falling down to the ground. **Luke 22:44**
>
> Who in the days of his flesh, when he had offered up prayers and supplications with strong crying and tears unto him that was able to save him from death, and was heard in that he feared; **Hebrews 5:7**

When we depend on our own strength to resist temptations, it is certain that as the magnetism of the temptation increases, we will give in to it. On a pressure gauge with readings 1 to 100, some may hold out to number 3 and others may hold out to number 9, and those who are the strongest willed might hold out to number 14. But regardless of the temptations of intense pressure that we may be able to survive, the pressure will eventually be so intense that we just cannot resist any longer. None of us can hold out to number 100 on the pressure gauge.

When the writer to the Hebrews stated that Jesus was tempted in all points as we are he was saying that at every point of pressure to give into temptations that we may be going through Jesus has also gone through. While we have a breaking point there was no point in His temptations that He encountered a breaking point. There was no force of temptation that was so intense that it would have caused Him to give in. He passed all breaking points that the strongest of us has ever reached. Because of His nature He could hold out forever.

> But was in all points tempted like as *we are, yet* without sin. **Hebrews 4:15**

The word *points*, according to *Strong's*, comes from the Greek word *pas*, which means "all." It is an adjective that can modify many nouns. The words *like as*, according to *Strong's*, "frequently denotes ... intensity."

> And now, Lord, behold their threatenings: and grant unto thy servants, that with all boldness they may speak thy word. **Acts 4:29**

The same Greek word that in Hebrews was translated "all points," in Acts 4 is translated "all boldness". It seems to suggest degrees of intensity with "all boldness" being the maximum.

While Proverbs tells us that a soft answer can turn away wrath, were these men hoping that with enough tactfulness these enemies of the gospel might go soft on them? No! They asked the Lord for not just a little bit of courage to gently face their opposition but for the highest intensity of boldness possible, not caringat all if their words provoked their enemies to wrath against them.

From this evidence, I don't think I am wrong to interpret "all points" as having something to do with the intensity of Jesus's temptation. This certainly is preferableto making it mean that Jesus experienced all the various kinds of temptations and struggles that are common to us. When we come to realize that the intensity of His temptation was much more extreme than any that we have faced, we then know that He's been "touched with the feeling of our infirmities."

It seems many Christians think the temptations of Jesus came from His fleshly appetites and emotions. Since He outsmarted His enemies in every trap, it shouldn't be difficult to believe that thepossibilityof Jesus allowing His emotions and appetites to ensnareHim was zero.Jesus feels for our infirmities not because He went through the same temptations we go through but because He is acutely aware of the weight of our burdens. We feel His feelings for us because we know He has gone through every point of intensity imaginable. When we are overcome by temptations, we can therefore draw comfort knowing that Jesus understands.

In this chapter, we have learned that the feelings and emotions that Jesus expressed were not that of a temptation to commit the sins that are common to our society. Rather, all His emotions were a reaction to experiencing for the first time the ugliness and repulsiveness of the sins of the whole world. We are comforted because we know the intensity of His temptation to resist receiving these sins was far greater than any temptation we have felt to surrender to sin's appeal. And equally as comforting as Jesus feeling the intensity of our temptations is knowing that Hehas shown us how to escape thesetraps that the enemy will use to try to draw us in to committing sin.

CHAPTER 22

EXEMPLIFIED THE WAY OF ESCAPE

We are inspired to believe for our decisive victory over temptations when we consider how Jesus handled Satan's temptations in the wilderness. Though the Bible clearly states that Jesus was tempted in the desert by Satan, I maintain that the appetites of Jesus's flesh never tempted Him?

We need to be aware of the meaning of *tempted* and *temptation*. Included in its definition in *Strong's Dictionary* are "to experience," "to prove," "to test," "to examine." Temptation is a test. A teacher gives students a test to see what they know and whether they have been paying attention to their lessons. Temptations test what is in our hearts.

Since we have learned that Jesus had no possibility of sinning, what did His endurance of temptation or testing prove? His temptation implies His character was examined as if under a microscope to see if His experiences proved that He was who He claimed to be. Jesus's experiences and trials were therefore occasions to test His unmatched ability to endure.

I've often heard, "If there was no possibility of Jesus giving in to temptation, how then was He tempted?" We usually think temptation refers to an enticement to sin. Because the Holy Spirit drove Jesus into the wilderness so the devil could tempt him, we have come to believe it must have been possible for Him to give in to the temptation to sin. We reason that if it wasn't possible for Him to sin, His temptation wasn't a real temptation.

> ¹³ Let no man say when he is tempted, I am tempted of God: for God cannot be tempted with evil, neither tempteth he any man: ¹⁴ But every man is tempted, when he is drawn away of his own lust, and enticed. **James 1:13-14**

I have shown from previous chapters that it was impossible for Jesus to be drawn away of his own lust because the sins of the flesh never appealed to Him.

> And it came to pass after these things, that God did tempt Abraham…**Genesis 22:1**

Though God tempts no one to sin yet He did tempt Abraham. This "tempting" was a testing of Abraham by the Lord to see if he would sin. It gave the Lord the occasion to test the integrity of character of Abraham's heart to see if he had developed in his trust and faith toward God? When God asked Abraham to sacrifice his son, he had an opportunity to prove that he, unlike in the past, would obey His command. Abraham promised to do it. However, making a promise doesn't count unless it is carried out and fulfilled.

God needed to put Abraham to the test because he had let God down on several occasions earlier in his life. He went against God's instructions when he took with him his father and his nephew. On two occasions, he lied to kings of other nations to protect his own life. In so doing, he put his wife, Sarah, at risk of being abused. He showed weakness of faith when he agreed with Sarah to take Hagar and "help God" follow through on His promise for a child.

Having learned from previous failures, Abraham received from the New Testamentwriters a glowing report of having recovered from past character flaws.

> [19] And being not weak in faith, he considered not his own body now dead, when he was about an hundred years old, neither yet the deadness of Sara's womb: [20]He staggered not at the promise of God through unbelief; but was strong in faith, giving glory to God; [21] And being fully persuaded that, what he had promised, he was able also to perform.**Romans 4:19–21**
>
> [17] By faith Abraham, when he was tried, offered up Isaac: and he that had received the promises offered up his only begotten son, [18]Of whom it was said, That in Isaac shall thy seed be called: [19]Accounting that God was able to raise him up, even from the dead; from whence also he received him in a figure.**Hebrews 11:17–19**

Similarly, God put Jesus to the test. But unlike Abraham, it was not to see if He would sin. He tested Jesus to demonstrateHe was who He claimed to be. This test would prove the essence of His character and being. Since only God could resist the intensity of this temptation, it would prove that Jesus was indeed the Son of God.

We know that testing of what truly is in our hearts could come at any time and therefore we must always be ready. In an earlier chapter I shared how the Lord delivered me from the temptation to lie for my boss. It happened again a few years later, in 1994, but this time at only a moment's notice, at another trucking job where I was a dispatcher as well as a driver.

When I took a telephone call from a client, my boss ordered me to tell him he wasn't in. I could have told the caller that my boss wasn't available, but because I knew he was available, I passed this call to him anyway. Afterward, my boss was very angry that I hadn't lied for him. I explained that if I could lie for him, I would leave him with the belief that if I felt it necessary, I would lie to him. That won his trust. Later, he asked me to do things he did not trust others to do.

In the same way God initiated this test of Jesus before Satan, He also initiated the testing of Job. God wanted to prove to Satan that Job, His servant, was faithful and that even the severest of tests would reveal his righteous heart. Job said,

> He knoweth the way I take: when he hath tried me, I shall come forth as gold. **Job 23:10**

The testing of Job did not cause his heart to become gold. While heat can make some substances stronger (iron into steel) the heat applied to gold is not the reason it's gold. Rather, heat removes the impurities in gold and reveals its true inner character. If it were anything else, the fire would reveal it. Similarly, Jesus's temptation provided practical proof to the world that He was of a different substance and character than Adam.

The Holy Spirit, not the devil, drove Jesus into the wilderness so the devil could tempt Him. The Spirit knew that the forty days of fasting would in the devil's mind leave Jesus somewhat vulnerable to his attacks. But instead, it would provide proof of what was in Jesus's heart.

Just prior to the wilderness temptations, Jesus heard God's voice from heaven saying:

> This is my beloved Son in whom I am well pleased. **Matthew 3:17**

This test of Jesus, unlike for Abraham, was for the benefit of others so they would have proof that Jesus was God's Son. When the people heard the voice come out of heaven, Jesus explained:

> This voice came not because of me, but for your sakes.**John 12:30**

This voice also caught the attention of Satan. I present no biblical evidence, but it could be that when he was Lucifer, Satan believed that Jesus was a created being. He may have believed that Jesus was no more the Son of God than he was and that this temptation of Jesus would be an opportunity to prove that He was not God's Son.

We recall how Satan was very quick to challenge God about Job's integrity while ignoring evidences of his righteousness. He believed that if Jesus felt neglected, like Job felt when he complained against God, He would not be able to resist the temptation to doubt His Father's care.

Just as God used the testing of Job to prove to Satan that Job was His faithful servant, He used this testing or temptation of Jesus to prove to Satan and the world that Jesus was His Son.

Satan knew that Jesus was sure He was the Son of God even before He heard His Father's voice. But he reasoned that when Jesus arrived at His most vulnerable point, He might begin to doubt His Father's care and question whether He was His Father's Son. Since it had worked with Eve to cause her to doubt the integrity of God's Word, and with the Prodigal son, whom we studied in an earlier chapter, to make him doubt his father's care, Satan, believing Jesus would have these doubts also, came up with a plan to bring these doubts to the surface.

Satan subtly introduced into Jesus's mind a thought that he hoped would begin His fall. With the same craftiness he displayed when asking Eve, "Hath God said …?" he said to Jesus:

> If thou be the Son of God, command that these stones be made bread. **Matthew 4:3**

Escaping Your Fallen Nature

Satan reasoned that since God seemingly neglected caring for Jesus's physical needs, Jesus would feel justified to use God's power through faith to meet those needs Himself. By performing the miracle of changing the stones into bread, He would've proved He had access to God's power. But at the same time, He would also have exhibited doubt, as Eve had, of His Father's care. If He doubted God's care, it followed at least in Satan's mind that He would've had at least a little bit of doubt as to whether He was God's Son. That's all that would be necessary to bring Jesus down.

> And he that doubteth is damned if he eat, because *he eateth* not of faith: for whatsoever *is* not of faith is sin. **Romans 14:23**

If we faced the same subtlety Satan used on Jesus, how would we react? If we went forty days without food, would we not begin to doubt God's care? We recall that God supernaturally provided food for Elijah. Because we know the Prodigal son doubted that his father would receive him back as his son, we might think that our heavenly Father had put us out of His family also!

Most of us would likely have taken Satan up on his challenge. Perhaps we would have called a pastor, the prayer line, or a friend to ask for confirmations that God had not rejected us because of a feeling of condemnation put on us by others. Our reaction would prove that we had permitted a doubt of God's care to enter our minds and possibly doubting we are anymore His children. The doubt would erase the peace and assurance that had earlier comforted us. That's what John the Baptist did when sending his followers to ask Jesus if He was the Messiah (see Matthew 11:2–6).

But what Satan didn't take into consideration was Jesus's relationship with His Father. The Holy Spirit drove Jesus into the wilderness as a test to prove that He was God's Son. Though He abstained from food, He never for one moment stopped partaking of what truly sustained Him: the words of His Father.

Because of Jesus's continual relationship with His Father, Satan discovered that He never once had any concern for His lack of physical sustenance. It was His unique nature that allowed Jesus to endure hunger and yet not be tempted to complain.

> ³¹ In the mean while his disciples prayed him, saying, Master, eat. ³²But he said unto them, I have meat to eat that ye know not of. ³⁴Jesus saith unto them, My meat is to do the will of him that sent me, and to finish his work.**John 4:31,32,34**

Jesus's disciples observed that He hadn't eaten for a long while. Thinking that He would be glad for food, they offered Him some. But Jesus used this occasion to teach them that doing the Father's will is priority. Just like the disciples, Satan didn't understand what truly sustained Him.

Satan threw everything he could at Jesus to make Him reach His breaking point only to learn that Jesus, unlike the rest of us, has no breaking point. Since only God Himself could have no breaking point, Jesus proved He was who He claimed to be by passing this test. The fact that Jesus came out of the wilderness unscathed proved that He was indeed the Son of God.

It seems many Christians believe that Jesus's temptation was that of enticing Him to use His divine powers to satisfy physical needs, but they miss the point! Jesus was never tempted in Hisheart to use divine powers. Not even for one second was the use of such power ever necessary. The temptations Satan offered Him had no appeal to Him.

> But he answered and said, It is written, Man shall not live by bread alone, but by every word that proceedeth out of the mouth of God. **Matthew 4:4**

Escaping Your Fallen Nature

Some think that Jesus's response to Satan by quoting the scripture was the reason that He was able to overcome His temptation. While it is true that hiding the Word of God in our hearts as David did (see Psalm 119:11) will help us not sin, Jesus's memory of God's Word was not what delivered Him from sinning. Rather, since it was not possible for Him to commit sin, His quoting the scriptures was simply His way of silencing Satan.

In mentioning the words that proceeded out of the mouth of God, Jesus was referring to His daily communion with His Father. Every moment, He lived by the refreshing words of His Father. While Jesus's physical strength and stamina to do ministry were aided by prayer, scripture, and the power of the Holy Spirit, His strength of character and integrity were due to His divine nature.

His divine nature was the substance of His being. It was a powerful, two-way flow of living water (which we studied in an earlier chapter) between Him and His Father. While it is scripture that stimulates us to partake of the divine nature to renew our minds (see 2 Peter 1:4) it was this flow between Him and His Father, of which Jesus continually partook, that sustained Him.

When Satan tempted Jesus to turn stones into bread, Jesus's relationship with His Father rendered Satan's temptation as no temptation at all. Only when His Father announced that the time had arrived to receive physical nourishment did He eat again. Because He was always filled with the presence of His Father He had no concern for physical or emotional lack. Therefore, He was never impatient with the fulfilling of needs. He always waited on the timing of His Father. While Jesus operated in the anointing of the Holy Spirit to meet the needs of others (see Acts 10:38), His own needs He left to the discretion, the leading, and the words of His Father.

Only the devil and those whom he deceived doubted Jesus's commitment to obeying His Father and remaining true to His own integrity. When he failed to trick Jesus, he tempted Him in two other areas. After the temple and the kingdoms of the world temptations failed to trip up Jesus, Satan finally realizedthat there were no weaknesses in Jesus. Jesus proved to be as resistant to the lust of the eyes and pride of life as He was to the lust of the flesh because, unlike the rest of us, He had no fallen nature against which to do battle.

While there were no weaknesses in Jesus whereby Satan could use His human nature to tempt and trip Him up, we, on the other hand, though we may have the born-again new nature of Jesus in us, constantly are in battle with our original fallen nature. Satan is always laying traps by which he lures us into doing wrong through the appetites of our flesh, our eyes, and our pride.

One trap that Satan has regularly set for me is that of appealing to my pride or to my sense of self-worth. Many times, while writing this book, I've been tempted to give up on bringing this book to completion. I realize that there's the possibility that if the book becomes more and more public so also will its author. I donot relish the thought of being in the spotlight.It is the message of the book, because it exalts Jesus, on which people's attention should be focused.

Realizing that it comes with the territory, hopefully any attention directed toward the book's author will be minimal. The attention that I've already garnered through my personal stories were incidental. In my original manuscript Itold only a few stories. But two professionals who had proof read my manuscript strongly recommended that I add many more stories as this would not only help illustrate my points but also increase credibility. Readers, then, would get the sense that I am just like them.

And yet from time to time, realizing it would eliminate this unwanted publicity, it has been a very strong temptation to not proceed with this new edition of this book (under a new title). But as quickly as these thoughts about quitting became a temptation, knowing full well that this was a trap set by Satan to prevent God's will from being fulfilled, with the Lord's help I have been able to overcome these temptations.

Escaping Your Fallen Nature

I am willing to face public scrutiny, if that's what it takes, for people to hear the message that God has called me to share. I've written this book and am making it available because I know that is what God wants me to do. I believe with all my heart that people need to hear the scripturally based message of this book so that they can have the assurance of their salvation.

This temptation to quit my book illustrates its main theme. Since this temptation originated with my original nature, my victory over this temptation proves that it is through God's powerful grace that *Escaping Your Fallen Nature* Entangling Your Life and Blocking Your Way can become a reality in your life also.

As I shared in a previous chapter, in my early life I was addicted to quitting. Though I didn't give all the details in that chapter I will give a few more now.

As I alluded to earlier, after quitting school in September of 1963 and then quitting several jobs, I left Winnipeg in the winter of 1964 to live with my grandparents in a village called Iona in southern Ontario. When I arrived, I was almost totally withdrawn. I would go to church with my grandmother but afterwards would never remain around long enough for people to meet me. There were a few times my grandmother got after me for being so antisocial. But I stubbornly refused to follow her advice.

But to help me get out of my negativity she convinced a neighboring farmer to hire me as a helping hand. I worked with him on his farm all that spring and summer. With all the credit going to my grandparents, that fall, having quit grade 10 in Winnipeg the year earlier, I tried again to get my grade 10, this time in St. Thomas which was about 15 miles from Iona. Every school day I rode the bus, attending all the classes right through to the Christmas break.

All throughout that semester I continued to be antisocial. I made almost no attempt, other than with one boy, to get to know the students and teachers. I always felt inferior to everybody. I remember writing on a piece of paper the words "things to do."

One of the boys discovered this note and then mocked me for coming up with such a line. This made me feel worse about myself.

But then things weren't any better at home. After all the encouragement and help grandma and grandpa had shown me I concluded that I was not worthy of staying at their house. In the last two months of that year I secluded myself from them. As soon as I came home from school I went upstairs to my room to work on my school assignments. And then when I came down for supper I would never enter in to conversation with them and answered their questions on how my day went with as few words as possible.

During those few months, I believed, and not even with the slightest bit of doubt, that I was the dumbest and stupidest person on the earth. I remember that there were many times, even with strong crying, that I complained to the Lord as to why He passed me by when He was handing out to others the gift of intelligence. I was consumed with these very negative destructive thoughts. The more I thought them, the greater was my depth of despair and discouragement. Throughout all this time I never once told anyone about this sense of inferiority.

But though I didn't recognize it at the time, one good thing about me was that I purposed in my heart that whenever I received a school assignment that I would work at it with all my might. Except for when I took time to eat supper, I spent all my time from the time I got home from school until late in the evening when I went to bed working hard on these assignments. I did it because I was hoping to at least make a passing grade. Except for believing that I did really well in drawing a map of the British Isles, I continued to believe, despite my efforts, that I was a miserable failure in all my subjects.

Though I wrote the Christmas exams, immediately afterwards I went to my grandparents and told them that I had decided to quit school and that I would be returning to Winnipeg. I was so quick and abrupt at announcing this that I was already gone before they had a chance to talk me out of it. A few weeks later my grandmother sent me my report card where I discovered that out of 32 students in my class I was the fourth highest with a 71 average – a total shock.

My point in sharing these details of what I was like back in my late teens is to give glory to the Lord for the overcoming grace that he has consistently shown me.It was because of my original fallen nature that I not only showed such negativity and fear in those early years of my life but also the temptations that I presently continue to face from time to time. But even as it was God that made a way for me to escape those life draining negative attitudes in my teen years, He reminds me that my escape from these traps set by Satan, which he sprung by stirring up my fallen nature, continues to come through the release of the Holy Spirit power from my born-again new nature.

The victory that Jesus won over the devil is the encouragement that I needed to believe that I too, through my new nature, can escape all the temptations and traps that the devil may want to put in front of me. It is the knowledge of what Jesus has done and of the Holy Spirit power that He has given to me through my new nature that inspires me to not give in to discouragement.

In this chapter, we have learned that Jesus was always ready for testing, that He could not be tricked by the devil,and that He had no need touse power. His temptations proved that He was, indeed, the Son of God.

If you are already a born-again believer, then because your newborn heart is of Jesus's nature, you can expect the anointing of the Holy Spirit to flow from out of you as it had flowed out of Jesus.Knowingthat you have a new nature that can conquer allyour temptations, even as Jesus exemplified in His life, you now have a source of encouragementto believe that *Escaping Your Fallen Nature Entangling Your Life and Blocking Your Way*is a realistic present day hope of being fulfilled.

CHAPTER 23

DELIVERED YOU INTO A NEW LIFE

We have studied in detail the character, integrity, and faithfulness of Jesus. The writer of the book of Hebrews said:

> ¹ Wherefore, holy brethren, partakers of the heavenly calling, consider the ... High Priest of our profession, Christ Jesus; ² Who was faithful ...
> **Hebrews 3:1–2**

Even as this writer convinced his readers to consider Jesus, I've shown that His credentials, unlike those of any other, warrants our full consideration also.

This nature that survived the most intense temptation anyone has facedis the nature of all born-again believers. The triumph of Jesus over the schemes of the devil, provingthat He was beyond the possibility of faltering,inspires and encourages all believers to believe for victory.

> He that shall endure unto the end, the same shall be saved. **Matthew 24:13**

Why wouldwe believers have confidence thatwe will escape our temptations ifwe concede that it was possiblethat Jesus could've given into His temptations? Since we have the same nature as Jesus, we can have complete assurance in the ability of our new nature to endure and overcome the devil's enticements.

If you are born again, you have that same ability not to fall prey to the devil's tricks. But if you are not yet born again, your study on how Jesus defeated His temptations has now made you aware of the nature of Jesus and His power to forgive your sins and heal your diseased heart.

On one occasion when Jesus was teaching in a crowded house, some men lowered their sick friend through the roof so that he would have access to Jesus's healing power. Though this man came for physical healing, Jesus knew that what he most needed was to be aware that He had the power to forgive him of his sins (see Luke 5:17–24). And when Jesus perceived his faith He then pronounced forgiveness upon him.

After hearing Jesus make this declaration of forgiveness a religious group, the Pharisees, asked, "Who is this which speaketh blasphemies? Who can forgive sins, but God alone?" They missed that Jesus's healing of this man's body corroborated His claim that He was the Son of God and that He, though the Son of Man, had the power to forgive.

Then Jesus taught them about forgiveness to show them that His power to forgive their sins has always been present and available (see Luke 5:17b). If these religious people had considered Jesus's offer of forgiveness, their lives, like this sick man, would have been totally transformed.

They were right in claiming that only God can forgive sins. Only He who is totally beyond the possibility of sinning can forgive sinners. If it were possible for Jesus to sin, then He would not have forgiven people until He had first paid for them. But even before He paid the price He granted forgiveness to those who trusted in Him.

In a popular song about being born again is the line, "Born again, there's really been a change in me." If you believe Jesus has forgiven your sins, there will be a radical change in your behavior.

> [26] Men's hearts failing them for fear, and for looking after those things which are coming on the earth: ... [34]And take heed to yourselves, lest at any time your hearts be overcharged with surfeiting, and drunkenness, and cares of this life, and so that day come upon you unawares. **Luke 21:26, 34**
>
> [4] But ye, brethren, are not in darkness, that that day should overtake you as a thief. [5] Ye are all the children of light, and the children of the day: we are not of the night, nor of darkness. **1 Thessalonians 5:4-5**

The day to which Jesus and Paul referred is the day that extreme tribulations arrive without warning, leaving those whose hearts are filled with fear and are consumed with the "cares of this life" completely unprepared. If you have not been able to overcome the temptation to hold on to bitterness toward others, how likely are you to cope when even greater injustices and pressures befall you? But if you know that your sins are forgiven and that you have a new heart, then that day and the troubles that come with it, Paul says, will not come upon you unawares to overtake you like a thief.

> [28] And when these things begin to come to pass, then look up, and lift up your heads; for your redemption draweth nigh ... [36] Watch ye therefore, and pray always, that ye may be accounted worthy to escape all these things that shall come to pass. **Luke 21: 28, 36**

In order "that ye may be accounted worthy to escape," Jesus instructsyou to look up, to lift up, to take heed, to watch, and to pray. He is especially trying to get the attention of those who have been careless about their salvation. Backsliders will come to realize that the Lord accounts them worthy when due to the stress on the earth their newborn nature prompts them to "lift up their heads." They will look to Jesus when they come to realize that the day of their redemption, after which there will be no further opportunity to escape, is drawing very near.

> [29] And he said, Come ... [30] But when he saw the wind boisterous, he was afraid; and beginning to sink, he cried, saying, Lord, save me. [31] And immediately Jesus stretched forth his hand, and caught him. **Matthew 14:29–31**

In another popular song there's the line, "Put your hand in the hand of the one who stilled the waters." This song identified this "one" as the man from Galilee, an obvious reference to Jesus. When Peter became troubled and began to sink, he looked to Jesus to rescue him. As he was about to go down under the water, Jesus quickly caught hold of His extended hand.

Jesus continues to still the waters and calm the seas of those with troubled hearts. Though He walked on the water to get to Peter, His method of getting to you is through the lifeboat of His written Word, as presented and explained in this book. Because you've learned these many truths, this lifeboat carrying Jesus is clearly in your view. Amid these turbulent waters that are threatening to drown you, you hear the compassionate voice of Jesus inviting you to "Come!"

Because you have allowed the Word of God to be planted into your heart the new pregnancy process has already begun. But this new life cannot be birthed until you, like Peter, say "Lord, save me." Since, with God's help, *Escaping Your Fallen Nature* is a very realistic probability, all that remains to complete this birthing process is to fully commit your life to Him. If this final birthing stage of the formation of Jesus has been completed,then you are alreadya born-again new creation.

Now that you've completed the reading of this book, ifyou know your heart has been made new or has been revived back to life, you need to connect and rejoice with other believers. If it's your desire I can be reached at <u>davidrpiper1@gmail.com</u>.

I trust that the truths explained in this book have been a help to you and that you are now celebrating the wonderful grace of God that brought these truths to your heart.Depending on the condition of your heart that I outlined in chapter 2, you are now rejoicing for one or more of the following blessings that the Lord has bestowed upon you:

1. For His faithfulness that released from your inner being rivers of Holy Spirit living water.
2. For His love that enabled you to overcome anxiety and the fear of losing your salvation.
3. For His mercy that forgave you of your backsliding and revived you back to life.
4. For His power that defeated your temptation to quit trusting in His loving care.
5. For His light that opened up your understanding of truth and set you free from deception.
6. For His grace that replaced your fallen nature with one thatproduceseternal joy and peace.

When you come to understand the many scriptures explained throughout this book about the power of your new nature, your defeats will turn into victories. Because much of what I've shared about these truthsrequiresmuch concentration to understand them, I recommend that you re-read this book. As you read it one or two more times, you will be inspired to celebrate your deliverance and will come to appreciate more fully that it was these scriptural truths that made escapingyourfallennature and receiving in its place the born-again new nature of Jesus a life changing reality.

For most of us, the process of deciding to become born again and receive the new nature of Jesus involved serious reflection and contemplation before we were willing to commit to Him and let Him be Lord over our lives. But regardless of the pains we went through, when the formation of Jesus in the womb of our hearts was completed and we were delivered from our labor, the birthing of His new nature in uscaused our sorrow to turn into joy.

In like manner, I have gone through labor pains in getting this book written and ready for publication. Even after the Lord planted in my mind seed thoughts and conceived in my heart the vision of writing it, it took many years before this book reached completion. There were several times that I considered aborting. But I am so thankful that the Lord helped me to persevere.

Now that the Lord has brought this book through the various birthing stages, especially of helping me through the hard labor of selectingappropriate marketing services, finally, it is delivered. All the labor I experienced is well worth it when realizing that for many of you the Lord, after inspiring you to believe that *Escaping Your Fallen Nature* Entangling Your Life and Blocking Your Way has always been His plan for you,has now also *Delivered You into a New Life*.

> Now unto him that is able to keep you from falling, and to present you faultless before the presence of his glory with exceeding joy. **Jude 1:24**

Escaping Your Fallen Nature

www.ingramcontent.com/pod-product-compliance
Lightning Source LLC
Chambersburg PA
CBHW052014070526
44584CB00016B/1748

www.ingramcontent.com/pod-product-compliance
Lightning Source LLC
Chambersburg PA
CBHW052014070526
44584CB00016B/1748